JUST WHO WE ARE

My Story of Grit, Grace, and Identity

A Memoir by

Robyn Stecher

Just Who We are

My story of grace, grit, and identity

A memoir

Incorgnito Publishing Press
1651 Devonshire Lane
Sarasota, FL 34236
888-859-0792

Contact@incorgnitobooks.com

FIRST EDITION

Printed in the United States of America

ISBN: 978-1944589776

10 9 8 7 6 5 4 3 2 1

For my parents
Bernie and Barbara

You gave me the gift
of knowing
that if I kept searching
I would find myself

For Joyce
for reminding me
not to be afraid

INTRODUCTION

*Life will go on
as long as there is someone to sing,
to dance,
to tell stories and to listen.*
~Oren Lyons

I stepped into my sixtieth year with a lot of questions. Where am I headed? How well have I lived? Did I do what I wanted to do? Have I gone where I wanted to go? Have I laughed enough? Have I loved with all my heart? Have I given enough? How will my son's life unfold? Am I becoming who I wanted to be?

I started writing about my fears and my fury, my joys and my losses, the ways I was broken and how I became whole. I wrote when I had a few stolen minutes in the morning or very late at night. I wrote on trains and planes, and sometimes in the car. I wrote when I doubted that what I had to say had merit, or that anyone would want to read what I had to say. I wrote until I didn't want to write another word. I'd walk away, and then I'd start again.

Mine are not stories of greatness like landing a plane in the Hudson River and saving everyone on board. I didn't overcome poverty to become a Wall Street mogul. I was raised in a mainstream, middle-class New England town. I wasn't special by way of winning Olympic medals or even being an exceptional student. When I was a teenager, I threatened to drop out of high school. I smoked pot, carried a knife, and hitchhiked. I never won a trophy. I wasn't always very pretty or overly smart. I quit a lot of things, but I came from a family of hard-working people, and somehow the embers of those values were enough to wake me up and ignite my ambition.

Armed with resourcefulness, I was determined to discover my purpose and find success.

My life didn't unfold the way I had imagined. When the unexpected came, stealthy and quiet, how fast it changed me. I might have crumbled, but I rose, demanding, "Show me what is possible."

My life's stories are about grit, grace and identity. My life has been beautiful and messy. I can't iron, fold, or make my stories any neater. I don't want to box them, burn them, bury them, forget them, trade them in, or label them for storage. I don't want to glorify them, either. I lived these stories to share them.

No hero, no one famous, no celebrity has more to share than what they have lived. If we stop telling the full-length versions of our truths, we become islands floating in seas that keep us distant.

We are all traveling together, finding out just who we are.

JUST WHO WE ARE

It is only with the heart that one can see rightly;
what is essential is invisible to the eye.
~Antoine De Saint-Exupery~

"Can we go on this show?" Daniel called out.

I didn't answer.

"MOM, can we go on this show?"

I was in the bathroom. The door was closed. Leaning into the mirror, I applied my mascara. On the other side of the door, I could hear the TV. Someone was about to win something big. Daniel was in his "game-show" phase, which had followed "The Muppets" phase and the "Presidents" phase. I didn't feel like answering. I wanted to be in the bathroom alone.

My son was obsessed. It didn't matter what show it was; he just wanted to be on a game show.

My parents, Bernie and Barbara, were ignoring him, too. I could hear my mother: "Bernie, where did I leave my pills?"

Barbara would keep asking, and Bernie wouldn't know. Daniel was 13. He was banging on the bathroom door. I didn't open it. I would stay in front of that mirror until he stopped.

We were in an unremarkable hotel room in Burlington, Vermont. We were there to pick up my niece Ashley, who was also 13, from circus camp. Afterward, we were all leaving for my parents' home on Cape Cod.

I was 47. There in the mirror, in the corners of my eyes, was the truth about the laughing and the crying, which came in equal amounts along the way. I liked those lines. They curled upwards and said something about my life.

Memories kept coming at me like water through a broken pipe.

I could see that smile I'd worn as I licked ice cream off my chin during those Cape Cod summers, long before Amy died when we were still a family of five. We would turn cartwheels on the grass and stand on our hands trying to outdo each other.

In the mirror, tears like black rain began to fall. I could feel my sister's fingers, wrapped in mine, when she was 34 and dying, with my soul crying out beneath the tyranny of the loss. My sister was gone, my marriage was over, and I was a single mother. My son, Daniel, had been born with a genetic anomaly. I wasn't a suburban mom as my mother had been, with a house to care for, three typical children, suppers to cook each night, and carpools to drive. I was minus a few kids and a husband, and more than one car. I had carved my identity from New York City in places too small for large dogs and where the concrete heats up in the summer like a clay oven and bakes you.

My college boyfriend had brought me to New York in 1977. Below the ornate ceiling of the Shubert Theater, I'd sat on a red velvet seat. The story of nineteen chorus dancers began an era for one of the longest-running shows on Broadway, and I'd memorized every word to every song in *A Chorus Line*. That had been the beginning of my affair with the city I would live in, love, and sometimes hate; it was a city that asked no forgiveness for the edgy flaws that, for me, didn't diminish her beauty.

My story wasn't like those of my friends from where I'd grown up in a suburb of Boston.

Now, I'd been divorced for seven years. My choice. Still, I wished Daniel's father and I could have saved the unfinished story we'd started. I missed the early years when we had a hammock in the living room and my garden on the rooftop, and we hung out with artists and relished scuba diving. I missed the romance of our beginning. I wished we could have shared the joy of parenting our son and that it would have been enough to save us.

On the day I left my marital home, it was raining. Everything I owned was packed into the 28 boxes that were loaded onto a moving truck. I closed the door to our once home behind me, locking out a decade of my life.

Being unmarried then, I'd thought things would get easier, but now, standing there in that bathroom in Burlington, Vermont, I saw the years covered in a veil of grief.

I listened to my parents in the other room going back and forth about misplaced eyeglasses and what we were going to eat for dinner. Soon, they would celebrate their wedding anniversary. I would never be married for fifty years. I wondered if I'd even remarry.

I remembered my father's voice from when I'd been young, coaching me as he'd run alongside my wobbly, new red bike—he must have been in his early thirties at the time. It had felt awkward at first, being so out of control, but after a while, my feet had stopped fighting. I trusted my arms would steer me. I just kept pedaling, and then I found myself flying along.

Chiseled from the bedrock of my careful traveling, there was my five-year-old faith. I wiped my nose with the back of my hand and splashed water on my face.

"MOOOOOOMMMMMMMM!" Daniel was calling.

I had to leave the bathroom.

I stepped out of the past and kneeled. I took Daniel's hand in mine.

"I love you," I whispered.

He let me hold him in my arms for a second. I sat on the edge of the bed. I ran my fingers through his hair. *My beautiful, complex son.*

"I really want to go on this show," he said.

"Don't you want to go to the pool?" He couldn't swim. I hated the smell of chlorine and the noise of other families.

"No," he answered.

Neither did I. We weren't like other families anyway. No, we weren't going to the pool.

It's just who we were.

BERNIE AND BARBARA

Grow old along with me! The best is yet to be...
~Robert Browning~

"Are you sure this is the road?"

My mother was in the driver's seat. My father was navigating.

"Yes, Barb, this is the road."

"I don't know... I don't remember this road."

"Well, this the only road, and *this* is the road."

My mother couldn't remember the route they had taken two days before on their journey northward from Massachusetts to Vermont.

"Let's stop for those muffins. We had the best muffins. Where was it? Bern?"

"I don't remember. We stopped a few times."

Bernie and Barbara met on a blind date in 1955. It was two weeks after my mother had been told by a tea leaf reader that she would fall in love and marry a redhead. Bernie was the redhead. He proposed to her on the back of a Howard Johnson's postcard. They were married within the year. She was 22, and he was 25.

I can't remember exactly when we started calling them Bernie and Barbara, but I think it was when Ashley referred to them as "Grandma B" and "Papa B." After that, they became "B and B," and their shared initials further consecrated the fact that they were inseparable. Their "card-sending generation" acknowledged every single friend's birthday and anniversary, and they always signed cards 'Bernie and Barbara.' They were apart only when Barbara gave birth to us, her three children. No one who knew them thought of one without the other.

At 72 and 74, they were king and queen of the road. The beginnings of Barbara's failing memory and Bernie's failing vision and hearing impairment seemed hazardous, but their independence, at all costs, had to remain unchallenged. They were still going places. This was good. As far back as I could remember, they'd made road trips. They had driven through most of the U.S. together. Without their car, my parents would have had no life.

I was five when we all went to a guy's house to check out Barbara's first car. That was when Bernie and Barbara couldn't afford more than a used, old clunker. Barbara's smiling face lit up like when we got a toy we *really* wanted. She would no longer be stuck at home with three children under the age of five. She took us to the town beach, Shopper's World (the mall), the kosher butcher's, and on other errands she needed to do. We visited her good friends from high school and college and played with their children.

On the ride back from Vermont to Cape Cod, I was forbidden from driving. For reasons I'll never know, Bernie or Barbara always drove. My niece Ashley and Daniel, both 13, were in the back seat. I was wedged back there with them, headphones securely over my ears. I was leaning on the car door. The kids were watching movies on a DVD player. It reminded me of when my sister Amy and my brother Steven were little. I'd be in the back seat of the car thinking my parents' fighting in the car would lead to their divorce. Back then, I would have loved headphones. They just didn't exist.

My mother was at the wheel. For most of the nine-hour drive, she was either gunning it or suddenly braking. When she occasionally forgot an exit, she traversed lanes to correct herself. For me, this was not conducive to even brief periods of dozing off, although the children miraculously slept through the near-misses. When we finally pulled into their driveway, it was an act of divine intervention that we were all still alive. I wanted a glass of wine or a shot of vodka.

Bernie and Barbara rid their home of palatable alcohol when my younger brother Steven was 16 and his car met up with the plate-glass window of a car dealership. The accident nearly killed him. The small amount of liquor still in the house was so old that I wouldn't risk drinking any of it. At midnight, I was wide awake, doing Ashley's camp laundry.

For the next two weeks, our collective eating habits would vary too much for a single, peaceful meal: one vegetarian who ate nothing with a face, one who ate nothing that walked or flew, and one who only drank fruits and vegetables. Ashley had been raised vegan by her California parents.

At 15, I'd declared myself a vegetarian after a summer stock theater experience where our meals resembled dog food. Barbara declared that she was not cooking special meals for me. My independence led me not to fear the kitchen...unless my mother was in it. This was still true. Even now, in Bernie and Barbara's home, I'd be terrified to show off my culinary skills.

In her domain, she controlled what came in and went out. My mother did the shopping because she didn't like when foreign things just "appeared" in the refrigerator. She would ask if we wanted anything from the store, but then she wouldn't remember what we'd asked for or that I hated foods like fat-free ice cream that are meant to contain fat. I drink my coffee with cream or half-and-half. Regular milk doesn't cut it.

Because we were Jewish, food was important. Growing up, we kept kosher, which meant we couldn't eat pork products or mix milk products with meat. We had many sets of dishes and silverware for meals with meat and other silverware for meals with milk. Barbara grew up a little kosher, but not all the way. When they married, she tolerated keeping a kosher home for Bernie. Bernie was kosher for his mother, my grandma Bessie, because if we weren't kosher, she wouldn't eat in our home. But Barbara loved eating lobster and shrimp, which weren't kosher foods. She taught Bernie about the epicurean delights he'd missed out on like lobster, shrimp, and Chinese food. We ate those foods at home on paper plates as well as pizza and subs (we called them grinders). When I was older, I thought being "paper-plate kosher" was so hypocritical.

Barbara cooked every weeknight. She liked her meat very well-done, but we weren't allowed to say it was burned. My favorite meal was macaroni and cheese from a box, which we very rarely ate. Her menu ideas came from magazines like *Good Housekeeping* and the little index-card box she kept in the kitchen. She saved recipes from her family and her friends. Friday night was Shabbat, which meant chicken, and then we went to temple. Saturday was date night for Bernie and Barbara, which usually meant pizza for us. Sunday was usually visiting day. We saw relatives or family friends, and we ate Chinese food or Jewish deli food. I loved chopped liver, corned beef, and pastrami on onion rolls. None of which I have had since I was 15.

That summer of 2005, when we were all together, I was 47, a capable executive with beneficiaries, a will, and an investment portfolio; people knew me to be highly responsible. I could do all the laundry, clean, cook, and take care of the children's every need, but I was smart enough to know, in Bernie and Barbara's home, not to answer their phone. Taking a message would result in failure. Long before answering machines, when we'd been very young, we'd been taught proper phone etiquette and how to write down messages. I rarely got it right. Barbara always had so many calls, and now endless appointments: temple, sisterhood, Hadassah, book club, mahjong, and volunteering to drive cancer patients.

Before I was old enough to drive and negotiating the use of the cars became the daily fight, the telephone in our home was the most important commodity. Because Barbara talked so much we couldn't share a single phone number, I got my own "princess phone" when I was 13. Her favorite punishment was to remove the phone from my room. It wasn't very effective. I would find the phone, plug it back in, and hide with it under my covers. Bernie was a smart man. He never got involved.

My father was the youngest child of Jewish Ukrainian and Lithuanian immigrants. My grandma Bessie was 12 when she was unexpectedly taken in the night and sent alone on a boat to America. She crossed the ocean, fleeing before the ghettos of Vilna would claim her. She didn't learn to read or write English. Her native language was Yiddish. Widowed at 30, with three young children, she worked fifteen-hour days in a basement for a Jewish caterer.

He was born a year after the Great Crash of '29, and throughout the Depression, the death of his father, and their ensuing poverty, Bernie still wouldn't be deterred from becoming educated. He worked numerous jobs from the time he was nine and on throughout college. Later, he was committed to his long career and taking care of his family. He wasn't extremely wealthy, but he was successful.

Instead of hearing bedtime stories, I wanted to hear about my parents' young lives. Barbara was an "only" child and admitted she was spoiled. Her father was both indulgent and overprotective. She was never allowed to learn how to ride a bike. Her mother Rose was suddenly taken to the hospital when Barbara was 20 and died unexpectedly the next day. I wondered what it would be like to be spoiled and to be an "only child." It sounded good to me, but I felt sorry for her because her mother had died. I don't think my mother ever got over it. She didn't have her mother to share her wedding day or to know her children. Her cousin told me that Rose, for whom I am named, was kind and a great cook.

It took a long time for me to realize how smart Barbara was. She whizzed through crossword puzzles, always beat us at Scrabble, and read two books a week. Later, I noticed she knew most of the answers on *Jeopardy*. She was a teacher for a short time but had left her job, like so many women of her generation, back when she became pregnant with me. Her father was insistent that no daughter of his was going to have children and work! I think she wanted a career, but felt she had no choice.

Bernie's stories about growing up poor and his many jobs intrigued me. I imagined it was awful. But he didn't describe it that way. He lived in a suburb of Boston in a Jewish ghetto. During regular visits from the welfare people, the family had to prove they were poor. Four of them lived on $100 a month to cover rent and food. They got public assistance for some basic food and yet he never really thought of himself as being deprived. There was one metal ship in a toy store window that he would longingly look at as he passed by each day, but it was very expensive. His sister, who had a job, would occasionally bring him little soldiers. But the metal ship would never be his.

Occasionally, they would have visits from gangs who came into their neighborhood. His mother wouldn't let him wear jeans or sneakers because "that's how the guys from the gangs dress," and according to her, it was a sign of being lower-class. How much lower-class could they have been? The highlight of his family's week was Saturday when they went to the movies—for a nickel. She insisted he wear ironed knickers and clean shirts. They didn't have money, but they had clean clothes and, even though they stood in bread lines, they always had food. My father, who got his first job at 11, didn't stop working until he was 83.

One day, when he was a teenager working in a dress factory, there were two tasks that needed to be completed before the end of the day.

One was to go to the post office and the other was to take some equipment to the basement. His coworker decided that Bernie would go to the post office while he took the equipment to the basement. When my father got back to the factory, police cars and an ambulance were outside. Inside, he learned that the elevator had malfunctioned and that his coworker had plummeted to his death. His boss's wife glared at him and said, "It should have been you." He was only 15.

When we were growing up, we used to go to the beach a lot. I loved it because Bernie, who didn't usually have a lot of time to play with us kids, would take us in the water with our floats, and we would build castles in the sand. Later, his grandchildren Ashley and Daniel would also love going to the beach with "Papa Bernie." He would take them out in the calm water of Cape Cod Bay and play with them or take them out in his little boat on the estuary near where he and Barbara lived.

When I was in middle school, my mother was usually mad at me. At the beach, I would scope out other families who looked worthy of my running away with them. I imagined my new family. I would be the princess, the youngest, maybe the "surprise" who had come long after older siblings. My adoptive mother would be sweet. She would hold me and stroke me. She would smell like fresh laundry. Nothing would stress her out, and I would make her happy. Nothing sad would happen.

But sad things did happen. When my younger brother Steven was in his late teens and I was in my early 20s, he was drinking heavily and using drugs. After meeting up with the car dealership window, which nearly cost him his life, he landed in rehab. Soon after Steven got out, someone who knew him was arrested on drug-dealing charges. He plea-bargained for a shorter sentence and ratted out my brother as an accomplice. Bernie appealed to the attorney general. I can't imagine how he felt, knowing that his son would be going to prison. The mandatory sentence for a drug offense in Massachusetts at that time was ten years—even for a first offense. My father pled with the judge. His son had been through rehab, he was clean, and he had a job. The judge was willing to reduce his sentence to a year in prison and nine years' probation.

It all came as a shock to me. None of us ever discussed it. Barbara never told anyone about it—not even her best friend. At family gatherings, my brother was just missing. Amy and I covered for our mother's sake. Steven was Barbara's favorite, or maybe she thought he needed more attention from her. Bernie visited him on most weekends. By then, I was already on my own in New York. I didn't understand him. How, with all the attention he had received—not to mention the sacrifices my parents had made for all of us to enjoy our many after-school activities and to provide for college educations—could he be so cavalier? It was like he was throwing it all away. I didn't try to find out what mattered to him. I made a lot of assumptions, and maybe I was wrong...but I did write to him. Later, I found a letter he wrote me from prison. He wrote about his mistakes, how he regretted the lost years, and what he had missed out on in his life. He asked about Daniel and Ashley. I wished I could hug him. But it would be a long time until we'd be able to do that. Later, he told me that "going away" had saved his life.

In my mid-forties, my sister and brother were both missing from my life, but the holes closed a little when I was with Daniel and Ashley. That road trip in 2005, from Burlington, Vermont to Cape Cod, was the last one I took with Bernie and Barbara. That summer was also the last time Ashley, Daniel, and I sat in the backseat of their car and laughed about their quirks and bickering. When August came to an end, Ashley went back to Santa Barbara, where she lived, and Daniel and I went back to New York.

I didn't know another hole was opening. Soon after that summer,

Barbara was diagnosed with mild cognitive impairment. She was in the unlucky ten percent of people her age who would face the beginning of the end of her working memory.

But Bernie, Mr. "King of the Road," came through. He wouldn't let those trips end. He took the wheel and made sure they kept going. Barbara hated the mean Cape Cod winters, so he bought a place in Florida, and they drove down there every winter. He would pack up the car to the point where he couldn't see out the back window, get Barbara and their dog Maggie inside, and off they would go. I used to imagine them bickering away on those long road trips; I feared for their safety and wondered if they would get lost, but their connection to each other was inseverable. Eventually, Bernie hired a driver so they could fly down and meet the car in Florida.

After she could no longer drive, Barbara's car sat in retirement collecting pine sap and needles. The idea of my mother giving up driving was tragic. After that, I think her world stopped turning. Bernie kept the car for years, as though by leaving it sitting there, he had not totally removed the freedom she once had. Eventually, he gave it to Steven.

The road trips ended, but at 89 years old, Bernie bought a new car. It is very safe. It keeps him on the right side of the line, and if he's too slow to respond, it brakes for him. It can see around corners and behind him. He drives alone now, and Barbara doesn't leave the house much, but he's still going places.

BOOMER WOMAN

Do not follow where the path may lead.
Go instead where there is no path and leave a trail.
~Ralph Waldo Emerson~

My class of beautiful, three- and four-year-old ballerinas wearing red lipstick, in fluffy tutus, twirled to the right. I twirled to the left. When I noticed that I was going the wrong way, the embarrassment wasn't enough to get me in line with them. I just kept dancing. My parents watched all the other little girls floating by, and I was standing with my finger up my nose. I wondered if they were mortified or if they knew I was destined to be different.

I sat at the edge of the sandbox in my short skirt with my naked, goose-pimply legs while the other children played. I felt cursed that a roguish boy named Brook was going to be my partner at our kindergarten "etiquette luncheon." I was scrappy and not pretty. Did my teacher think I was a tomboy and roguish, too? When we arrived at the restaurant, it was the fanciest place I'd ever seen. There were crystal chandeliers and white linens. It looked like somewhere that princesses met princes, but I didn't feel like a princess and Brooke was no prince. As he pulled out my chair for me (part of the etiquette training), he could barely get it to move along the carpet. By the age of five, I was already honing my skills at helping others achieve their potential. How could I help him? I didn't want us to fail our manners test. I could gently kick him under the table if he wasn't properly executing on the finger bowl or putting the napkin on his lap. I wanted for us to be just as perfect as the prettier girls and less scruffy boys, but I knew we weren't.

When I was eight, my mother and I were late to my piano recital. I was running up the walk to my teacher's home, and I fell. My tights were torn, my knee skinned and bloody. I was a mess; I was mortified. My mother tried to console me, but it was pointless. My piano teacher's living room was full of her students and their mothers. I walked in and tried to pull it together, but I couldn't be comforted. The teacher took me into her den, away from everyone, and sympathetically assured me that it was fine. She would change the order so I could go last. This did not help because the most advanced students were going last. When I sat at the piano, all I could think of was how the boy who had gone before me was much better than me. I started to play but couldn't remember my piece. I fumbled and tried to start from the beginning. It was futile. I stopped. My hands fell limp on the keys.

My teacher ushered me back to the den. I went into the bathroom and stayed there for a long time—crying. After that, I quit the lessons, but I played the piano for fun. Later, I quit flute, French, Spanish, Hebrew, gymnastics, art classes, private school, *and* dancing. I abandoned anything I wasn't naturally very good at. But years after my divorce, the first thing I bought when I had a little money was a piano. It was my emancipation gift to myself, a reminder that I could play for joy because I chose to. I'm not sure now if I was a quitter or if maybe I just moved on from what wasn't working for me.

Early on, I had figured out how to make use of my father's cinematography talent. I enlisted him to get out his 8mm camera and shoot my movies. I cast my brother and sister in my directorial masterpieces, ordering them to "act" more convincingly and demanding "cuts" and breaks in the action when things weren't going my way. I also made good use of his Wollensak reel-to-reel tape recorder. I would wait for him to cue me, and *click*, the reels started turning. I would squeal happily when I heard the playback and heard my voice narrating my descriptive fairy tales. I was 10 when *Funny Girl* was released. It was my favorite movie. I went digging around in my mother's closet, searching for a gown, a wig, and a fur hat. I came down our front stairway, performing my best Barbra Streisand rendition of Nicky Arnstein. My parents called me Sarah Bernhardt. She was a famous French actress, "queen of the pose and princess of the gesture."

Most of the time in elementary school when everyone else was quiet, I was daydreaming, scheming, or chattering away. I was sent to the coat closet, sequestered from others in penance for being "bold" enough to depart from the rules. Later, I figured out that I wasn't "bad;" my imagination was just more powerful than whatever the teacher was teaching. According to my mother, I daydreamed too much. She was sure I had ADHD, but no one knew what to call it back then.

My girlfriends and I would lie outside eating the sweet bottoms off the grass. We checked our chins to see if the buttercups reflected yellow, which would mean a boy liked us. Day after day in the heat of summer, I looked up at the sky and thought endlessly about my future husband and the maid I would have. (Having a maid meant I wouldn't have to do the chores my mother asked of me.) My stories included a secret desire for international travel and going places like New York City, which I'd seen in movies. I had a burning sense that, beyond life in our suburban development, there was more.

By the time I was a sophomore in high school, my body was not made for winning medals and trophies. When it came to physical competition, anything below my collarbone still required "lack of co-ordination" forgiveness. When we were being picked to play sports, I would feign illnesses to get a note excusing me from the "lineup". I wasn't worthy of any position on any team.

In the mid-Seventies, kids were dying of drug overdoses. I smoked cigarettes and pot, hitchhiked, carried a knife, and didn't wear a bra. I was in the guidance counselor's office regularly. "What's the problem?" I was asked. "You're so bright, and you aren't doing well in your classes." I had no answers. I was most content when I was hanging out with my friends, writing poetry, learning how to play guitar, and listening to Don McLean, Frank Zappa, and Joni Mitchell. I just wanted to get out of school.

I suffered the misery of having too little confidence and no outlet for my creativity. I wanted to escape the malls, the druggies, my friends, and even my own ennui. For my junior year, I convinced my parents to send me to a private girls' school for the performing arts. Private school wasn't on my parents' agenda or in their budget, but they saw it as an answer to my anguish. The Tudor buildings and sprawling lawns on campus looked grand. I was accepted. We were reading Chaucer and studying the work of George Eliot. This was very different from the public high school. The standard there was to be no less than exceptional, and this was much more than I was willing to give. My grades were average. I argued with my teachers and sought refuge in the drama department.

The drama teacher, Mr. Lindberg, was directing a rarely per-formed play by A.A. Milne based on the early classic, The Wind in the Willows. I thought his choice was lame and had no interest in auditioning. My disdain brought an unexpected surprise. He asked me to codirect the play. Finally, I had met an adult who didn't think I was an underachiever. He saw the part of me that shined—my imag-ination. When the play was over, he gave me a gift. It was a book in which he had inscribed his gratitude to "The Divine Ms. R." He believed I had the ability to lead, even though I had no idea I would lead anyone anywhere that didn't include trouble.

FINDING KATHY

You said you 'n me was gonna get outta town,
and for once just really let our hair down.
Well, darlin', watch out, 'cause my hair is comin' down!
~Thelma and Louise~

Given my less-than-motivated high school academic performance, I went to a marginal college in Connecticut. It was the best school I could get into at the time. I majored in drama, which was appropriate. Being an actress seemed much more interesting than my idea of an office job, where I would have to sit at a desk and type.

I met Kathy in acting class. She sat down next to me. I looked at her and blurted out, "You have the most beautiful eyes!" It was the beginning of our lifelong friendship, and we were a fierce duo. She had long, black curly hair and a fiery Italian personality. She was like Cher, and I was like Bette Midler—only smaller, and I couldn't sing. We figured out that we weren't going to get anywhere as actresses in Connecticut. Together, we plotted to move to New York City. We auditioned for the Stella Adler Conservatory acting school through NYU. We were both accepted. At first, because there was no housing, we were offered rooms in the infamous Chelsea Hotel. When we found out the punk rocker from the Sex Pistols, Sid Vicious, had been murdered there, we had to convince our parents to let us live in an apartment.

It was the spring of 1978, and we had little time before September when school began. Kathy was from Washington Township, New

Jersey; I was from Framingham, Massachusetts. Because she lived closer to the city, she had to find us the apartment. Kathy went walking around Greenwich Village near NYU. She noticed a guy hanging out in front of a building on Waverly Place and asked him if there were any available apartments. He just shook his head no. She flashed a hundred-dollar bill and, suddenly, an apartment was "going to be available." The superintendents had to be bribed with "key money" for a tipoff about an empty apartment. This was cheaper than hiring a broker. Money talked.

The apartment was a cockroach-infested miracle. I had no idea how cool it was that we were going to be living in the middle of Greenwich Village, right off Washington Square Park.

With the U-Haul trailing behind the car, Barbara and Bernie made the road trip to drop me off. After we got all of my stuff up into the apartment, they looked around. Their faces said it all. To them, this was the strangest choice anyone could make. It was going to take a few weeks for us to get the place inhabitable. We had to paint, clean, and hire exterminators. I'm sure my parents thought I wouldn't stay. Back home, roaches were something people smoked—not something that shared our kitchen—but, for the first time, my spirit soared. I was home! The rent was $380 a month, and often, we didn't have hot water. Today, that apartment would rent for more than ten times what we paid for it, and I'm sure the tenants have hot water.

The rebellion that made me a defiant child served me well in a place where drug dealers and murderers were equal occupants of the daily news. David Berkowitz, the "Son of Sam" serial killer, had just been apprehended. I'm not sure my parents knew about it, but guys like him didn't scare me enough for me to be frightened of the city. I returned to my parents' house for holidays and short visits, but it would no longer be my home. Later, I asked if they ever worried about me. Bernie said, "No, not that I remember." I think he was in denial. He was just avoiding thinking about me. If they'd known about some of the things I was doing, they would have worried or hauled me back. Maybe parents didn't worry then, or not in the way we do now.

Kathy and I learned to cook with help from her traditional Italian mother, Gloria, who lived in New Jersey. Gloria was always generous with groceries and brought us delicious food that she made. My favorite was her eggplant parmigiana. I had a charge account at a fancy Italian specialty food store. We ate brie, cooked fresh pasta, and ate rich, delicious desserts like crème brûlée—nothing I had grown up eating. That gourmet dream lasted until I didn't pay the bill for a couple of months. The store cut me off.

Kathy and I believed we had traveled lifetimes together and that our union was bound by an eternal contract. Even when we were on different continents, we stayed connected through the love letters we would write each other and the phone dates we would make, calling collect to overseas phone booths and getting away without paying. No matter how much we partied or which boyfriends broke our hearts, Kathy and I took care of each other. We shared everything—money, food, clothing, and our double bed.

Kathy was a talented singer. She performed in small cabarets and eventually mounted her own shows in the Village and SoHo. I was her producer. We loved all kinds of music. We visited museums and devoured the poetry of Cummings, Neruda, and Eliot. We were seduced by strong women writers: Sylvia Plath, Erica Jong, Marilyn French, Anais Nin, and Ayn Rand.

We regularly went to small, Off-Broadway plays. We saw Sam Shepard in the theater right before he won the Pulitzer in 1979 for *Buried Child*. *The Elephant Man* had just made its Broadway debut. The theater was changing, challenging audiences with themes about hardship, struggle, and redemption. Stephen Sondheim's

Sweeney Todd was provocative with edgy lyrics, dissonant melody lines, and a dark, twisted plot of revenge and love. As I sat in the theater with my mother and Kathy watching Len Cariou and Angela Lansbury bring on Tony Award performances, it never occurred to me that I would one day work on behalf of an actor as famous as Mr. Cariou.

The Village was a place where you could get very lost or find yourself. The street life, shops, clothing, musicians, drug dealers, guys playing pickup basketball, tattoo parlors, sex shops, food, dancing, bookstores, and Hare Krishnas chanting in their small parades made life there unlike any other place I'd experienced. I learned the hard way to ignore men who told me I looked like a model. One day, a guy followed me into my foyer and promised me I would make a lot of money if I let him take my picture with a wet tee-shirt. I wasn't dumb enough to think it was for real. The thought crossed my mind that he could rape me. My pocketbook was stolen a couple of times because I hung it on the back of my chair at a restaurant and didn't pay attention. Even when I felt like it would beat me, or I was lonely and life felt harder than I'd imagined it could be, the currency of New York City was possibility.

By my junior year at NYU, I knew I didn't want to "suffer for my art." Professional acting didn't feel like my path anymore. I changed my major to creative writing and literature. Kathy remained in acting school. She'd gone to beauty school before we met so she'd have a backup profession. I had nothing but my street-smarts; I had to stay focused so I would get good grades and find a good job. By day, my intellectual alter ego kept me sequestered in NYU's Bobst Library studying modern and postmodern literary works for my dissertation. By Friday night, I'd be ready to let loose.

In the late Seventies, the drinking age was 18. Kathy and I danced and drugged in the iconic clubs: Studio 54, Xenon, Ice Palace, and

Max's Kansas City. We prepped a whole week for those Saturday nights. We borrowed clothes from each other and bought Paul Mitchell "Spritz Forte" (hair glue in a spray bottle) by the gallon. We'd be soaked in sweat from dancing, but our hairstyles would remain intact. We went with enough money for one drink and cab fare home. All night, guys would buy us drinks.

Disco wear was never acceptable in the daytime, but for the clubs, the bigger the hair and the more outlandish, bosomy, and shimmery the outfit, the better. A man in a white shirt with his collar turned up, a satin jacket, his shirt unbuttoned to his waist, and a medallion resting on his tanned chest...that was hot. Women wore gold lamé, leopard skin, sequined bandeau tops, fat belts, stretch halter jumpsuits with shoulder pads, and lots of iridescent glimmering stuff. Our platform shoes gave us the needed lift to compete. I was the beneficiary of Kathy's beautician's license; she rocked my hairstyles and makeup. Getting past the bouncers was a sport. Being rejected at the door would be a whole week's work wasted. The clubs opened at 11 p.m. We'd party all night and get home by the time the sun was rising.

We spent hours making our own mixtapes on dual-cassette tape recorders. If we weren't practicing our dance moves in the living room, we were working out. Jane Fonda was our idol. I had the Reebok high-top sneakers and leg warmers, but I couldn't keep up with the moves in aerobics class. I didn't have the coordination for it, so I wandered into the weight room where the guys worked out. I got a few looks that seemed to ask, "Who does she think she is?" Thin was in, and I wasn't intimidated; I was going to be "ripped."

Sex was available in unlimited ways and quantities. We were free to choose, but we weren't always choosing wisely. Sometimes we were shutting down, putting out, and shutting up. A roll in bed with a stranger was a gamble for an STD, but it could also be steamy.

Date rape wasn't talked about much. It happened more than most women acknowledged.

Always fashion-forward, we sported "mullets." Then, we cut our long hair into shag-style layers; Kathy wore hers wildly curly, and I blow-dried mine into carefully pulled coifs to give it the "Farah Fawcett look." *Charlie's Angels* and Brooke Shields (nothing came between her and her "Calvins") were setting the mainstream fashion standard. In the early Eighties, Betsy Johnson, Patricia Field, and Norma Kamali were trendsetters. At the same time, Patti Smith and Robert Mapplethorpe were challenging the mainstream music and art of the time, digging up the underground that would become the bedrock for the New Wave punk and art movements.

The fuel crisis that produced lines at the gas stations back in the town where I'd grown up was always in the news. As serious as it was, it seemed inconsequential to us. If Kathy and I did any driving, we borrowed Gloria's big, red 1977 Cadillac, which we nicknamed "the boat," and took our bad-ass selves cruising around the city. Our usual mode of transportation was the subway, filthy and slow, with broken windows and graffiti-covered walls, and filled with the stench of the homeless.

Washington Square Park was the place where dealers congregated, but it was also our backyard. They were part of the scenery. We just walked past them and ignored their customary greetings: "Good smoke!" "Nice ass." We were regularly grabbed in places strangers shouldn't touch. We flipped them the finger and just kept walking.

We wandered around the cobblestone streets and industrial buildings of SoHo. Artists who weren't yet discovered, and whose work would later become highly valued, mingled in new galleries that popped up, emerging high-end clothing stores, and bars that became hot with entertainment-industry types, models, and Wall Street's super-rich. The Lower East Side was still mostly tenements known for housing beat poets, struggling musicians, writers, and the homeless subculture of squatters and addicts.

One afternoon, I was mugged at knifepoint in our apartment; I heard something in the hallway, but I ignored it. Then I heard the unlocked door open. I approached the man standing there to tell him he had the wrong apartment. He pulled out a switchblade and didn't say a word. He advanced. I backed down the hallway, never taking my eyes off of him. He asked me if I had any money. I grabbed my purse from a table and gave it to him. I stayed silent.

"Give me your jewelry."

I handed him the necklace and bracelet I was wearing. "Okay," I said. "Now go."

"Don't scream, and you won't get hurt. What else you got around here?"

I heard him say "scream," and it triggered me to call for my neighbor...

"STAAAANLEEEEY　! HELP!"

Stanley was a 70-year-old, bon-vivant textile designer. His big standard poodle always at his side, Stanley was no superhero, but he could have called the cops. Stanley, however, wasn't home.

My assailant didn't like that I'd yelled for help. When his fist hit my face, I felt the warm gush of blood from my nose.

"Why are you doing this?" I asked through my hand, which was now covering my face.

"I'm a drug addict. I need the money."

Was I really interviewing my assailant?

He cut the cord from the blinds with his knife and told me to sit in a chair. He tied my hands behind me and left. I think his intention was that I wouldn't immediately be able to call the police.

I got loose quickly and called 911. The cops came, and I offered them a beer.

"You're the one that could use the drink," one of them said.

If I'd had a gun, I would have shot my attacker. I wonder how that would have felt years later, telling the *alternative* ending to this story. I'd live with a little PTSD, my nose gets broken, and he dies. I'm happier with the truth. He got away, and the cops couldn't be bothered with trying to find him. He probably died of a drug overdose, and my life went on.

New York City was emerging from the tough economic times of the Seventies. Despite my mugging, the Village was considered relatively safe, but the East Village along with "Alphabet City," "The Bowery," "Meatpacking," and Harlem were all off-limits. It was impossible to believe that those neighborhoods would one day be among the most sought-after and expensive real estate in the city.

The day MTV launched on cable in 1981 was as important to us as the launch of a space shuttle. The idea of a 24-hour, all music, commercial-free music video network was a huge media innovation. I went out and bought our new "modern" TV; the color screen was twenty-three inches and it weighed seventy-five pounds. A guy named Isaac sold it to me and gave me a good deal for the promise of a date. He and I eventually became good friends.

Fame (nominated for six Oscars) was the second-highest-grossing film that year, and a must-see for any aspiring actor or theater devotee. Its multiracial cast and behind-the-scenes look at LaGuardia High School for the Arts launched Irene Cara's career. "What a Feeling" was our theme song, setting us free as we belted out its lyrics.

Jennifer Beals' character, Alex, in *Flashdance* made a powerful statement about what was possible for a tough young girl who worked in a coal mine and dreamed of being a dancer. Her audition for a prestigious school of ballet lacked evidence of any formal training, but her outrageous, modern breakdancing won her acceptance.

Her sexy boldness offered those of us who weren't overly gorgeous, well-off, or perfect at anything the possibility of beating the odds. Both Cara and Beals were women of color. These films showcased a new kind of beauty.

Betty Freidan helmed the "women's movement," which was strengthening, and Gloria Steinem glamorized it. A new generation of us was coming on board. The Seventies and Eighties began delivering strong women in multiple sectors: politics, journalism, publishing, and law. But women were still pushing against a tidal wave of marginalization as well as physical and verbal abuse. Strong, leading women were now pouring into America's living rooms via TV, and at the same time were constantly sexually objectified. It was just the beginning of women taking their place in directing and producing, but more than twenty-five years would pass before a female director would win an Academy Award.

The warning of television's duplicitous role in American life had been forecast in the 1976 film, *Network*. The film's lead character, Howard Beale, has a mental breakdown on the air. He had an epiphany that his decades-long identity as a trusted network anchor was a lie, as was the concept of network news. A young female programmer (Faye Dunaway) negotiated for control of a new segment, allowing Beale to rant, uncensored, live on television. Ratings soared. Unheard of at the time, the film foreshadowed the eventual format of "unscripted" or "reality" TV.

We couldn't have imagined choosing from thousands of broadcast and digital options that we would one day watch on screens that wouldn't even be TVs. For us, TV was the epicenter of entertainment, yet limited to three networks and the beginning of cable. *Saturday Night Live* with its original cast of Gilda Radner, Jane Curtain, Lorraine Newman, Bill Murray, John Belushi, Steve Martin, and Garrett Morris, was hilarious and cutting edge because they dared to openly parody every part of our culture. Not even our president was spared. If we were home, we would have friends over, get stoned, and tune in.

CNN launched in 1980, bringing the world to the U.S. in real time. The networks would begin to profit in the formerly unprofitable news space. Women were finally breaking into the male-dominated genre, too. Barbara Walters, Carole Simpson, Connie Chung, and Katie Couric would co-anchor the news. Diane Sawyer and Leslie Stahl would win awards for their broadcast journalism. But those positions challenged women to compete with men who were held to different standards. Christine Craft won the nation's attention in the late Eighties with one of the first high-profile sex-discrimination cases when she was fired from a local news anchor position in Kansas City (at the age of 38) for not being young enough or pretty enough, and not being "deferential" to men.

TV, movies, music, magazines, and books influenced us and gave Kathy and me the idea that, as women in our generation, we'd be fighting stereotypes. But we also felt that we might have unprecedented possibilities. We were "Boomers," but had no idea what being part of this generation would mean until later.

In 1979, my junior year of college, I landed a summer job traveling overseas with a charter travel company. I had spent two summers (before I'd moved to New York) stuffing envelopes in a fifth-floor walk-up, alone with a radio in an old building in Boston. I didn't like my job, which was mindless, but I liked my lunch hour when I would walk around Faneuil Hall. I was determined to get something out of that experience, and I had a plan. The next summer, I was going to convince the owner, who my father knew, to allow me to travel to the Far East for the company. It was a long shot, but I was going. When the time came, he explained that sending a 19-year-old overseas was unheard of.

"I'm smart, good with people, and I know what the company does. I can do it. I'm mature for my age." What was really mature for my age were my big breasts. I was unrelenting. He finally said yes.

For three months, I stayed in Hong Kong and traveled to China, South Korea, Japan, and Thailand. I was the youngest of my team. We were the liaisons between the travelers from the U.S. and the local tour companies. My leadership skills became apparent when one passenger had a heart attack and I had to manage 350 anxious people, much older than me, readying to board a plane. A riot nearly broke out.

Few young, female Americans were traveling in Asia alone, but our partner tour operators in Hong Kong were memorable and kind. I had outgrown the hitchhiking and knife-carrying days of my teen years. Now, I was humbled by the world I was experiencing and the many cultures I was learning about. I traveled through Thailand (my favorite), South Korea (where I was strip-searched), Tokyo (where I felt isolated—a lot like the movie *Lost in Translation*), and China (which in 1979 few Americans had yet visited). When I stepped off the train in Guangzhou, Chinese people were lined up just to see the Americans coming off the trains. My reddish curly hair and big feet were of special interest.

I went to places I'd dreamed of going when I'd been that little girl twirling buttercups, lying on the grass in my friend's backyard, and imagining my life far away from our suburban development.

When my journey to the Orient began, I met a guy on the flight to Hong Kong. I think he was in his late twenties. He was starting an import/export business. He would come and go, staying with me in my hotel room when he was in Hong Kong. I liked it when he was there. He told me stories about his travels, and he knew a lot about the history of Asian art and culture. He took me to the best local places where most Americans would never get to eat. At the end of my trip, he was leaving for Bali. He wanted me to go with him.

My dutiful inner voice kicked in. *You have to go back home to Kathy and your apartment in New York, and finish school. What would your parents say? You can't just go with him.*

It was one of those decisions that would have changed the rest of my life. Doors open, doors close. But I wasn't destined to make that trip. So many things would have been different for me. I wouldn't have met Alan, so I wouldn't have Daniel in my life, and I might not have had my career. Maybe I wouldn't have lived in New York City. There were a handful of times when I might have gone left instead of right. Where would those choices have led me?

What would butterfly catching in Bali have been like? Sometimes I wonder.

BUY A GOOD SUIT

*A wise woman knows how to summon her courage
and do what is right, rather than what is easy.*
~Suze Orman~

I returned to New York for my senior year and graduated from NYU in 1980. My father's sage and encouraging words on graduation day were mixed with his pride and a challenge.

"If you like your life here and you want to stay, you'll figure out how to pay your bills."

Jimmy Carter had waltzed us into one of the worst recessions in history with fuel shortages, the Iran hostage crisis, unemployment at nearly ten percent, and interest rates at double digits. Steady work and a decent paycheck were my biggest priorities; staying in the city I loved was my goal. Regardless of my decent college pedigree, a liberal arts-educated woman without a clear professional path was less marketable than a graduate from Katharine Gibbs, the secretarial college. I had been thrown out of typing class in sixth grade for writing "The quick brown fox fucked the lazy dog." I'd also convinced myself that I'd never have to type.

I was a hybrid: a former aspiring actress who was part hippie and part writer with little to write about. Major publishers were fierce titans in an industry that relegated young, hopeful female writers to editorial jobs that required typing and paid less than $10,000 a year. I wrote essays and eloquent, long letters for my true loves. Kathy was my muse and my ear for the poems and short stories that wouldn't have a public audience. The idea of publishing seemed impossible. In the 1980s, Barnes & Noble became a mall staple, and it was my favorite store in Greenwich Village. Besides shoe shopping on 8th Street, I loved buying books, but writing one I would publish seemed impossible.

One day, I dressed up in a nice suit and went down to Merrill Lynch to apply for a stockbroker training program. I wasn't interested in a career on Wall Street, but I knew the money was good. When I arrived, I got into a line where men were waiting to fill out their applications. When I got to the front, I was told that women had to get in another line, type eighty words a minute, and pass a shorthand test. Men were being interviewed for the training programs. Women would be the secretaries for the men. I couldn't pass a typing test or take shorthand, so I was in the wrong line either way.

I thought about reaching out to the travel company I had worked for the year before, but that wasn't my dream. It would have been fun traveling overseas again, but eventually, I'd choose to come home. The way I'd been raised, the values I'd been born into, would lead me to a home that was mine in a place I knew—the modest, one-bedroom Greenwich Village apartment where Kathy and I had grown accustomed to the mice and roaches. There, if we had little else, we still had each other. I wanted a career that would afford me my dream: to wear nice clothes, eat in any restaurant, travel the world, treat my friends and family generously, and live somewhere in New York City with a view of Central Park or the East River.

I started calling travel agencies listed in the Yellow Pages. When a man answered the phone during one call, he said that if I could beat him at backgammon, he'd hire me. Strange, yes, but I was up for it. Kathy came along and waited downstairs. The office had paneling on the walls, and the windows were opaque with grime. I could tell the sun never shined through. I played backgammon well enough, but he kicked my ass. Still, he hired me. My boss's name was David. He was odd, but not mean or rude. I stayed at that dinky office for a year and a half. We were writing airline tickets for diamond dealers. (Back then, airline tickets were handwritten and kept in a safe.) I always felt like we were hiding something, though from whom I wasn't sure. I think he paid me $150 a week off the books, but it was a job.

I decided to apply to law school. I took the LSAT and was accepted at a small New York City school, but Bernie made it clear that he wasn't paying for more education. His suggestion to move home and commute to a Boston school was a nonstarter. My life in New York was to be protected at all costs.

Scenes from my previous loser jobs played in my head. When I was 15, middle class was not classy enough for my tastes, my allowance didn't cover my love of shopping for clothes, and my mother was adamant that I work. My first job was for a Hickory Farms cheese store. My assignment was to roll a cheddar-cheese-like mash into a ball and then roll that in nuts to make their famous "cheese logs." I came home stinking of the place. My next job was a step up. I worked at Herman's World of Sporting Goods. It was there that my bosses figured out I was a terrible cashier, so they made me their accessory. They would check out expensive ski equipment and high-end sporting goods at my register for significantly discounted prices. I guess they figured I was a good target since my drawer would never balance anyway. I knew this was wrong and asked to be moved to the sales floor. That was way more fun and not illegal. Next, I tried waiting tables three times and failed miserably. I had severe issues keeping track of all the orders in the fast-paced, diner-like joints where I worked that served both cocktails and food. Eventually, I got a job at a Marshalls, which was a better fit because I loved clothes, but I spent my paychecks long before the money made it home. The worst job I had was as a chambermaid. Deplorable. I worked with a woman who smoked cigarettes and drank swigs of some unknown substance while she ordered me to clean filthy rooms, which included the remains of broken liquor bottles, soiled sheets, and disgusting bathrooms. My mother would be parked in the car when I came out. "How was work?" she'd ask. Was she kidding? What in God's name could I have told her? She knew it wasn't good.

My post-college successes were won in millimeters. I finally got a job through an employment agency. I was a receptionist for a meat trader. My boss would ship sides of beef from all over the world on big container ships and sell them to supermarkets and other large-volume meat buyers. He liked me and promoted me. My job had nothing to do with the meat; I got dressed up every day and acted like I was his secretary. He had a better job for me. He had a mistress, and I was his shill. He forgave my lack of typing and shorthand skills. Despite the girlfriend, he still tried to French-kiss me and grabbed me repeatedly. He was also a screamer. One day, I'd had enough. I went out to lunch and didn't return. Quitting wasn't something foreign to me, but quitting a job was different. This wasn't something encouraged by my parents—especially my father, who had worked since he was nine and had been on welfare growing up. I went home and hurled my failed self onto the couch. I called my mother, sobbing, but she was in a meeting.

The next day, I became an entrepreneur. I bought three *really* good suits: a black Pierre Cardin, a white Jones New York, and a green Albert Nipon. I couldn't afford even one of them, but I'd recently acquired a credit card, and no one was going to talk me out of it. I maxed it out. My business strategy was that if I invested in those suits, I'd at least look like I was worthy of consideration by a potential employer. I'd get a good job and pay off the card.

After failing typing tests and being told I was unemployable, I was finally hired for a temp job at a production company. The boss walked by my desk.

"What are you doing here?"

"I'm the temp. Someone told me to sit here and answer phones."

"Who do you think you are, dressed like that? When you work in production, you might have to plunge toilets."

The boss called me into his office and told me I should look for a job with a little "power" in it—maybe go to work for a talent agent. I didn't know exactly what a talent agent did, but he'd said it with so much conviction. Toilet plunging didn't seem like a fun way to become a TV producer. The job was all wrong for me, but I still loved my suits.

Now I was unemployed again. I was a failure, but I didn't want to act that way. I threw a fox stole Kathy's mother had given her over the black Pierre Cardin suit and marched off to a lecture at NYU. Tom Wolfe was speaking. The film *The Right Stuff*, based on the book he had written, had just been released.

An older man sitting behind me leaned forward and told me he liked my suit. I thought he was disgusting and politely rejected his offer to take me out for a drink. Then he asked me if I wanted to meet Tom Wolfe. That worked better. If he knew Tom Wolfe, I thought, maybe I should be nice to him. He asked me what I did for a living, and I told him I was a TV producer. (I figured that sounded good even though I didn't know what a TV producer did.)

He challenged me.

"What do you produce?"

"Well, I'm not producing yet, but I will be. TV, I hope."

"I was a TV producer. Who do you know?"

He had me.

"Nobody," I said, remembering the toilet plunger story. He said that he had a Rolodex and contacts in the business.

"What about that drink?" he asked.

I was a little afraid of the quid pro quo—but I went. The old man told me he'd been a TV producer in the 1940s and 1950s, in the days of live TV, for a program called *Studio One Television*. Now he owned a talent agency, and he represented Tom Wolfe.

I chose a nearby bar where the bartender knew me.

The old man was one of the first talent agents who, with his wife, represented performers for commercials, film, and television. His lengthy client list boasted all of the TV-commercial stars I had grown up watching, including Madge the Manicurist. For forty years, the actress Jan Miner was responsible for Palmolive being the #1 dish-washing detergent. I later learned she was paid hundreds of thou-sands of dollars to be "Madge." That was serious money in 1982. She was his biggest client. I wasn't certain of what the old man saw in *me* beyond my pretty face and that suit, but he offered me a job as his assistant.

I spent the next three years working for him.

The good news was that he didn't care if I could type or take shorthand, and I had found a job I liked. The bad news was that I had to accompany him all over town visiting advertising agencies and bars where the people we were meeting didn't like him. I convinced him he had to pay for my dry cleaning because I left work smelling like the fat, stinky cigars he smoked. He didn't behave well, either. He regularly smacked my butt and tried to shove his tongue in my mouth. I would make light of it and tell him to cut it out. We had work to do. It was annoying, but I "filed" it. I had better things to focus on.

The best thing that happened was when he tossed me a script for an animated series. He left me alone in the office with his scary wife, who hated me. I'm not sure what was more threatening—her voice or her long, red fingernails.

The first challenge was that I had to rack up the client's voice demo reels on the old "reel-to-reel" machine. If I made a mistake, the tape that was threaded through a series of little wheels would snap and break. This wasn't good. Asking his witchy wife for help would make things worse. Every once in a while, she would come in and give me a dirty look. *Are you still here?* By the morning, I had listened to the reels, and I'd matched all of the characters in the script with the actors I thought could voice them.

Even though Lester took all the credit, we booked three of the main roles for the series, which was called *ThunderCats*. This was fast and fun and didn't take as long as movie or theatrical deals. I was excited and wanted to do more of those castings. Eventually, the old man promoted me to be an agent. I began to focus mostly on voice performers in commercials. I was lucky that my desk, now at the other end of the office, was far away from his. I'd been relocated to sit next to Marilyn, a veteran agent who was willing to mentor me. She was a pro—soft-spoken, calculating, and elegant. She was nothing like the old man. I listened while she charmed the clients and made great deals. There weren't very many female agents to begin with, and she was black. I thought she was brave. I wanted to be like her. I started to figure out that most of the people the old man did business with thought he was eccentric and obnoxious. At 25, I respected what he had accomplished, but I thought his small business was limited. It was time to see what other opportunities might be out there.

I handwrote a letter to his biggest competitor, the founder of an up-and-coming talent agency that was dominating the New York commercials business. The old man disliked him, and

I wanted to know more. I got a call and a compliment on my beautiful handwriting. When I met the agency owner, he spoke quietly and thoughtfully and asked me a lot of questions about my life and my family. It was obvious he took his business very seriously, and success was of great importance to him. We met for a while, but he told me that because I didn't have a clientele that would follow me, I wasn't a strong candidate.

I thought I could easily build a client list. He just didn't know it. I didn't think an interview that had lasted over an hour should have resulted in outright rejection.

I sat on my couch at home. There must be other agencies to try.

A week later, I got a call at my office. The voice on the other end of the phone introduced himself as "Scott."

"Can you talk?"

He worked with the man I had just met. He explained that he knew I had visited the *ThunderCats* recording sessions and had been friendly with his clients who were also on the series. I thought I was in trouble, but he suggested that we meet. I learned it wasn't a bad thing. He liked that I was outgoing and "aggressive." (In the male-dominated industry of the 1980s, this was a compliment.) I was making myself known. He suggested I return for another meeting.

I met with Scott and his partner Steve. They both advocated for my hiring. I was offered $5,000 less than what the old man was paying. That was a lot of money. I tried to negotiate, but it was "take it or leave it." I was in no position to take $5,000 less. I was in no position to leave it.

One big incentive was that Scott was gay. At least he wouldn't sexually harass me.

THE SON YOUR FATHER DREAMED YOU'D BE

Most parents would hope the whole thing goes away,
or pray that their sons land on their feet soon enough.
~André Aciman~

One day, when I was in my late twenties, I saw my friend Marc sitting in the lobby where I worked. I hadn't seen him in a couple of years.

"Marc?" I moved closer so that I could hug him, but he backed away and looked down. His face was covered with red blotches. He told me a dish had blown up; it had been a "bad accident."

"I'm here to do a catering job. I am in catering now."

We stood there awkwardly looking at each other. It took me a minute to put it together, but I had seen it before—the irregular reddish-purple splotches were telltale signs of Kaposi's sarcoma, a deadly AIDS-related cancer.

When I met Marc, I was 19. His face was angelic, and his body was hot. I liked the way he spelled his name with a "c" and the way his teeth lined up in a perfect smile when his full lips parted into a grin. His eyes were playful, like light dancing on water. On the days we went to class together at NYU, we ate chocolate chip cookies in Washington Square Park. We shared the tri-colore salad and an eggplant rollatini appetizer, which were the least expensive items on the menu at a small, romantic place nearby called Volare. We got caught passing notes and laughed at our serious literature professor while he lectured on Rilke and the *Duino Elegies*. On weekends, we often hung out in his apartment on West 72nd Street. We cooked poached shrimp and asparagus with hollandaise sauce, drank cheap Verdicchio, and dined al fresco in his tiny garden. We walked in Central Park and talked about our dreams. He wanted to be an actor. I wanted to be a writer.

After months of hanging out, we went to a party one night. I drank and smoked enough to take him by the hand into the bedroom.

"C'mon," I coaxed him with a sexy smile.

At the doorway, he stopped. He touched my face and pointed across the room to a handsome man wearing a suit. The man was twice our age. "I'm in love with him."

Marc's purple knee socks, funky sunglasses, loafers, and pink shorts should have tipped me off, but I hadn't seen it coming.

Even though he broke my heart, the walks in the park and the soirees didn't end. After we graduated, he tried to pursue acting. I just wanted to get my bills paid so I could stay in New York City. By the mid-1980s, we had drifted apart. Maybe it was because we didn't have a lot of time for the kind of fun we'd had before, back when all the time in the world was ours for the taking.

It was less than a year after I'd seen him in my office when his partner called to share the details of Marc's memorial service. Marc was probably 28 when he died. My beautiful, talented friend had been taken by the mysterious sickness that was claiming gay men's lives.

By the time the disease had a name, it was too late to stop it. The GMHC (Gay Men's Health Crisis) was founded to provide a resource center for education and support related to the epidemic of AIDS. Pamphlets and posters were displayed all over Greenwich Village. Gay activism was rounding another corner. The existing discrimination against gay people and "their" disease was primarily ravaging two major U.S. cities: New York and San Francisco. The few doctors who were specializing in AIDS-related infectious diseases were overwhelmed. Demands for a cure or vaccination were slow to bring action. The affected population was too narrow a demographic, and the large pharmaceutical companies didn't yet have enough data to prove that the first drugs being introduced were effective.

Shows with gay themes were winning Tony Awards: *A Chorus Line*, *La Cage aux Folles*, *The Normal Heart*, *Torch Song Trilogy*, and *The Boys in the Band*. But by the late 1980s, the discos and nightclubs in the city started closing down. The music died along with the countless young men who had given their lives to the epidemic that decimated them.

My colleague Scott and I became good friends. Born into the first generation of openly gay men, he paid dearly. He provided support and cosigned the health directives of men whose families had abandoned them and who were far too young to be thinking of the end of their lives. For years, he cared for his partner Lee, who had been neglected by his own family. Scott and I, and Scott's friend Orly, sat vigil by Lee's side into the early hours of an August morning when his fight ended, and he quietly passed on.

Two years after Lee died, high atop Scott's shoulders at the Gay Pride Parade in Greenwich Village, my son Daniel laughed at the floats and the outlandish outfits and outbursts of joy happening around us. At five, he didn't know just how significant this celebration was.

Scott's story of inner conflict, hiding for fear of being "outed," is the typical narrative for middle-aged gay men. As a child, he was bullied and hurt, and yet, later, he was armed with a certain determination that his identity would not be limited by his shame. The entertainment industry was a safe haven. He was my mentor and taught me what I needed to know about our business so that I could succeed. Mostly, Scott taught me about being generous and fierce, and to have courage. He was a tough guy and a strong advocate, but he may not have been the man his father dreamed he'd be. His parents didn't always celebrate those parts of him I loved—his romanticism and his heart, which he offered in whole to so many who were lost to the decade of death.

My son is older now than my Marc was when we were in our early twenties and hung out in Washington Square Park. I can't imagine Daniel's friends, suddenly and in large numbers, dying.

When I walk through the park, I think of Marc and how we laughed about the notes we passed. I think of the big chocolate chip cookies, his beautiful smile, and how I forgave him—not once, but twice—for breaking my heart. I still miss him. I have walked the block where he lived and stopped in front of his building. I imagine us in that apartment, goofing around, and remember all those Upper West Side afternoons we shared. I wonder what we'd say to each other now. I would thank him for the dreams we shared, the meals we cooked, the walks we took, and the way we laughed when New York City was still new and we were discovering ourselves. He taught me to love a man in a way I had never loved before. I wonder who he might have become.

BROOKLYN

Brooklyn of ample hills was mine,
I too walk'd the streets of Manhattan island,
and bathed in the waters around it,
I too felt the curious abrupt questionings stir within me...
~Walt Whitman~

By the mid-1980s, the clubs were closing. The music was changing. Socializing was different, but so was I.

I was coming of age at a time that was turbulent and often confusing. The women's movement was going full tilt, and the AIDS epidemic was just beginning, taking thousands of lives. Cocaine, crack, heroin, and pills of every variety, once reserved for the underground, were now—along with massive quantities of alcohol—readily available forms of recreation. Finding ourselves in the vortex of this, Kathy and I were forging ahead by figuring out how we fit in and who we aspired to be. We struggled with setbacks, balancing our social lives and love lives as well as our aspirations. Trying to keep our balance wasn't easy. Men were usually at the epicenter of our dramatic crescendos and our deepest dives.

The year before I graduated from college, I fell in love. I met my boyfriend at a dance club, and our chemistry was like Krazy Glue. We were inseparable. He was handsome, romantic, and fun. He was the love of my life...or so I thought. Kathy was away in London at graduate school, studying acting. Within a year, he moved into the Waverly Place apartment with me, and then we announced our engagement.

Our wedding would be the following year. When I met his parents, they interrogated me. It was worse than a job interview. My pursuit of a career, in lieu of staying home to be the wife and mother of their son's children, made me a bad prospect. A more demure, conservative woman from a much wealthier family would have made the grade, but as it was, they didn't attempt to hide their disdain.

When they realized we were serious and had every intention of being married, they invited my parents to their home for what we thought was a wedding-planning visit. Instead, it was an intervention. They announced over dinner that not only were they unsupportive of our relationship, but they also wouldn't invite a single person to our wedding.

As my parents were leaving, I felt so embarrassed and hurt that I didn't know what to say to them. I was ashamed and felt responsible for naively walking them into an ambush. My fiancé's father had been adamant; he made it clear he was going to get his way.

To my parents' credit, they were willing to go on with the wedding. His parents forced him to choose—them or me. The stress of their disapproval cut a deep gash in his relationship with them.

I knew that if we married, we'd have lifelong difficulties. His parents had a lot of control—they were very well off, and my fiancé worked for his father. He was insistent that he would always choose me over them, and I was sure he would eventually resent me. It was reminiscent of *Romeo and Juliet,* and I foresaw our fatal ending.

Two months before the wedding, I called my father to tell him. I had to cancel. His voice was gentle: "It's a drop in the bucket if you'll have a life of pain." The beautiful wedding dress my mother had bought me went to a consignment shop. I felt guilty and sorry for the loss of what should have been a joyful time for all of us. Their unrelenting support was loving, but they probably felt relief, too.

Over the next year, he and I stayed together, but he coped with his parents' contempt by using large quantities of cocaine and alcohol, and by gambling. His parents were quick to blame me, but I saved his life when I insisted he go to rehab.

A month later, when he got out, we tried to make it work, but it was over.

I was heartbroken.

Kathy and I always had boyfriends, and being alone didn't feel right to us. I'm not exactly sure why. Was it the era, our anthropological design to mate, or maybe we were just young and couldn't see the great value of finding out who we were if we decided to be alone? After the breakup, I casually dated some guys, but by the time I was 28, I didn't know what to look for. When it came to marriage, I wasn't sure I was listening to the right voice. Marrying and having children was the "typical" thing to do, but many women of our generation were also forging ahead with careers and bypassing starting families—especially in major cities, where women were waiting much longer before "settling down."

Alan and I met when I was 28 at a place called Mary Lou's, a busy Greenwich Village bar and restaurant where models and artists hung out. He and his good friend Howard sat down next to me. They seemed nice enough. Alan was quick to make it clear that his buddy had a girlfriend.

Alan's eyes were blue like a cloudless sky. I hoped he thought I was pretty. I dragged on my Dunhill cigarette and turned my head, letting a slow and steady stream of smoke trickle from my lips. When I turned back, I asked him if he minded the smoke.

"I hate it."

I liked his honesty, or so I thought.

I found out he was an artist and a photographer. He lived in Brooklyn, and he was about to celebrate his 39th birthday. It was cold out that night, and he offered to drive me home. I lived around the corner, but I said okay. He parked outside my building. The heat of our breath and the smoke from a joint we shared fogged the windows of his car. He placed his foot on the windshield and drew a fish in the shape it left. He made me laugh and then kissed me.

After we started dating, I quit cigarettes.

Months of my stuffing a change of clothes into a bag and spending nights at his place made my city friends curious. "How's it going with that guy?"

I would laugh and say, "Yeah, well, he's from *Brooklyn*."

Brooklyn then was uncool and nothing like Greenwich Village. Park Slope was the Brooklyn neighborhood where Alan lived. Later, it became *the* Gold Coast of the borough, but it would be another twenty years before an influx of city dwellers would make the neighborhood and its real estate valuable. At the time, it was very middle class. There were many older people there, mostly Italian and Irish families who had originally settled "the slope" in the early part of the century. Young couples with babies were just beginning to move in.

I wanted to be sure Alan was the one, and I wasn't so *sure* about Brooklyn. With every trip to his house, I thought of myself as a city defector. I couldn't imagine the neighborhood's future celebrity. The building Alan owned was built in the 1870s. When he bought it, it was mostly "raw" square footage. It was the kind of place only a young artist with very little money would agree to buy.

The buildings on that corner weren't fancy or desired, as they later became. They were mostly dilapidated, their warrior exteriors a good front for what little was left inside. I had seen pictures from the early 1970s when Alan had moved in. A step on the wrong plank would have sent him plummeting to the basement. He was a sculptor and a photographer who would make do just by having the space, where he could be creative. A whole floor of the building was his designated "art studio." Before I moved in, he had renovated a storefront and a small apartment to create income, which was smart. He lived on the top two floors. I wondered if he would ever renovate them.

It was bohemian and rough, but it appealed to the "artsy" part of me.

When I first started going to Brooklyn, a few little cafes dotted the main drag. I rationalized that Prospect Park was only two blocks away with its sweeping willows and lawns. We made picnics and went to weekend concerts. We took long walks there and rode our bikes along its perimeter. Like Central Park, it had a zoo and a carousel. We would hop on his motorcycle and ride into the city to visit galleries and hang out with his artist friends. We both liked the same music, good restaurants, red wine, getting tanned, and traveling to warm places with beautiful beaches.

Being with Alan was an adventure; he was intriguing. He had been to Woodstock. In the Seventies, when most Americans wouldn't have considered it, he traveled to the Middle East. He was a sculptor, using plastic to make visual art. He had consulted with the U.S. Olympic Committee to help create a safer luge mask. He was a photographer and an inventor of sorts. But what characterized him most was how he loved his Brooklyn pedigree; when the Brooklyn Bridge was being renovated for its centennial, he bought up some of the original granite and made "Bridgestones" a keepsake he sold. He spoke with a thick Brooklyn accent, which at first I thought was kind of funny because he sounded like Robert De Niro in *Taxi Driver*, but it grew on me.

A year after we met, I left my beloved Greenwich Village apartment and moved in with him. It wasn't an easy decision, but I was in love. As I walked the block from the F train down Ninth Street to his home, the neighbor kids waved and smiled at me as if to say, "Yay! You are one of us now!" I felt initiated, and my ambivalence started to fade. Alan made planters for me, and I created a roof garden. I picked up garbage from the sidewalk and yelled at the same homeless guy who regularly pissed on the building. I was becoming one of them, and yet, it was still unclear exactly how I would fit in.

A CROOKED SMILE

A smile is a curve that sets everything straight.
~Phyllis Diller~

One day, I was doing sit-ups. My temple swelled with pressure as my head touched the floor and flattened when I raised it. Alan took me to his friend, who was a radiologist. After that, a series of tests revealed I had a golf-ball-sized benign vascular tumor. It had been growing in my left temple. As it expanded, its ganglion of veins stubbornly grew around the bone of my cranium. I'd been unaware of it until it began bulging in the space it had dug next to my left eye. It was not cancerous, but it had to come out.

The news of the tumor and its impending removal came just weeks prior to our leaving for the Caribbean for a scuba diving trip we'd planned. I was determined that the diagnosis was not going to interfere. *We were going.*

On the second night of the trip, we left our hotel room and headed for a restaurant. Alan was edgy. When we got to the place, he was fidgeting, and he rejected the first table we were offered. I wasn't sure what was on his mind. I thought maybe he wanted to talk about the turmoil of the doctor's visits and the unwanted visitor in my head.

But after we sat down, he cleared his throat a few times, leaned over, and quietly asked if I would marry him. I was surprised. He offered a simple band of diamonds and rubies, and I said yes. Undeterred by the threat that my mysterious tumor could cause a stroke that would kill or permanently maim me, we were both brave—or seriously in denial.

When we returned from Tortola, I had a lot of calls to make. I first announced to my family and best friend that Alan had proposed and that we were thinking of getting married sooner rather than later. Alan and I had been together for a year and a half. It didn't seem like we needed a long engagement.

Then, I began seeking opinions about the "management" of my tumor. My options were few:

1. An experimental technique utilizing lasers and radioactive "pummeling"

2. An old-fashioned "excision" requiring a scalpel, stitches, a long hospital stay, and weeks of recovery

The experimental approach seemed risky. The aggressive and self-assured neurosurgeons at the NYU Medical Center couldn't convince me of why my head should offer target practice for some newly developed and rarely performed procedure. What if this "stuff" they were shooting into me missed the vascular anomaly and careened into my brain? I wasn't intrigued or sold on it.

We were told that the tumor wasn't going to explode and that I could put off surgery, but not for very long. Still, I wasn't immediately opting for a surgery that "might" leave my face paralyzed for some unknown period of time and would ruin my wedding pictures.

We planned to get married within six months. Our honeymoon would be a two-week diving trip to the Cayman Islands. That trip wasn't negotiable. I'd invested in learning to dive, thinking Alan and I weren't the type who'd be playing tennis or golf. We loved going to islands with beautiful beaches. The scuba lessons had been hard because I'd always been afraid of drowning and hated getting water up my nose, but I'd managed them because Alan loved diving. I just hoped that diving and vascular tumors were copacetic.

Alan and I picked a venue on Fifth Avenue—around the corner from my former apartment, close to the bar where we had met. We planned a beautiful, semi-traditional ceremony and added a twist—a rock band that had never played a wedding. On April 24, 1990, Alan and I, and the tumor that no one could see, walked down the aisle. And then that summer, we went diving as planned.

By October, it had been a year since I'd learned of the resident hiding in my head. A week before the surgery, José, my trusted hairstylist, chopped off my long, curly hair. With each snip, I grew quieter. My hair was part of my identity. It had changed as my life had changed. Short, long, red, blonde, asymmetrical, curly, and straight. Now, chunks of my mane lay on the floor. I had been warned that if I left it long, the care of my hair around the incision would become an issue. So, I just cut it off. I figured it would be easier to care for if short, and it would grow back.

Dr. Biller had carefully explained how he would make the incision. It would run neatly along my ear and inch its way into my scalp, and there it would remain hidden. I placed one finger at the base of my ear and another a few inches above it and guessed the incision might be about eight inches.

I don't remember much about the surgery, or even the exact date—just that it was an October day in 1990.

"Are you okay?" I heard a woman's voice from far away.

"ARE YOU OKAY?" This time, her voice was louder.

I tried to open my eyes, but it felt like there were heavy sandbags on them. I couldn't move my head. Was I okay? I didn't know. My mouth was dry. I couldn't make sound come out of my lips. But I heard words in my head, so I could still think—my brain was working.

I wanted to say, "My head hurts." But I couldn't speak. I just moaned.

"I know," the nurses said. "You had quite the surgery."

I reached for her hand. My head felt like someone had cut through it with a chainsaw. I needed to hold on to someone. I later found out the surgery had taken six hours.

After the egg-sized tumor was removed, thirty stitches were used to close me up. While I'd been under anesthesia, a nurse had corn-rowed my hair so that the incision could be made. I raised my hand to touch my head, which felt like a bowling ball. It was wrapped in layers of gauze. There was an intravenous line in my right arm and a tube draped by my shoulder.

After the morphine kicked in, things were better.

Alan was there when I got to my room. Even in my hazy condition, I whispered to him to get me a private room. The thought of sharing a room was awful. I think he took one look at me, and it hit him. The surgery had been very serious. I'm not sure how, but he managed to get me the private room. Kathy was traveling overseas, so she couldn't be there, but my two friends Scott and Mary came to visit. They were making jokes about how I looked. My head was mummified.

Ten days later, I was released. Food interested me less than dou-ble doses of painkillers. I'd experienced something that would be hard to explain. I could barely open my mouth, and most of my nu-trition was delivered through a straw. The left side of my face didn't work; my eye was droopy. I couldn't raise my eyebrow. With each passing day, I would try to get the left side of my mouth to rise with equal enthusiasm as my right. Nothing. I had half of a smile.

As I emerged from a cocoon of gauze, the outside world felt over-whelming and loud.

"The facial nerve has not been damaged," said Dr. Biller, breath-ing on my face as he examined me. "Sutures are coming along."

He was the expert. What choice did I have but to believe him? I was curious to see what the incision looked like, but I was not ready to look. Not yet.

Surgeons don't make promises. He didn't know when I would be able to open my mouth wide enough to eat an apple or get my teeth cleaned. The latter was not the most important thing to me; I was just trying to make sense of what I couldn't have been prepared for. My uncertainty was the source of my faith. I would get through this. I would smile again.

My recovery required me to stay home from work for six weeks. Before the surgery, this recommendation had seemed like an eternity. I had worked nonstop for the past ten years. My career and job at the talent agency were the primary focus of my life. I wanted to return and keep growing.

As the weeks at home passed, my membership in the "Yuppie" (young, upwardly-mobile professional) club suddenly seemed less important. The career I was so committed to, the workouts I'd missed, the car we would buy...they were all diminished by the surgery. My new best friend was Percocet, and I wandered in search of greater meanings for my life. At 32, I was facing my mortality.

I learned about tarot and my astrological chart. According to the cosmos, Saturn makes its full orbit every 29.5 years, thus journeying back to the exact place where it aligns astrologically to the time you were born. Most people experience introspection and questioning at this point. It's a time when young people begin their journey into adulthood, leaving behind what is no longer useful and questing for what's next.

I had already been on my own for fourteen years. I had followed through with the conventional choices I'd been raised to equate with stability and success—a job and marriage. Before the surgery, I'd wanted to rise to the top of my profession, make a beautiful home, and share life's unknowns with my husband. All that had seemed like enough. Now, lucky to be alive, some part of me *still* didn't feel whole.

I kept remembering fragments of conversations with Alan about children. The sound bites started as whispers and grew louder. Whenever we had discussed it in the past, I'd been reluctant. Having a baby wasn't important to me. He was almost 42, and he wanted children while he was still relatively young and healthy so that he could be involved and enjoy them. *Was it crazy for me to be entertaining this?* If I did get pregnant, having a baby would be the only thing I would ever do in my life that would be irrevocable. Marriages can end and careers can change, but babies are forever. That was a fact. It was huge.

I wasn't sure if this was behind the void I was feeling, but something in me was not complete.

Two months after my surgery, I was back to work. I was coming out of the fog of the painkillers and the isolation of weeks spent alone. I felt grateful to be feeling good, but my life wasn't peaceful. Things had taken on a sense of urgency I couldn't quiet. I would lie in bed and stare at the cracks in the ceiling, thinking it would fall down on me. This bohemian home wasn't feeling "hip" anymore. It was feeling dumpy. The thought of having a baby hadn't left me, and if we were going to even consider it, we definitely needed to renovate.

We could refinance the current mortgage and use the money to make our home more comfortable, and we could add another bedroom. We made a plan to live in the space and do the work in sections. We would just keep moving around the two floors. We had 2,500 square feet to work with; it would take a year. It felt like something to look forward to, something we would do together to make Alan's building into our home.

It was early January when the work began. I slowly climbed the stairs to the first landing. I heard banging and men speaking in Spanish. I climbed the next set of stairs. I approached the place where we cooked our meals, where we usually ate and talked and slept. There was just rubble. The walls were gone. Men pushed past me, carting wheelbarrows of plaster shards. Piles of 100-year-old wood and dust were everywhere. I stepped in my high heels over the mess. The exposed guts of the far wall were shocking. It had been demolished so fast. The wood was yellowish and rotted. It smelled musty from being sealed for so long. I made my way toward Alan, who stood with the contractor in the middle of what had once been the kitchen. I wanted a reassuring hug. He handed me an old newspaper they had found in the wall as if this were something that might sweep the horrified look from my face.

"Look at this!" I noticed the date on the top of the paper—it was from the 1950s.

Yeah, cool! I thought, but the chaos was more than I could stomach. I handed the paper back to him and sought refuge in our bedroom, which had not yet been gutted.

A couple of weeks later, I tried to reconcile how this blown-out hole would become our home again. My surgery had only been three months earlier. I questioned our sanity. Was it too soon to do this? Was I strong enough? How would we cope with the ongoing upheaval? Alan was letting go of his hippie past with its macramé potholders, spider plants, and hammock in the middle of the living room. I was letting go of my single, capricious past. My identity as his wife drew me into a new level of adulthood. As the house became the upgraded home we had imagined, we were both letting go of our carefree pasts. After only nine months of being married, I wondered if my dream of marriage was just something I had concocted from movies and romantic novels. The more the building changed, the more I saw how Alan was becoming more controlling, and I was acquiescing. I thought that maybe it was his adjustment to this new life, departing the life he had made there for so many years without me.

For weeks, when I returned from work, there'd be a bunch of guys I didn't know banging and hauling debris until well into the night. Alan was resourceful with his quirky, homemade remedies, trying to convince me that everything would be okay like with the "kitchen" he rigged from a sheet of drywall, a rice cooker, a microwave, and a hotpot. He didn't want to discuss my discomfort and fears about the environment being so dirty, news of asbestos being dangerous, or what unknowns lived within the floors and walls of this antique building we were ripping apart.

I looked at Pottery Barn catalogues and dreamed of a pristine, new, upscale life.

One morning, I sat on the bed, and from behind the plastic, make-shift wall, I surveyed the mess. I didn't know if I should laugh or cry, or what I should feel. It wasn't the best time to tell Alan about the one thing we hadn't planned for. The pregnancy test I held in my hand was "positive."

THERE'S SOMETHING ABOUT DANIEL

Daniel (Hebrew): "With God as my judge."

The delivery had been "uneventful." *Uneventful*. What a strange word for a birth. It was language I later read in Daniel's hospital record.

The birth was a planned C-section. I climbed up on the table with a fetal monitor strapped around my middle. I was told our baby was "doing great". There were some low-level contractions, but I didn't feel them. I didn't go into labor. No awe, fear, or surprise first pains. I'd been given an epidural, and I mostly remember being cold and shivering uncontrollably.

I was tented, and our obstetrician described in detail what he was doing. Breathing through an oxygen mask, I could only feel some pushing and pulling. I could see the masked faces of the doctors and nurses, past my raised knees, and then, our baby being lifted out of me. He was carried across the delivery room to the corner, where he was cleaned up and swaddled. I don't remember him crying. He just squirmed a little and let out a high-pitched squeal. It wasn't a robust declaration. It was an inquiry as if he was asking permission to be there. A stream of urine arced from his tiny, naked body and soaked the doctor's pants. Our proper obstetrician didn't wear scrubs; he was wearing dress pants. He held our baby out in front of him to avoid a further soaking. Then, he carefully handed the baby off to Alan. That done, the doctor bent over, rolled up his pants, and continued doing whatever obstetricians do after they deliver babies. My eyes followed my son as he was being moved around the delivery room. He was cleaned and wrapped. There was whispering over in the corner, and he disappeared behind a huddle of nurses.

I was mired in the trappings of surgical stirrups, epidural paralysis, tubing, and an oxygen mask. Alan's eyes went soft, and his hands trembled as he held our baby for the first time. My husband was 43. He had done a lot of things, but neither of us had experienced anything like this. Until this moment, he hadn't known the baby I had come to love long before this day.

For months, I wondered what the ultrasound technicians saw, chattering away with their enthusiastic babble that everything "looked great!" In the low-resolution, grayish blur of the sonograms, they pointed out our baby's face, his hands, and his feet. I tried to see the glory in those eerie pictures. After we found out he was a boy, I was content just knowing I would soon meet "my son." I would later say those words with propriety, the way I'd practiced saying "my husband" when Alan and I had first been married. I felt our son kicking and rolling and twitching as he moved inside me. Together, we hobbled up and down stairs with swollen ankles and a bladder that couldn't wait one more minute. At night, I laid in bed, rubbed my belly, and sang to him, wondering, *Who are you?*

"Is everything okay?" I mumbled through the mask.

The sound of my hoarse voice surprised me. Alan just nodded. He didn't speak. I tracked the nurse who came and took my son out of my view. A huddle of doctors and nurses stood with their backs to us, whispering. Alan was still by my side. I stretched to see what they were doing. My legs were suspended in stirrups. It was too quiet.

My obstetrician asked, "Doing okay?" and before I could say anything, he added, "We are just going to finish you up." Only half of me could feel the pulling as I was being sewn back together. I was still cold and shaking. I wanted the doctor to hurry so that I could hold my baby. The only sounds were the beeps of the monitors, the rush of my breath through the oxygen mask, and the accent of the anesthesiologist's voice behind me, asking again if I was okay. I nodded, but tears streamed down my face.

I had never given birth before. I didn't know if I was okay. I had never been in a delivery room. I'd thought there would be more noise.

When they wheeled me into the recovery room, a nurse with thick, sweet perfume and dark hair on her lip took our baby from Alan and handed him to me. I had never felt anything like what I felt in that moment. He was very sleepy; his head rested on my chest. Our son had dark hair, and his face reminded me of my Grandma Bessie. There was peace for a minute. Then, without warning, the nurse swooped down like a vulture and seized him. As she lifted him away from me, she said that she was taking him to be "warmed." He was too cold. It happened so fast that I couldn't protest. I looked at Alan as if to say, "Do something." We were both overcome with confusion. I didn't remember reading anything about babies being too cold. With our baby in her arms, the nurse disappeared. I looked at Alan with desperation, but he didn't say anything.

The pediatrician we had interviewed a month earlier walked in. Someone must have called her. She explained that, although everything seemed fine, there were some things about our baby that were unusual. He had been born with only one umbilical artery, which meant he might have renal or brain damage. His left hip was dislocated. He had some features that she described as "dysmorphic." This meant he didn't look like other babies. His face looked "different." There was no robust cry of declaration to say: "I am here!" She was concerned that his lungs were underdeveloped. All this, she explained, meant a team of neonatal specialists would intervene. But it was the geneticists, with their uninvited forensics, who scared me most. They were in search of a syndrome or diagnosis. If they found it, what would that mean? A life sentence of unknowns from which there'd be no return? Our pediatrician told us that an orthopedist would be in to see about his hip in the morning. This mini-militia of medical personnel and all the terminology flying at me were just annoyances. I nodded when they spoke, and their words floated away like the autumn leaves that fell outside. I only remember wanting my baby back in my arms.

Night fell. It was time for Alan to leave. *What was taking the nurses so long? Where was my son?* The curtains that separated the woman next to me were drawn, but I lay there for hours listening to her quietly talking to her baby. I was fighting the drugs, trying to stay awake in case they brought my own baby back.

Hours later, a nurse handed my son to me. "You need to feed him."

I think it was around 2 a.m. I was swimming up, up, up through the morphine as my uterus contracted with labor-like cramps. This was another thing I hadn't read about. I felt like someone was ripping me open, and I would pass out from the pain of it. I had my son, but I didn't know how to feed him. My hands were bound with tape, shackled by the IVs. Because of the pain of the incision and the contractions, I couldn't sit up. My baby seemed so tired. I carefully pulled my hospital gown down to expose my breast. He turned away, and I closed my eyes. I held him tightly. I had never held a newborn baby. It was like the smell of baking cookies, hot chocolate, caramel, or vanilla. I had him in my arms, fragile like a bird I'd once rescued in my backyard and nursed back to life. Whatever the pediatrician had been trying to tell us earlier, we would all be fine. Nothing was wrong. No one would take him away now; no, now we would just go to sleep.

A voice startled me. I wasn't sure if I was dreaming. It wasn't the sweet angel of new mothers who had come to help guide me through the surreal. The nurse loomed over me. There was sweat on her forehead. "Did he eat?" she barked at me. It seemed like all these nurses were much larger than me, big-breasted, and had the same dark hair on their upper lips. This one spoke like a drill sergeant. I moved my head from side to side. I couldn't speak. She reached over and lifted my son off of me, shaking her head in pity. That was it. I had failed. I was being punished for not knowing how to feed him. I tried to call after her, but I couldn't make the words come. I wanted to get up, but I was tethered to all kinds of equipment. The nurse who'd taken him away didn't turn back; they were gone in seconds. Fighting the drugs and the pain, I tried to reach for the phone to call Alan, but I couldn't make the stretch, and then I resigned myself to the tidal wave of tears that took over and the sleep that swept me under.

The next morning, I was exhausted and wished Alan could be there. He was at home supervising the renovation that was still underway. With our baby coming home soon, he was fighting with the contractor to get the work done as soon as possible.

A social worker came to speak with me. I glared at her as she introduced herself and asked, in the same way that elementary school teachers speak to their first-grade students, "Are you okay?"

I didn't answer immediately. Then I said, "I need to find my son."

"They have him in neonatal care. Everything is going to be okay."

That word "okay" was getting annoying.

"His glucose levels fell, and they just want to run some tests. Let's talk." She moved closer to me.

"No, no, I don't want to talk." My voice was wavering. "I just want to see my baby."

"They—are—just—running—some—tests," she said slowly and calculatingly as if she were speaking to a wild animal.

"What kinds of tests?" I demanded.

"I can try to find out for you," she said.

"No. *No!* I am his mother, and *I* will find out." Except... I couldn't move from my bed.

I closed my eyes, and that was when the tears started. She sat in silence, her hands folded on her lap.

"Can you please, please, get me to my baby?" I whispered.

She asked if I had spoken with my pediatrician. No. But I needed to call her. I also needed help. I couldn't dial the phone. I couldn't walk. The social worker asked if I had her number.

I whispered her name. "Please, call her. *Please.*"

Later that morning, one of the nurses put me into a wheelchair. If she hadn't, I would have crawled down the hallway to find my son. I pushed myself toward the double doors marked NICU (Neonatal Intensive Care Unit). The bright lights, the smell, the energy level... everything about it was intense. I guessed that was why it was called "intensive care." I surveyed the bays of little plastic houses called "isolettes" and tried not to look too closely at any of them. The babies were too small, with too many tubes and ventilators and IVs coming and going from them. It seemed like all those whooshes and the beeping were pushing back death's waiting door. Then, I saw my baby. A needle was protruding from his small forehead. He was crying. His little body was jerking and jolting. I didn't know if he felt pain, rage, or loneliness. He wore only a disposable diaper. *I had so many baby outfits at home.* There was no blanket covering him.

I needed to get him out of there. Fast. He should be asleep in his new crib with the dancing bears overhead. I needed to find out who was in charge. I looked, but everyone was busy. There was no one to ask, and I started to cry. I could only imagine picking him up and carrying him out of there, but I couldn't even stand up. I wasn't sure if I was supposed to, but I reached into the hole, to where I could touch him.

I spoke to him. "It's okay, baby. It's okay. I'll get you out of there. Don't cry."

I looked down at the IV needle taped to my hand. I didn't even know his name, but he knew me. His tiny finger wrapped itself around mine. I didn't want to let go. A nurse came over and startled me. She barely looked at me as she reached into his little plastic house to check something. I could think the words, but I couldn't speak. I had so many questions. I just sat there in the wheelchair in silence for a long time, crying and staring at my son. Another nurse eventually came over and put her hand on my shoulder.

"Don't worry," she said.

The presiding neonatologist made the rules. Meetings with him were arranged by request in advance, and they were very few and far between. He was busy saving the lives of *his* babies, and this was *his* unit. I learned early on that the nurses did what he said; they couldn't and wouldn't answer questions. "I'll ask" was the usual response. He gave the orders; they were obedient. But I didn't understand how housing my son in a plastic box devoid of his mother's contact could be helping him.

What kept me from staying in bed, asking for more drugs, and putting a pillow over my head? Why do some mothers feel nothing for their babies in those first weeks? Why does a penguin risk its life to shelter a single egg in sub-zero, Antarctic conditions? I was unaware of what was happening in the news. I had no idea what was happening at work, who had called, or who wanted to visit. I didn't know whether it was night or day, or what day it was. I didn't even know whether my son's room was ready for him to come home. I was lost in a private, silent war with the hospital, and this love I had never felt before.

My doctor was kind and understood that I didn't want to leave without my son. Because I'd had surgery, he was able to approve my staying in the hospital longer than the usual few days. As often as I could, I wheeled and eventually walked down the hall dragging my IV pole. I stood outside the door for an hour or more hoping the nurses would let me in early. I wanted to feed my son *my* milk—not their formula. I was so stressed out, I couldn't produce breast milk. I battled with the evil pump that pinched and hurt. I would limp down the hall with my meager offerings, hoping to impress the nurses, but they were too busy to notice me. They couldn't stop and talk. They pointed to the fridge where I was supposed to deposit the milk, and I stalled so that I could be closer to my baby. If someone did see me standing there, the usual response was, "Visiting hours are over. You can come back in the morning." I would force a smile and limp back to my room.

In the days that followed, we learned about O2 levels, blue episodes, and bilirubin; these were terms I hadn't read in any of my books about having babies. I stood by while my son's heels were pricked numerous times a day for blood. I kept an eye on his monitors. He was taken for CAT scans and MRIs. I didn't know where he was in the hospital or who was holding him. I tried not to think about him being alone. I thought my heart would stop, but maybe it forgot its pain so that it could just keep beating.

When I was told I had to leave the hospital and that my son wasn't going home with me, I closed my eyes and prayed for the strength to walk away. I asked a God I had forgotten if it was possible for my baby to know that even though I was away from the hospital, I was always with him and I'd be back.

Every day, I traveled from Brooklyn to the hospital in the city. It took about an hour. It was exhausting. I wasn't sleeping, and then I would sit at the hospital all day. Ten days passed, but it felt like a month. On the day we were told we could take our son home, we had yet to name him. He became Daniel—the courageous one

70

who walked into the lion's den. It means "with God as my judge." A middle name never occurred to us. We dressed him in his blue knit outfit, its little feet still too long and its arms flapping by his sides, and carried him outside to freedom. Although we'd no longer be at the mercy of the neonatal care unit, we were stumbling into territory that no one could have prepared us for.

Beneath the blue outfit, a Velcro harness secured our baby's dislocated left hip. An apnea monitor was taped to his chest; it would wake us and warn us of his irregular breathing. He still didn't eat well, and he cried a lot. He was tiny and yellow from jaundice. I was both scared and excited as we carried him into the house. We were finally home. I imagined that it would soon be filled with Daniel's cooing and restful hours in our new rocking chair. I wasn't prepared for the colicky days and the night terrors, or the screaming from ear infections.

I bathed him carefully in our kitchen sink, trying to steer clear of the medical devices he was rigged with. I was afraid to fall asleep and couldn't forget the parting words of that neonatologist: "We think it's genetic. We've done all kinds of tests. We've checked his kidneys, heart, and brain, and they checked out, but there's something different about your son. Time will tell. I'm not sure."

GETTING PAST NO

"No": used to express the negative of an
alternative choice or possibility
~Merriam-Webster Dictionary~

At night, I'd flip through child development books. Other babies had roly-poly faces with aligned features. Daniel didn't. My son's face was different... His face was small, and he had huge eyes. To me, he looked wise. Those eyes had a knowing gaze. Even if his head was floppy and he was tiny, he was beautiful to me. Sleep wasn't his favorite thing. He woke frequently and would cry for hours. Starting at three months, he was plagued by ear infections. He also had difficulty with digestion. He kept throwing up everything he drank. Since the day we'd brought him home, a sleep monitor woke us every ten minutes. I couldn't shake the thought that our son, lying next to me in our bed, wouldn't make it through the night.

For the next few months, we shuttled back and forth to various doctors, but with each visit, I got more defensive. I was sure our son would be fine, but questions kept emerging about his development.

When Daniel was five months old, I returned to work. Each morning, our nanny would come, and I'd leave feeling I was betraying him. I had negotiated less time in the office, but my commute alone took an hour in either direction. I was still gone the whole day. I passed on dinners and work-related outings so that I could rush back to the other part of my life—my baby, my husband, our life together. My determination to rise to the top of my profession frayed with each step I took away from my son. Precious hours that could have been spent with him felt unbearable as I left him behind.

Our pediatrician was also a pulmonologist. She tried to convince us that Daniel would outgrow the sleep apnea and the monitor. A pediatric gastrointestinal specialist diagnosed reflux, which caused his stomach upset. We needed to try different baby formulas. Finally, it was organic goat milk that helped. Daniel smiled, but he was floppy and couldn't sit up. Instead of creeping, he rolled, and by the time he was six months old, instead of using his arms and legs to try to crawl, he dragged himself across the floor. He was very small. He didn't resemble me or my husband, and his right arm would sometimes stiffen. His right eye turned in. His hip had relocated with the harness he still wore. By the time he was ten months old, our pediatrician was concerned that he was missing milestones; he didn't sit up on time, he didn't use words on time, he didn't crawl or roll over... She suggested we visit a neurologist.

Sending us to a neurologist meant she suspected that my son's brain wasn't developing normally. I was scared. I didn't want to go.

I brought Daniel to a local pediatrician in Brooklyn, hoping to hear a different opinion. Within a few minutes, he offered, "I know what's wrong with your baby." *Really? The best doctors in New York City didn't seem to have anything conclusive to tell us.*

"Yes," he said most assuredly. "Your son is brain-damaged." I stood with Daniel in my arms and stared at the doctor. I wanted to scream, *"Are you crazy?"* 'Damaged' was the last word I would have used. *NO. We are not damaged, and we won't ever be damaged.* I had established this in that hospital where he'd been born. I walked out of the office with Daniel in my arms. *What a fucking freak.* But, on the way out, I felt my legs wobbling. *What if he's right?*

We eventually brought Daniel to a neurologist, who diagnosed him with "low muscle tone" (hypotonia). He asked if a genetic work-up had been done.

"Yes," I said. "All the tests were inconclusive."

"There are new tests being developed, and keep in touch with your geneticist. Maybe she can eventually discover something."

I wasn't sure I wanted her to "discover something."

"Your son will reach milestones on his own timeline. Motivation is going to be a big factor, but with physical therapy, we will see how he develops."

The doctor seemed nice enough, but there was a hesitation there, too—an unspoken concern he wasn't sharing. I could feel it. He wasn't saying much, but he encouraged us to help Daniel by expecting him to "work" to get his toys, providing opportunities for him to move rather than handing them to him.

It felt cruel at first, but later I realized that "motivation" is a strong factor in everyone's development. We reached out to a physical therapist. The goal was to increase Daniel's strength and coordination. But observing her "playing" with a big ball and mats, encouraging my son to do what was hard for him, angered me. Daniel would become frustrated and cry. I wanted to banish her from our home. She encouraged me to integrate some techniques for improving his strength and mobility, but I didn't want to be his therapist. I wanted to be his mother. I didn't want to dwell on Daniel's *accomplishments* or getting him to reach *goals*; I wanted to be in the moment with him. The professionals could do the work.

By the time Daniel reached his first birthday, we had assembled a small army of specialists: a pediatrician, geneticist, neurologist, orthopedist, ophthalmologist, urologist, ENT, gastroenterologist, and physical therapist. With every "developmental milestone" he missed, with every opinion we sought out, there were no answers... just the weighing and reweighing of little information. Time, we were told, would tell us what we yearned to know. Locked in the mystery of a genetic aberration that no one could identify, week by week, our son was excluded from what was considered typical. It was a word I would learn to forgive. It was a limited word, and it meant "average." We would always be different. It's who we were. That's what I told myself and anyone who would listen.

Well-intentioned people told stories of how their "normal" children hadn't walked or spoken "on schedule." If Daniel did everything "late," that was okay with us. When he was twenty months, I had finished tying his shoes and backed away from him. He wobbled for a few seconds before he put one foot in front of the other and tumbled forward into my arms. That qualified. Those were his first steps! Many months passed before he could walk on his own, but I believed he would do far more than walk. He would run.

When Daniel was two, I started thinking about preschool. I made an appointment for a classroom visit. Compared with the other children, Daniel was in his own world. He wasn't as physically capable—he wobbled when he walked and fell a lot. He drooled uncontrollably, too, but he had an impressive wardrobe with matching bandanas to keep his shirts dry. To get up, he had to put his hands in front of him and, with his butt in the air, push as hard as he could...and then he'd fall. He just couldn't stand up. Because he couldn't walk capably, he was unable to get a toy and play, or get a book and "read" like the other two-year-olds who busied themselves around him. On the sidelines of the room, I watched my son sitting alone, trying to swim in a swirling sea that was going to drown him. He seemed content, but I wanted to scoop him up and run. *I made a mistake. I was wrong. We never should have come. What did I do?* After about fifteen minutes, the teacher walked over to me and touched my shoulder. She asked me to step outside.

"This is not the right school for your son. As you see, he is just not like the other children. Perhaps you could contact the board of education and they can help you with an early-intervention placement."

Her words just drifted away.

My eyes glazed over. Alan and I walked home in silence. We'd both thought he would be fine. Our son would outgrow all of this. This teacher didn't know him. There would be somewhere else, I was sure.

But there wasn't anywhere else. I made appointments at two more local preschools. The kind smiles of the directors belied the truth. The answer was, "No."

We waited. When Daniel was two and a half, we took him for a neuropsychological evaluation. And then came a barrage of information. He had expressive language, but he didn't speak in phrases. Each labored word of his speech was unrecognizable. I kept a book in which I listed all of his "words"—they weren't really words so much as approximations of words...just sounds. I wrote down the corresponding meanings so I could be his interpreter. I was the only one who understood what he was saying. The low muscle tone in his face and mouth made "placement" and "articulation" a challenge. His speech was considered significantly impaired. He would require speech therapy. To help with all of his fine motor issues, he would also need occupational therapy. He couldn't hold his cup or a spoon or fork. When he played, he had an awkward way of using his hands; he couldn't hold a crayon, and he didn't like the feeling of Play-Doh or getting his hands messy. He was unstable and fell a lot because he lacked core strength, and his physical therapy would have to continue. On top of all that, he had sensory integration issues, which meant that even a little wind would feel like a turbine engine, light was blinding, and stepping off a small curb felt like coming off a mountain. The testing revealed that he had a high "verbal expressive IQ," which meant that he was intelligent, but all of the other deficits (as they were referred to) were interfering with his progress. If he attended a "special" preschool, he would receive all of his therapies at school.

I got a list from the board of education. The schools were called "programs." Alan and I began visiting, but there seemed to be no appropriate setting. The children were "classified" by the board of education into specific "impairing conditions"—those with speech impairment, significant cognitive delay, or various other challenges—emotional or physical challenges, or severe physical limitations. Alan's regular response was that none of the professionals with whom we interacted "know what they are doing." We were both exhausted by the scrutiny. Alan's love for Daniel was best shown through his protection of him. He had no patience in general, and zero patience for people he perceived as being critical or judgmental of his son. He would regularly insist that Daniel was "on his own clock" and leave it at that.

The director of Special Sprouts (a special-education preschool next door to where we lived) was getting into her car. I walked over to her and explained that my son had been observed by a social worker at her school, but that he had been rejected from her program. I was sure he would be a good fit if only she would give him a chance. I was begging. Soon afterward, we were invited back for another interview, and he passed. I saved a letter from his first teacher there, who wrote, *"Daniel, you are a very special child and I can tell already, you will go on to do great things in your life."*

Almost 3, Daniel was sweet and funny. He loved all kinds of music just like we did and would bob his head to the beat of whatever we were listening to. Generally happy and animated, even if we didn't understand something he was trying to tell us, he was quick to try to make us understand by either gesturing or repeating it until we just had to keep guessing. Daniel wouldn't give up. His hair was long and curly. His huge eyes and long eyelashes were unique and beautiful to me, but doctors don't describe features as "beautiful"...to them, Daniel's were "unusual" or "atypical." Later, those eyes would unlock the mystery of his genetic identity. Fingers, toes...no inch of him was left uninvestigated. I was consumed by guilt as I left for work each day. I knew very little about why my son's development was so slow. He was bright and engaging, yet his specialists wanted to define him by applying "norms" that included his physical "functioning" and "characteristics." He couldn't be compared to average children his age. He wasn't like them!

We didn't have the internet then. Research was nearly impossible. I was sure of only one thing: If I had more time with my son, it would be better than leaving him behind each day. I bargained with myself, churning with strategies as to how I could stay home. Alan was concerned that we needed the income from my work, but I couldn't keep up with the appearances and the demands of my job when, every morning, I was leaving the most important part of my life behind.

AMY

If you want to sing out, sing out
And if you want to be free, be free
'Cause there's a million things to be
You know that there are.

~Cat Stevens~

It was January of 1994. The sun was sinking in a winter sky when I walked into my son's room to put away his laundry. I held a shirt close to my cheek and remembered his baby smell. His clothes seemed so much bigger now that he was two.

The phone rang. Amy was calling from California.

"Ya know that pain I've been having in my leg?... I've been seeing a chiropractor... I went for some x-rays... The radiologist called my doctor right away. There's a problem with my hip... They found a lesion. The x-rays showed that the bone is deteriorated. I have to go for a bone scan."

"Wait, what? Stop. What do you mean deteriorated?"

"Well, I had a pain in my sternum for a while, but they said it was some benign thing."

"What pain in your sternum? For how long?"

"Since right after Ashley was born."

"You didn't tell me."

"Oh, well... I thought I did. I guess I told Mom... The doctor said there are only a couple of things that would do that to bone. A weird bone disease, maybe osteoporosis...or...cancer. He's pretty sure it's not osteoporosis, but it has to be ruled out."

I heard her daughter, Ashley, crying in the background. She'd just turned two and was waking up from a nap.

"I better go," she said. "Don't worry. I'll talk to you soon."

This made no sense. How could it be cancer? It couldn't be cancer. One in seven people would die of cancer. I remembered that statistic from somewhere. Her primary care doctor barely knew her, though. Amy was healthy and strong. There was no cancer in our family. She wasn't sick. What about those "seven warning signs" in pamphlets in doctor's offices urging patients to inspect moles and watch for shortness of breath, and cautioning them against sudden weight changes and tiredness?

Amy called a few days later to say that the bone scan had picked up numerous "hot spots" in her lungs, liver, and hip. A biopsy had been ordered. Her voice was hoarse and tired. "Well, at least the waiting is over. At least we know."

Inside, I was howling like a wounded dog, but I couldn't let her hear that. There was just silence.

"You need to find the higher good in this," she said.

There were six or maybe nine months left. That's what they'd told her.

It was a collision with the unthinkable. I bargained with a God I had long ago accepted didn't necessarily intervene in personal matters—a God I wasn't sure would hear my plea for my sister's life. I went to the library to do research. I called the American Cancer Society. I got in touch with Silent Unity and requested a prayer vigil.

A few days later, Amy and I were talking.

"I wonder if people will pull away from me because I am sick?" she asked me.

I couldn't believe it. "No, Amy. No, people will not pull away from you.

This is crazy. No one who loves you would do that. I will be here for you no matter what..."

She had been at her best friend's home. Another woman was visiting with her twins. The moms and children were all running on the lawn except Amy, who couldn't run. She told me she felt ashamed because they all looked so beautiful and healthy, and she wanted to scream, "I CAN'T RUN. I HAVE CANCER. I HAVE CANCER." She said nothing and watched while the other adults laughed and the kids played.

I booked a flight to Santa Barbara. Alan didn't want to be left alone with Daniel even though we had help. He was concerned about the expense, but I counted the days until my trip in February. I felt so far away from my sister. Until I got there, we would only have phone calls, or I could send letters.

The smells of New York seemed more intense: hot dogs, roasted nuts, homeless people, exhaust fumes, sewer gas, and perfume. Bricks were redder. The blue of the sky was more noticeable. The taxis seemed more yellow, and the subway seats were dirtier. Daniel's questions took longer to answer. His laughter was louder, and every step I took felt heavier. Amy was only 34.

Her Ivy League education trumped my acceptance to NYU. She was the smarter one, the steadfast one, and the one who'd been able to smoke large quantities of pot and still get A's. She'd always been the "good" one. She was the one our parents didn't worry about. When she'd broken the rules, it had been done in secret or chalked up to "individuation." My rebellion had kept me in constant trouble with our parents. Maybe I'd been no less guilty, just more foolish to have gotten caught.

On the day I arrived, a month from that day she'd told me about the cancer, Amy's husband Jamey met me at the Santa Barbara airport. They'd been married almost four years, but I hardly knew him.

When we got to the house, Amy was in the living room. She looked up at me and grinned. Beautiful Amy. I hadn't been expecting her crutches, but she explained that too much pressure on her right leg might cause her hip to fracture. Eight months earlier, we had been lying in a bed on Cape Cod and talking about whatever you talk about when you think you have your whole life in front of you. At the time, she'd seemed okay, but she hadn't ridden bikes with me because she was in pain. She'd been limping, too, but had insisted it was from carrying Ashley everywhere.

That August was our last family vacation because she had cancer. We just didn't know it.

Amy and Jamey had just finished renovating and decorating their new home. Purple and green paint calmed the rooms. Ashley's stenciled closet and shades were the latest touch. Amy and Ashley had been busy planting flowers, bringing life back to the long-forgotten yard, which had been neglected by its previous owners.

The next day, Amy wanted to take me somewhere special. She said it was a surprise. I had to drive. She was worse off than I had imagined, but I tried to be entertaining. I wanted to distract her. She sat quietly in the car with her eyes closed, fingers locked in her lap. Ashley's chatter filled the silence. The word 'cancer' surfaced occasionally, mixing with her sing-songy, two-year-old voice.

Amy directed me to a cul-de-sac. We parked by the entrance to a path. She pointed toward the woods, and I followed her. She hobbled on her crutches through the mud and into the eucalyptus grove. I worried that she would fall. Ashley pranced ahead of us. There was no sound but the crunching of sticks and leaves beneath our feet. The eucalyptus trees smelled fresh. Sunlight streamed through the branches. Amy pointed. I looked up. There was a wave of monarch butterflies fluttering in the air. They were perched by the thousands on the trees and all around us on the ground. We sat on a log and just watched them for a long time. I had never seen anything like it. The whole forest was vibrating. She directed me to hike over a small hill—to go ahead, she'd wait for me. I made my way up the incline and, just over the rise, a meadow spread out as far as I could see. At the end of it was a cliff where the Pacific Ocean crashed below. It was stunning. I understood what had brought her from New England to this part of California. She had long ago left the snowy winters that made New England so pretty and the sticky August humidity that brought the mosquitoes and restless nights. The tall buildings that defined the landscape of Boston, and the grittiness and fast pace of a city, didn't feed her soul. When she left the town where we grew up, she headed for San Diego. She left everything she knew to discover who she might be. After she met Jamey, they made their way to Santa Barbara. It was the expanse of wide-open spaces, places to hike, and boundless nature—where the air is clear and the ocean's powerful surf meets the unique beauty of the rugged California coast—that made this the place where her spirit soared. This was where she belonged.

Later, Amy and Ashley were playing in the yard. She was using her crutches to pick up and throw a ball. I was thinking about the butterflies. Some butterflies live for only two weeks; some of the rarest and most beautiful live only twenty-four hours. I was on the phone with Alan. My life in New York seemed far away. I missed Daniel. It was the first time I had been away since he was born. Alan sounded tense, but that was the way he had been for a while. He didn't like that I had left even though I had cooked a week's worth of meals in advance and he had our nanny's help with Daniel. *Damn, he's really clueless. My sister is dying.* The glass muffled Ashley and Amy's mingling laughter.

Neighbors brought food and plants and mowed the lawn. Friends came regularly to check in to offer support or something from their garden.

We went to the health food store. A woman stopped to say hello and noticed the crutches. I heard Amy's sweet voice saying, "I have cancer." I wished she could have said anything but that.

The next day, we took Ashley to her preschool. It was at the home of a friend. As soon as Amy made her way down the driveway, five of the other parents approached and hugged her. She looked them straight-on, smiled, and nodded as if she'd be better soon. I pushed Ashley on a swing and sang to her.

The diagnosis was adenocarcinoma, a rare form of aggressive cancer typically found in much older people. Cells taken from her lung biopsy were poorly differentiated. It had metastasized from its unknown primary site into her sternum, hips, liver, and lung. *How does a single, tiny mutant cell become so devastating?* Her oncologist felt there was no immediate benefit to undergoing chemotherapy or radiation. The toxic chemicals would only destroy what "healthy" months were left. He was only concerned with ensuring Amy's comfort.

I noticed the pictures on his desk—his wife and his two boys. I wanted to ask, "What caused this? How long has Amy lived with this cancer, and how long did it take to eat away at her bones? Could she have stopped this? Could this have been diagnosed earlier?" Her first symptoms appeared two years before, and that would mean there was very little time left.

The oncology office, the signs for the radiology department, the room where people sat while chemo dripped silently, the word 'cancer'...all of it, once reserved for someone else's tragedy, was now ours.

We walked down the hall of the hospital. "No cure." Those words just kept playing on a loop in my head. I walked ahead of her because I didn't want her to see that I was crying.

The doctor had recommended a HANDICAPPED placard for her

car. When Amy noticed the expiration date for six months later, she chuckled. "Well, I guess he thinks I'm not going to live very long."

That night, we went to a restaurant for her birthday. We were celebrating with her three closest friends. Amy wanted to ask each of us a question. I was the last to go. She asked me about the most risqué place where I'd had sex. In 1985, when my boyfriend was in rehab, he and I went into the bathroom of his room and very, very quietly had sex on the toilet, risking that, if we got caught, he'd get thrown out. Even in the candlelight, I could see her face turn red.

Her new orthopedist urged her to consider hip replacement and radiation. *Who would help with the house and Ashley?* I could try to come back, but I lived so far away. I wanted to offer more. I wanted her to have anything and everything so that she could be more comfortable. Maybe outside help? I quickly learned, though, that "comfortable" for my sister wasn't the same as "comfortable" for me. She was adamantly opposed to a stranger coming into their home and taking over with Ashley.

The next day, we all went to the zoo. Amy rode in a rented wheelchair.

When we were little and someone rode past in a wheelchair, we would whisper and wonder what was "wrong." Could anyone imagine that my sister had terminal cancer? I wanted to scream, "This can't be true!"

I stared out the window of the plane. I didn't know when I would be back. I knew the only thing I could give her, more than things money could buy and more than the help I thought she needed, was to let her know I believed she would survive this.

Amy was nineteen months younger than me. Our brother Steven was fourteen months younger than her. She was the middle child, the quiet one who clung to our mom while she made the beds. After Steven was born, Amy and I shared a bedroom. In our new room,

Amy and I took naps together. We giggled and talked when we were supposed to be sleeping.

There was never any doubt about who was the older sister. Especially when we played "beauty parlor." Once, I "set" her hair with a head-full of Vaseline, which I used for "setting gel." When Barbara discovered us, she was furious. She grilled my sister as to what had happened.

"Robyn wanted to do it, and I said yes."

I should have known better, but it was so fun. I was fascinated with the beauty parlor. The women went each week and had their hair done. They sat with rollers under dryers and came out looking so pretty. I loved it when we got to go with her. We played on the floor with the bobby pins and hairclips. After my debut as a hairdresser, it took days to get the tenacious goo out of our hair.

I was almost five and Amy was three and a half when we moved from our small house to a bigger house. We each had our own room, and there was a wooded backyard with a brook. For a long time, we weren't allowed to play near it. We collected turtles and scavenged around in the woods. We found treasures like sparkling mica rocks, and once in a while, a snake or a bone.

We had new neighbors to play with. We collected troll dolls and bags of fabric scraps and bickered over who had the best Barbie clothes. We pretended to be Batman and Robin. (I always had to be "Robin.") There were days of raking piles of leaves, playing dress-up, hopscotch, Wiffle ball, building snow forts, and tobogganing. We went ice skating and bowling, and we loved going to the movies. We went to overnight camps and day camps. I held her in my arms when she was scared. We went to the beach on hot weekends and vacationed with our family on Cape Cod.

At our Nana and Papa's house, we slept together in a small bed. There was a print of Gauguin's *Dance*, and we giggled because the people in it were naked. She would cry because she missed our parents. I held her. Until she was in her early teens, she didn't go to sleep without first saying to me, "Good night, sleep tight; don't let the bedbugs bite." I taught her to smoke cigarettes and pot.

During our college years, we weren't as close. Amy had gone to school in western Massachusetts, and I had gone to New York City. I missed her. Both Amy and my friend Kathy were in London for semesters abroad, but they had yet to connect. One night, I was on the corner in Greenwich Village at the payphone near our apartment. I dialed the number of Kathy's payphone in London at exactly the time we had agreed to speak. After Kathy picked up, she said, "Oh my God! I think I see your sister. There's Amy!" It was so random. My sister was just walking by at the exact same time I had called. I remember there being a big moon out that night and thinking that despite our different choices, my sister and I could both see that moon even on different continents. I felt that we were connected by a force I couldn't describe. I didn't like feeling the distance that had crept between us.

All this kept me from sleep as the plane carried me back to New York. I had the same faith in Amy as I would trust a compass. She never seemed lost. But now she was on the other side of something I couldn't imagine, and no matter how much I wanted to cross over, the cancer was there, like a spiral of barbed wire, keeping me out.

FOR SURE, THERE WILL
BE UNCERTAINTY

*I have been driven many times upon my
knees by the overwhelming conviction
that I had nowhere else to go.
My own wisdom and that of all about me
seemed insufficient for that day.*
~Abraham Lincoln~

I was struggling with conflicting identities: I was the caring mother, the giving sister, the sacrificing wife, and the loving daughter. I was the dutiful talent agent who donned her armor, wore a suit, got to work, and honored her commitments to her clients, her growing career, and her family's financial needs. My parts were being stretched like a rubber band that would snap. A therapist I consulted said, "Your plate isn't full. It's cracking."

Alan was becoming increasingly aggressive. If I didn't comply with his demands, he would become hostile. One day, I came home with a leather jacket. When he saw it, he started an inquisition: How could I afford this jacket? How could I spend this money? *Was he accusing me of stealing from him?* We didn't have a formal agreement about our finances. He worked and had an income. Each week, I withdrew from the business account only what I needed for our household expenses and small expenditures like my haircuts and Daniel's clothing. I'd found the jacket at a small local store on sale and paid for it with my own credit card. I had just wanted something nice for myself, and it wasn't expensive. I could have paid it off. I stood there listening, but I wanted to tell Alan to just shut up. His position was that I was *irresponsible*, and I should have consulted him. His anger was disproportionate to the situation. His use of the word "irresponsible" was laughable, too, but I couldn't laugh. I was afraid. I kept quiet. He was yelling loudly, very close to me, and his face was flushed with rage. He could be "heavy-handed" at times, but I'd rationalized that he had a lot going on and wasn't talking much about his fears. I "understood" his emotional reactivity. I had grown up with a mother who regularly raged without warning. I had the tools for this. I would be okay. Or would I? This wasn't the first time. *If he got angry enough, if I provoked him, would he hurt me*? I had to tread carefully. *Would he punch me? Would he harm Daniel? No. Never.* I couldn't imagine that. I had to put those thoughts aside. He was just stressed out.

I thought I should talk to someone, so I found a therapist in the neighborhood. Her name was Deena. She was soft-spoken and calm, the kind of woman you want to hug right away. In her office, I welcomed her boxes of tissues. The more we talked, the more I uncovered the part of the equation I didn't want to face. My husband wasn't emotionally stable. We had been married less than four years, but so much had changed since those times when we'd been jumping on his motorcycle, visiting galleries, and just tooling around. I tried to be a good wife, fulfilling my husband's expectations that I would support him and shoulder all of the childcare, which meant research, strategizing for Daniel, following up with all of his therapists and his school, managing our way through bouts of relentless croup and ear infections that seemed to linger on. I shopped for our food and cooked our meals, and I worked full-time with an hour commute on either end. We were going into the city to specialists' offices twice a week. Still, I felt that as much as I did, it wasn't enough. I didn't see how I never stopped. I didn't see how I had disappeared. There was no time to think about myself. Alan was insistent that I lacked the wisdom which he, at 43, had acquired. According to him, one day I would understand things I couldn't possibly know now. I was confused by this regular affront. Still, I would try to please him.

With every fifty-minute therapy session, it became clearer that something was missing. There was no one there for me. My family was far away. Alan had become absorbed with his business and obsessed with his own health. My sister's cancer had catapulted him into believing that he, too, would die of cancer. I wasn't sure his concerns were well-founded given he had no family history of it, and I wasn't willing to entertain it.

Deena asked me if I knew anything about the psychiatric term "narcissism." I had no idea what she was talking about. I knew it as a literary term. She explained that narcissists have extreme responses to even small, perceived offenses. They lose control of their emotional equilibrium. They get triggered when they believe their needs aren't being met, and then they act vindictively. She asked me about my mother. I put my hands over my face and remained silent. I couldn't get into it. She asked me to bring a picture of her to our next session. The next week, I came with the picture. In it, I was five, sitting at our kitchen table with a pencil in my mouth, daydreaming—as if I were contemplating something I was going to write. My mother was standing over me. She had a sponge in her hand. Clearly, she wanted to clean the table, and I was in her way. Her face was stern and mean. I wondered why my father took that picture. Was he trying to capture that insatiable, imaginative spirit of mine? The wistful look on my face was a stark contradiction to my mother's need to get the table clean. Of course, I didn't remember the scene. Deena asked me what I saw. I was seeing more than just that moment in time; I was looking at that relationship through a lens I hadn't looked through before.

In Deena's office, peeling back the layers of my life revealed how I ached for so much more than I was getting. Both my mother and Alan weren't available. And if they were...the only way they knew to show it was so much less than what I wished for. I felt disconnected from both of them. I had to take care of myself so I could be present with my son, but how was I going to do this? Leave Alan? Daniel was only three. What about work? Deena and I talked about my job. If I left, I'd be financially dependent on Alan. I was unsure I should put myself in that position, especially knowing his behavior had been so unstable, but for the time being, Daniel had to remain in the forefront of my life. I had to prioritize him—not forever, but for now. My sister had six, maybe nine months to live. I would make concessions, leaving my career aspirations in the past. If our marriage could weather this, I would try to make it work. But I wasn't sure.

I wrote a heartfelt letter to my bosses and planned to leave the company. Within the month. I cleaned out my office. The boxed memories of my decade-long career landed in storage in our basement. I didn't wonder what I'd miss or what would happen. The satisfactions of money or promotion, the need to matter or be acknowledged, all disappeared the day I walked out that door. Many clients and colleagues were kind and supportive. Those who knew me well understood why I had to leave. I would miss people, but I wasn't sure how any of them would fit into my future life.

I was a trained hunter. My finely-honed skills to "achieve" at my workplace were an important source of my success. I would discover there was more. Now, the harvesting of love, finding something to put my faith in, and coming home to myself would become my work. I had mastered how to detach emotionally. In therapy, I would collapse into a stew of feelings. I was building a bridge back to my heart, but it was going to be a long journey. My workplace camaraderie and the community where I was respected were gone. I had spent years grinding away to get somewhere, and now I felt like I was nowhere. I missed my sister as she fought a disease that was ravaging her body. *How soon would her life end? How would this affect those of us who loved her—especially her daughter and her husband?* With only the U.S. postal service and the telephone, I struggled to connect with her.

There were many uncertainties about my sister, my marriage, and my son's future, but in the moments that Daniel and I shared, there was beauty and joy. I was excited to start this new chapter, but getting ready to go out with him on weekday mornings was odd. I would stand in front of my closet looking at my suits hanging neatly and my high-heeled shoes carefully arranged on the floor and wonder if I'd ever wear them again. It didn't matter. I wasn't getting dressed to be seen. I had my hair cut very short and didn't care if it was messy. I didn't bother with makeup. *What to wear?* Loose clothing and sandals. I wanted to fit in. I didn't know just how ironic that was, because no matter what I wore, I was never going to fit in. I focused on the cherished time I would share with my son.

Each morning, I dropped Daniel off at his special-education preschool and returned home to help Alan with his new business. It was 1994. Apple and Pixar were pioneering the use of "Computer Aided Design" (CAD) in full-length feature films like *Toy Story*. Alan was one of the few people in the country who had embraced the technology. He was instrumental in bringing this technology into the architectural sector. (There were only two companies at that time that were introducing CAD into architecture, though it's now a standard for the industry. Alan had the license to work for one of them.) Day after day, the pressure of having only one income, the many unknowns of whether his business would be a success, our son's unique circumstances, and my sadness about my sister's cancer hammered away at us. By noon, I couldn't wait to get out of the house to pick up Daniel at school.

At the playground, I felt like an outsider. I wasn't a regular. I had missed two years of weekdays and didn't blend into either of the groups: the nannies who congregated with children they cared for or the parents of the "typical" children who pushed them on swings and watched them effortlessly coming down the slide. Having an atypical child made me different, too. I was no longer "mainstream." I don't remember feeling loss or sadness. I just remember feeling that Daniel and I were a team. When I looked into his eyes, I saw pure love.

I searched for someone with a toddler who was unsteady, another child who couldn't jump or climb. The parents were speaking among themselves in little clusters. *Do they triumph over each step, each easy stride, each climb of a stair, or each tumble, knowing their child will get up?* In my heart, I knew the answer. I kept to myself and pushed my son on the swings. He was two and a half and couldn't walk more than a few feet yet.

I would buckle Daniel into his seat on the back of my bike and head off to the park. Those afternoons were magical. We would stop and listen to the Caribbean guys drumming, or we would go to the carousel or the zoo. No one knew where we were. I felt so free.

At home, I retreated into Daniel's laughter, twirling him in my arms and dancing to his favorite Raffi songs. His tiny voice peaked in soprano squeals as he stumbled around the house flapping his hands and singing. We played with his favorite *Sesame Street* toys, did puzzles together, and "read" for hours. As soon as I would finish one book, he wanted another. We shared a world that was only ours.

Our favorite place to go in the neighborhood was Barnes & Noble, just a few blocks from our house. Once, we were looking at some books on a table. I turned away for a minute, and he was gone. Panic rose from my feet into my heart. The sound that came out of my mouth was feral. "DAAAAANIELLLL!!!" Everyone around me just stared at me. I became frantic. *Where was he?* There was an escalator nearby, but no. He wouldn't have been able to negotiate it. I kept hearing my voice, shrill and unrelenting, calling for him. I couldn't see him. I tried asking people if they saw him. I was shaking, and I wasn't making sense. It must've been ten minutes. I was ready to call the police.

"Mommy?" I heard his tiny voice.

I reeled around. He was sitting on the floor, peeking out from under the table where I had been looking at the books. I knelt down and dissolved into him, clutching him. The two of us on the floor and my sobbing must have made it appear as if I were losing it.

"Where were you?" I demanded.

"Reading."

Thank God.

I held him close and then pushed back, my hands on his shoulders. "Okay. Here's the rule: If you can't see me, you are in the wrong place."

"Can I have this?" He held it out for me to see: *Pat the Bunny*.

"Yes. Yes, you can have it."

I was so grateful that he hadn't been abducted, I would have bought him ten books.

"Come." I took his hand. "Let's go home."

MISSING PIECES

How soon will we accept this opportunity
to be fully alive before we die?
~Steven Levine~

A few months after her diagnosis, Amy had hip replacement surgery. After her recovery, she was traveling north to a women's cancer retreat in Tiburon, California. There, she would get a respite from her daily life. She was excited about it. I felt especially good that I could visit. While she was gone, I'd be helping Jamey and Ashley in whatever way I could.

Alan had reluctantly agreed to my going, but not without a fight. I was using airline miles my parents had gifted me, but since I had left my job, every decision had to be approved by him.

The morning I was leaving, I was waiting by the window and looking out for the car service to take me to the airport. I heard the car horn beeping. Simultaneously, I heard Alan calling out from the other room. It sounded like he was having a heart attack. I ran to him. He was doubled over in pain. I called out the window to the driver to leave—I wasn't going. I was frustrated and annoyed, but I had to shift into the moment. I didn't know what was happening.

I took Alan to the hospital. He was having a kidney-stone attack. *Why now? WHY?* We were entangled in a tightly wound knot: his needs versus mine. I felt ridiculous when I called Jamey to let him know I couldn't come. This was so wrong. It was a really shitty excuse compared with my sister's cancer. Alan and I were in a game of tug of war—and I was unable to just leave him and go. The nanny would have taken care of Daniel, but Alan expected me to stay with him. The saddest part was that I *believed* I had to stay with him and that I had no choice. I had let my sister down.

A few weeks later, I left. It was a short visit, but I remember how quickly Amy's cancer was progressing and how hard it was for her to get around. We went to a county fair, and Amy was hobbling slowly on her crutches. I encouraged Ashley to ride her first pony and eat cotton candy. I wondered if she'd remember it. She was an inquisitive and strong-willed toddler. She'd be okay, I thought. She would find her way... Too soon, I got on the small plane to L.A., where I'd make my connection, and I watched Ashley and Amy getting smaller and smaller as they waved at me. I didn't know when I'd be back.

The months passed. I didn't get to visit Amy that summer. She was communicating sporadically. I hoped for an invitation from her, but it didn't come. Bernie and Barbara were lost. Their daughter had a few months at best. We didn't talk about it. Not in those terms. I couldn't communicate with them, and the breach was widening between Alan and me. His moods were increasingly erratic. He was angry most of the time. I couldn't turn to him for anything. I just had to keep the peace.

During our annual August family vacation with my parents, I didn't want them to know how much stress I was experiencing. Being with Alan was like walking on broken glass, and I was careful not to incite any arguments around Daniel. There was nothing fun about the five of us hanging out in a house by the beach while my marriage was disintegrating and my sister was 2,500 miles away, suffering and isolating herself. One night, we called so we could all say hello, but she was tired and didn't want to talk for long. I felt emotionally stranded with no provisions.

In October, I convinced Alan that there was no choice. I needed to go back to California.

It had been six months since I had seen Amy. She had been hospitalized for a course of whole-body radiation. Her doctors were amazed at her determination to get home to be with her family. The night before I left, I got a call from her doctor. Her cancer had spread. It was in her brain now; he said the scan looked like someone had taken a paintbrush and flicked it. Specks everywhere. There wouldn't be much time.

When I arrived, she was in bed. She was much thinner. The scarf on her head hid the loss of her hair, but her freckles still warmed her face. I could hear the birds outside the window. I walked slowly toward her and sat on her bed. I leaned over, wanting to pull her close, but she winced. I longed to have her throw her arms around me and squeeze. She was lying still as if she were paralyzed.

A sweet smile stretched across her thin face. She hugged me with her eyes.

"Don't you think I look good bald?" She winked.

I squeezed her hand.

"I brought you some earrings. Do you still wear earrings?"

She took them from me and put them on. "What do you think?"

"Perfect—they are you."

She took off the scarf. "Don't you think I have a well-shaped head?"

"Oh yeah. Yeah, Amy, you definitely have a well-shaped head."

One morning, I set my video camera up on her dresser so I could record our conversation. If her doctor was right, this might be the last chance we would have to talk. We shared stories. In hers, I was mean to her, had hurt her, and pushed her away. Memory is not a straight line. I remembered different stories—loving my sister and being protective like she was my favorite puppy or a coveted doll. I feared since we were little that we would be separated. Once when we were playing, suddenly she couldn't walk. I thought she was fooling around, but when I realized it was true, I went screaming into the house. Our parents took her to the hospital. It was a virus. I could still remember standing outside the hospital, looking up at the bricks and windows. She was in there somewhere. I was crying, "Please give me back my sister."

It was almost Halloween, and Ashley wanted to dress up as an "angel witch." We spent afternoons on Amy's bed, reading and playing. I taught Ashley a camp song. We sang it in the round.

I love the mountains
I love the rolling hills
I love the flowers
I love the daffodils
I love the fireside
When all the lights are low
Boom de-ah-da
Boom de-ah-da
Boom de-ah-da.

During that visit, my calls with Alan were draining. He complained about being overwhelmed and alone. He showed little interest in how my sister was or how I was doing. I had planned to be away for five days. Before I'd left, as I had before, I cooked meals and set things up with our nanny for her to work longer hours. *What more could he want?* The day before I was scheduled to return home, Alan insisted I leave right away. My heart sank. I was concerned about Daniel. If Alan was burning out, I should leave to be home with my son. *It was only a day, for God's sake...was he for real?* I was embarrassed to tell my sister. With each call, I tried to keep it from her, but she overheard Alan and me fighting. When she asked if everything was okay, I didn't want to share the details. I just nodded. She wasn't convinced; she didn't like what she was hearing.

I was sitting on her bed when I told her, "I have to go."

All she could say was, "Fuck."

I took her hand. "The day is coming... I will leave him. *I will.*" She was my witness. Given how advanced her cancer was, I wasn't sure if that was the last thing I would ever say to her.

A month later, Jamey called to let us know that Amy was drifting, and it was unclear how long she had.

This time, I didn't know how many weeks I'd be gone. I asked a cousin for help with the airline ticket. Alan would have to deal. I had to get on that plane.

Bernie and Barbara were staying with Amy and Jamey. I was staying with Amy's friend. On the first night we were together, Bernie unpacked the projector he had brought. The 8mm movies rolled out years of our childhood birthday parties clicking away. In the movies, we waved, but the handheld lights were so bright we covered our faces. We were dressed in our pretty party dresses and special shoes, and our mom's cakes would make their debut.

It was a common first-born privilege that there was more footage of me. Amy had usually felt second-best, and that made me sad. We laughed and commented on the house where we'd grown up, which looked so much smaller now. New coats of paint, new shutters, different landscaping, new dining room drapes, new carpeting, and new wallpaper appeared in the movies. That was the last visit my sister and I would have together in the home where we had been little girls.

I was sitting in Amy's garden, feeling alone. Our brother Steven was in Massachusetts and unable to come. I wished things could have been different with him. I toggled between hating him for not being there and trying to have compassion toward him. His life was complicated. It always had been. Long before the drinking and the drugs, when he was a child, he was different than us. He didn't do as well in school, and then he dropped out of college. He was closer to Amy now but had remained distant from me, maybe because I was more critical or because I was the oldest and acted more parental toward him. Meanwhile, my husband was checked out. Our parents were holding on to shreds of hope. Our family was like a box of puzzle pieces that didn't fit together.

One morning after we had been there for a week, I woke up early. The same as I'd done every day since I'd arrived, I went over to Amy's house. Jamey was at work. Ashley was at school, and Bernie and Barbara were out shopping. I sat next to Amy and took her hand in mine.

She appeared to be sleeping. "Hi, Rob," she whispered. She didn't open her eyes. She was drifting in and out. "How ya doin'?"

"I'm okay." I leaned over and kissed her cheek. Her voice was barely more than a whisper. She began sharing her plans. She wanted to be cremated. She wanted Ashley and Jamey to have her ashes. She wanted a memorial bench, but she was unsure of where; there were a few places she had in mind. We talked about different options for her memorial service. She and Jamey had already met with a cantor whom she had chosen to officiate. She wasn't into religion, but a Jewish officiant felt right to her. I sat by her side, listening like we were planning a party, as though we had discussed all of this before, but we hadn't. When it was time, I would make the phone calls.

Every once in a while, she would slide into sleep and then come back. As the hours passed, we went through her address books. I read her the names. She barely had the strength to respond, so I just kept reading. She would doze off for a few seconds and then pull herself back. She wouldn't let up on finishing. We agreed the memorial service would be on the Wilcox Property, a cliffside preserve overlooking the Pacific Ocean. I would call her favorite restaurant to arrange a catered lunch at her home.

When nine days had passed, I didn't remember that it was Thanksgiving. I didn't remember that it was Bernie and Barbara's 39th anniversary. I imagined the day they'd left for Santa Barbara the previous week. Did they say anything to each other as they laid their black clothing into their suitcase?

That afternoon, I drove to the ocean, sat in the car, and wrote. Mom and Dad had left. Jamey had taken Ashley out.

I returned hours later. There was no movement, no sound. It was as if the house were wrapped in cotton. I approached her bedroom. Amy was still. I went to her side and held her hand. My tears landed on our joined fingers.

I don't remember making the calls she had asked me to make. Maybe I did make them, or maybe someone else made them. After her memorial service, I heard, "I'm sorry," over and over again, and people were hugging me, but I could feel nothing.

I had to leave.

"I'll be back for your birthday," I promised Ashley.

In January, she would be turning three.

IN LIEU OF FLOWERS, REMEMBER LIFE IS SHORT

Be patient toward all that is unsolved in your
heart and try to love the questions...
like locked rooms and like books that are now
written in a very foreign tongue....
Live everything. Live the questions...
~Rainer Maria Rilke~

When I got back to New York, I felt like I was being tossed around in waves that lifted me and threw me down against a rocky ocean bottom. As soon as I'd catch my breath, it was forced out of me. As I scrambled to get up, I'd be knocked down. I'd drag myself to the shore, but the waves would come again. I limped through the months until I could eventually withstand the waves; they didn't pummel me anymore. One day, the threat of them was gone. A part of me was missing, but I could stand up, and the grief wouldn't take me down.

As promised, two months later, Daniel and I returned for Ashley's birthday. When we walked into Jamey's home, the echo of my footsteps on the wood floors reminded me that Amy was gone. I sat on the chair by the window and remembered the day we'd gone to see the butterflies and how I'd watched Ashley and Amy playing outside with the ball.

Amy was one of the kindest, smartest, wisest, funniest people I had known. She had dedicated her life to teaching children who were both deaf and diagnosed with extreme spectrum disorders. When I'd asked her if she *really* thought she was making a difference, she'd looked at me incredulously. "Of course I'm making a difference." *How did she know?* She just believed it. She loved her work.

In those last weeks with her, I tried to reconcile myself with the questions. *Why did she only get 34 years? Why did she have to go? Are there people who are so special they just need less time here?* I wanted answers. I wanted to make sense of it. I couldn't.

The next morning, Jamey made us pancakes. *How is he getting up in the morning?* Ashley wanted to have tea parties and to play with Daniel. Her make-believe world was the perfect escape. As she served us "pretend" tea and biscuits from her little wood stove, she asked, "Where is my mama?"

I answered, "She is here with us. We just can't see her."

I wanted to tell Ashley that she would be given many gifts, and that life would offer her more than she could ever imagine—that she would travel to faraway places and, just like her mom, change lives along the way. I wanted to say, "Never stop believing in what you dream of. Your mom will always be there for you." But the truth was that Ashley was three, and all those thoughts were not as important as the moment. I sipped my "pretend" tea and tried not to cry. I could only love her, right then and there. I didn't know when I would see her again. I had to believe life would get easier for her and Jamey. Eventually, Amy's wish for them would come true. There would be a new family for Ashley. Jamey would remarry, and Ashley would have sisters. Amy would forever be a part of all of us. Ashley would never walk alone.

I looked through Amy's clothes, hanging exactly as they had been hanging on Thanksgiving. I touched her skirts and tops, scarves, and sweaters. I ran my hands over them. I smelled them. Jamey had asked me if I wanted anything. I took a top and a skirt I'd bought for her last birthday and a black sweatshirt from The Gap. It moved with me six times. I would keep it until my mind was gone and I couldn't even remember it was hers.

Back in New York, the creative and life-loving parts of me were shriveling up like dead leaves that fall in autumn. My nights were long and dark. As our relationship had become more estranged, Alan and I had begun going to therapy. The appointments became a vicious cycle of arguing and defending ourselves. I didn't recognize the man I had married. He was seeing a psychiatrist to address his "mood swings." The doctor was willing to share very little except that Alan was being medicated for manic-depressive disorder. The drugs would calm the extreme highs and lift the lows. He toggled around acting like a zombie, and then he'd wake up, and the nastiness would surface again.

Parts of me were being swept away like the tide going out, and the rest of me was being swallowed by quicksand. Some days, I thought about taking Daniel, getting in the car, and disappearing, but my son's voice led me back. I had to stay the course. I needed a plan.

During the next six months, there was nowhere to hide, but I could write. My words filled pages, and those pages became my glue. Writing kept my brokenness from disintegrating into a powder that would have blown away. I wrote a manuscript about the end of my sister's life, intending to give it to Ashley when she was older. I wrote love letters to my son. I penned long missives to my husband asking his understanding. My words were lost on him. I was invisible.

Clinging to driftwood in a churning sea, I finally worked up the courage to send an essay about my life with Daniel, now three years old, to "disabilities" publications and one mainstream magazine. In the mid-1990s, there were very few personal narratives being published in magazines and just as few books about children and families with "special needs."

Rejection letters came, but I didn't give up. When the acceptance letter arrived from a major magazine with a sizable offer, I was amazed. The most widely read mainstream magazine in the world was publishing my article. I couldn't believe it. I felt sure Amy, ever-present, had helmed this unexpected surprise. Eventually, the editor sent a photographer and planned a big spread. I wasn't sure when it would be on newsstands, but my voice would be heard. Other families with unique children would know they weren't alone.

A year later, Daniel and I were in the local supermarket. The cashier who knew us pointed to the magazine rack. It was the Family Circle Mother's Day issue. When I saw it, I wished Amy could have held it in her hands.

A SCHOOL FOR DANIEL

Everybody is a genius.
But if you judge a fish by its ability to climb a tree,
it will live its whole life believing that it is stupid.
~Albert Einstein~

Daniel was still in preschool, and I had to find the right kindergarten for him. We hoped the board of education could offer us a public school that could meet all of our son's educational, social, and therapeutic requirements. Most parents don't think of kindergarten in terms of "placements" and "programs," but we had no choice. The idea of an "individualized education plan" (an IEP) sounded attentive and responsible, but it was written by specialists who observed Daniel only once and didn't know him. They would dictate the support that his new school would be required to supply. I went to meetings at the board of education, armed with pictures of Daniel so the attendees who had not met my son would at least see the person we were discussing. He was determined to express himself, but his language skills were still delayed, his speech was inarticulate, and his fine motor skills had only marginally improved. Holding a fork, drinking from a cup...even the simplest uses of his hands made the idea of even tying his shoes or handwriting improbable. We didn't know how his gross motor challenges would affect him. He walked and moved awkwardly, and would probably never play a team sport—although that was the last thing I was worried about. He was very small, and he wore braces on his feet to help support his balance. He would likely need a lot of support throughout his elementary school years.

We looked at a couple of recommended public schools, but their "inclusion" programs weren't well established. I was skeptical as to how a classroom of thirty children and a small group of "special education" students were going to be best served by only two teachers and a classroom aide.

I discovered that the private special-education schools specialized in educating specific types of children. The NYC board of education culled information from both observations and testing, and classified children whose educational needs could not be met in mainstream classrooms. They classified Daniel as "speech-impaired" with other "disabling conditions" and provided us a list of possible schools that could be right for him. If none were a good fit, or if Daniel was not accepted to any of them, we had the option of finding another school we felt would serve our son's needs. The cost of the tuition and transportation would be our responsibility; we would then "sue" for the costs to be reimbursed. The process involved hearings that took place at the board of education building, and we would need an attorney to represent us.

We eventually found a private school in Manhattan. It was a 45-minute ride in traffic from our home, and Daniel would require a bus. Because the board of education had not yet approved him to attend the school, we would have to transport him and pay the tuition ourselves. Preparing for our case would become a full-time job, and this was only *kindergarten*. I couldn't imagine twelve years of this.

We learned early that, even with resources and the best specialists advising us, special-education environments are far from "one size fits all." Every child is unique. The start of their education begins the process of discovering which environments and teaching methods best serve their education. Add therapies such as speech, occupational, and physical therapy to this equation, assuming the school even provides such therapies, and it's a bit of a guessing game whether a certain school will be right for any given child.

A few months into the process, we had our doubts about Daniel continuing at his chosen school, but he would have to finish out the year. The educational plan was substandard and didn't address or support our son's obvious intelligence. Because he was more motor-impaired than the other students, the school wanted to separate him into a "class" with one other child. I was infuriated, but anger can be motivating. Having been a talent agent for ten years, advocating and marketing came second nature to me. Because I was in a business geared toward perception and how to create value around talent, I was prepared. I saw in my son what no one else saw. I saw his potential.

First grade was coming up fast, but I would find another school.

For those who lack imagination, complex people are difficult to understand. The word "disability" is, by definition, limiting. The prefix "dis" means "not" or "deprived of," and usually means "unable." I've never liked it. Daniel wasn't a poster child for what he would "overcome." We are all given gifts and liabilities. If we are lucky, someone recognizes the shiny parts, but the darkest parts of us are still there. We wouldn't be who we *are* if not for all those parts conspiring to make us unique. Whatever our son was given (and we had no idea what "it" was), he was illuminating. There was *something* about Daniel. His speech was barely intelligible, but I would gently ask him to repeat and piece the words together. I was able to hear his thoughts even if he couldn't articulate the words correctly, and I understood.

With September looming, we visited a number of schools, but Daniel was denied acceptance to most of them. His therapeutic needs exceeded what they could offer. Our attorney suggested a school on Long Island that specialized in speech and language development where he could get physical, occupational, and speech therapy onsite. He could attend the school for first through third grade, and it was possible they would expand beyond that. There were six children in a class, and he would have an aide to help him.

Initially, the distance seemed too far, but the work of its founder was groundbreaking in communication and speech "disorders." That school would provide the attention and language immersion that would set the foundation for our son's unique learning needs. But with additional children being picked up and traffic, it would be a two-hour bus ride from our home in each direction. Imagining my son on a bus for four hours a day made it a difficult decision, but I felt we had no choice. They accepted him at our interview.

I pored through the results of tests designed for children who were not like him—tests designed to describe his deficits. I read the reports that cost thousands of dollars, and I filed them, sometimes laughing in disbelief and sometimes crying. They included comments to the effect that he would have great difficulty reading and learning. Phrases jumped out such as "global neurological impairment," "pervasive developmental delay," "high expressive verbal IQ," "speech and language impaired," "fine and gross motor impaired," "learning disabled," and "attentional issues." These descriptions were all familiar to me; there was nothing new. But Daniel was not the child in those pages.

Daniel was enrolled in a dance and music class. The other children were able-bodied and could easily follow all of the teacher's directions. I knew it would be more difficult for Daniel, but he wasn't shy. I didn't want to sequester him from opportunities for socializing and fun. One afternoon, I got there early to pick him up. Each child was asked to walk along some cardboard blocks that symbolized the Great Wall of China. Two or three children quickly pranced barefoot upon the blocks and, within seconds, ran to the end. When it was Daniel's turn, he took a step up onto the first block. Daniel's ankle braces required that he keep his sneakers on. He steadied himself, took three steps, and I heard the thud of his knees hitting the floor. He tried to balance himself but fell again. He got up, moved the blocks back into place, and stepped back onto them. For the other children, this might have taken seconds, but for Daniel, it took minutes. I held my breath. There was silence, and then all of the kids started cheering him on. "You can do it, Daniel!" Once again, he began to walk on the blocks, but he couldn't balance. He fell. I heard his little voice saying, "I can do this. I can do this." He was on the floor, and one more time, up he went. I wanted to run to him and hold out my hand, just as I had when we'd walked along the sidewalk together, but I remained still. After a few tries, he finished. The teacher hugged him, and everyone was clapping. On that day in Brooklyn, I discovered who my son was. The answers to his uncertain future wouldn't come from pages of reports. The answers would come from Daniel. If there was a syndrome or some medical terminology underlying his complexities but we could never discover a way to label him or name it, I would be content in knowing Daniel was Daniel. He would find his way.

TWENTY-EIGHT BOXES

You're only one defining decision away
from a totally different life.
~Mike Batterson~

In the fall of 1996, I was 38. I sat alone in a synagogue in Brooklyn. I hadn't attended services in years. Yom Kippur is the most solemn and introspective of the Jewish High Holy Days. It is the day we humble ourselves and ask—not once, but three times throughout each service—to be truthful, to go inward, and to be witnessed as we find that for which we seek forgiveness. I was feeling so alone. Surrounded by hundreds of strangers, I was confronting the truth. I was in a marriage that was over for me. It had been two years since I had held my sister's hand and promised I'd leave my husband.

As I was listening to the prayers that had been chanted for thousands of years, sanctifying this day of humility, I prayed silently: *If there is a power greater than me, please see I am struggling. Offer me a sign, anything, so that I might forgive myself and find clarity and freedom from my pain. If I owe my husband anything more, show me what it is. I want to remain faithful to the promises of my wedding day, but we have changed. I have changed. Life is too short, and I have to leave him. Part of me is dying. I must salvage myself from the wreckage. I am alive and here for Daniel. Please lead me to do what would serve the highest good for us and especially for my son, whom I love so deeply.*

If I left, Alan would believe I was betraying him; he would hate me for it. He would do everything he could to make it difficult. But I could return to work. I could create an independent life so that I could provide for my son. I wept through most of the service.

Right before I left the temple, I went into the ladies' room. There was a sign on the wall: "If you are being abused, there's help." It went on to list all the ways that domestic abuse manifests. I stood there reading and rereading it. And then I hurried out.

Whether you believe in angels or the power of the universe or God—or luck or none of these forces at all—and whether you believe in divine intervention or just coincidence, when I returned home, the phone rang. A stranger's voice said that I had been suggested for a newly created position at a large, prestigious talent agency. He asked if I would consider an interview. I was silent as I listened. I was in shock. I told him I was flattered and grateful for the call, and that I would think about it.

One thing was certain—the man who called was definitely not Jewish. No Jew would call on Yom Kippur. *But why now? How was this happening? Who had referred me? How did this person know me? What if I took the interview? What if I got the job? Then what? Was my sister in another dimension, somehow involved in this?* The idea of pursuing this opportunity was both curious and terrifying, and it was an answer to my prayers.

The building on West 57th Street housed one of the best-known talent agencies in the world. I hadn't been in an office for three years, but I got dressed on the day of the interview with a certain confidence as if I were being led. Good thing I had kept my suits. Classics. I picked a favorite—a chartreuse Tahari. I questioned the color, but I went for it. Green is the symbol of life and renewal. Done.

The offices were fancier and more corporate than the building I had worked in before. If I got the job, I would be helping to build a department like the one I'd left three years earlier. I watched the numbers in the elevator going up.

The interview went well. During the decade I had been active in the entertainment industry, my credibility and reputation in my area of specialty had become well established. If I wanted it, the job was mine.

On the train back to Brooklyn, I wondered how this could work. I didn't know how to explain to a potential employer that I had a child with complex needs. I wanted him to know, but I didn't want special treatment. I would have to prove I could manage the pressures of building a business, but I wanted reassurance that I would have the leeway to care for my son. Unexpected needs would arise.

If I went back to work, I could leave Alan. He didn't want me to go, but I knew we were incapable of fixing our broken marriage. His anger was non-negotiable, and my pleas for rational behavior went unheard. We'd fallen into a familiar pattern: I would gather strength and then crumble in retreat. I learned from reading and talking with Deena how common it is for women in abusive relationships to lose their identities in the cycle of manipulation. I had become the poster child for that. I couldn't think straight. No matter what I did, my life was going to be difficult. I decided I would call and say, "No."

I called, but I didn't say "No." Instead, I said, "I'd like to have another meeting."

I could stake my claim with this—I'd be financially independent. Eventually, I could move out and start a new life. It was emancipating and scary at the same time. I had nothing, no money, just my personal belongings, but I had everything to gain if I could reclaim my life.

What about Daniel? Did I have what it would take to support him through what would surely be an egregious divorce? Was it fair?

When I announced to Alan that I had been offered the job, he said, "If you take that job, you are proving how determined you are to end this marriage."

Exactly as I'd predicted. So be it.

I went into our bedroom and starting shaking, knowing this declaration was the beginning of the end.

The initial job offer was for a lot less money than I'd asked for, but it was a good opportunity. The prestige of the agency was an important consideration. I had been gone from the business for long enough that I knew the time was now. I was doing the right thing. This would be an excellent credential, and I'd quickly prove myself.

Daniel, now seven, would need new routines. I prepared lengthy and detailed lists of snacks, activities, and hour-by-hour instructions designed to avoid any confusion for our caregiver in advance of beginning our new lifestyle. I was in charge of all communications with the school as well as organizing and attending doctors' visits. When I got home, I would take over with dinner and whatever needs Daniel had. We didn't miss a single bedtime story.

My days were exhausting. But no matter what, I made it to Daniel's school, an hour away, for talent shows, holiday shows, awards ceremonies, and parent/teacher meetings. And every night, I ran from work to the subway for the hour ride home so that Daniel and I could spend as much time together as possible.

Usually, I was walking into a minefield with Alan, but whenever I wasn't sure how I was going to keep it together, I would close my eyes and hear Daniel's voice: "Can we have pizza?" "Can we have ice cream?" "Can we watch [a certain movie]?" "Can I have [a certain game]?" "Can you read to me?" "Can you come in and say goodnight?" He led me to the only place I felt secure—the steady heartbeat of my love for him.

Within months of my taking the job, my life with Alan became unsustainable. He threatened me a few times. I sought out an attorney to begin the process of serving him divorce papers. I was shaking as she educated me, discussing the steps that needed to be taken.

I wanted to be educated about the law and what I would be entitled to. The attorney forewarned me that, because Alan had owned the building prior to our marriage and we didn't have a lot of shared assets, the small financial settlement I might receive could end up being spent entirely on legal services. And, even if I were eligible for it, I wasn't so sure I'd ever see a child-support payment. I couldn't afford to move out, but I needed boundaries. She suggested that we negotiate a separation agreement. The house was large enough, and we could live on separate floors. She also urged me to seek an order of protection. This was not something I had ever considered. It felt so extreme. Having Alan served was going to be a very deliberate assault against him—that sounds like an ironic way to describe it, but there would be a court record of it. This was serious. At the time, I was very confused and not so sure I should do it, but I pushed myself when a friend said, "One of these days, he might push you down those stairs."

I didn't want to go, but on a cloudy day, I left for family court. I sat in an unfamiliar, cold waiting room with wooden benches. A lot of people were there and so many children. Every conversation echoed off the walls. I tried to reconcile how I'd gotten there. I felt so different than these people. But was I? They were seeking refuge or justice from a judge just like I was.

After Alan was served the order of protection, he was infuriated, and he insisted I had invented the entire allegation. He was also adamant that I was wrong to want to divorce him and that I was at fault. He made it clear that he would fight me, and he wasn't paying for my decision to leave.

I couldn't afford my attorney, but I scraped together the retainer from the small amounts of money I could still access in our joint bank accounts. As soon as he saw the withdrawals, Alan closed the accounts. The lawyers went back and forth, but we had an agreement that we would take turns caring for Daniel every other weekend. I just hoped it would end soon, and that I would have enough money at the end of it all to pay my attorney.

For a year, we lived in the house together. In order to relocate, I needed to establish my work history and credit. The rental market in Park Slope was getting expensive and tight. The neighborhood had become highly sought after, so I couldn't afford a suitable two-bedroom nearby. On a rainy day, I took Daniel into the city and found the only one-bedroom apartment I could reasonably afford, in a safe, full-service building. My credit wasn't very good, but if I came up with a $10,000 security deposit, the management company was willing to offer me a lease. My father agreed to loan me the money.

I started packing. I would be moving in two weeks. Our agreement had stated that Daniel would reside with me and have visitation one night a week and every other weekend with Alan. Then, without warning, Alan announced he wasn't signing it and demanded to get joint custody of Daniel; he insisted that every other week, Daniel would reside with him. It was a faulty proposition. Given Alan's anger toward me, his inability to co-parent, his moodiness, his lack of organization, and his general demeanor of being depressed and overwhelmed, I knew he made this demand to hurt me, and without regard for his son.

My attorney argued for my sole custody, but Alan was adamant that, if I didn't agree, he would see me in court. My friends thought he wouldn't be able to handle the multitude of needs presented. He was just punishing me by taking my son in a situation that required more than the typical resources, patience, and stamina of parenting. But there wasn't any choice. I would have to arrange two school buses—one for Brooklyn, for when Daniel was with Alan, and one for Manhattan, for when Daniel was with me. I also had to find a nanny willing to work in two separate households in distant parts of the city. It was implausible. What about Daniel? It would be highly stress-ful for an eight-year-old child who already faced enough challenges to move between homes. Yet, Alan was unrelenting.

The September day in 1999 when I left Brooklyn, it was raining. The movers loaded the twenty-eight boxes containing everything I owned onto the truck. I watched as the movers drove away. I didn't take my key. I turned back once and looked at the lintels and the thousands of red bricks occupying the corner that had been our home. Alan would change the lock within the hour.

Each of the boxes was labeled carefully as if the bubble wrap could protect the good memories and the labels might explain the remnants of my broken life. Only the baby pictures and the video-tapes of Daniel really mattered to me.

I couldn't afford a car service, so I took the train uptown. My chest felt like someone had taken a rusty blade and carved out my heart. I prayed Alan would bring Daniel to me that weekend as promised. I wondered what my son would think as he waited for my return in those hours after school. I had always promised when I left the house, "Mommy always comes home." It was the one day, I didn't come home.

My friend Joyce met me at the new apartment with a big hug. We went to work unpacking. I was grateful I didn't have to be alone. With each dish, glass, fork, knife, and spoon we unpacked, it was becoming more real. I had done it. After we were finished, I stared at the yet-to-be-unpacked boxes awaiting dressers and storage for our clothing, books, toys, and pictures. I looked out at the rain. Joyce held me in her arms.

There was a playground in the back. I would be closer to work. The views were good. Our apartment number was 2020—clear vi-sion. We wouldn't have furniture, but we had a mattress Daniel and I could share. I made the bed.

FAITH

Faith is the belief in that for which there is no evidence.
~Unknown~

The first night Alan brought Daniel to the new apartment, I met him in the front lobby. He looked so small. The entryway was two stories high, sweeping and enormous. It was like a big hotel. We went to a pizza place on First Avenue. He was quieter than usual and confused.

"Why are we living here now? Where is our furniture? Who are those men at the front door?"

"Our furniture is coming. The men are doormen; they make sure we stay safe."

"When is the furniture coming?"

"I'm not sure, but soon."

"Where will we sleep?"

"On the bed."

"Will you read to me?"

"Yes, I will always read to you."

"Where will I have my birthday party?"

"We will figure it out."

The next month, Daniel would be nine. Of course we would have a birthday party. My parents came every year for his birthday, and they were already planning to visit. I could use my father's help assembling furniture as I would get furniture by then.

The truth was that I couldn't afford furniture, but I believed we would eventually have what we needed. Meanwhile, the doormen became Daniel's friends. Daniel would chatter away with them when he got off the bus, and they looked out for us. Neither of us had ever had doormen, but their watchful and protective eyes and ears were invaluable when I wanted to know if Daniel had gotten home okay or if the nanny had arrived. The pizza guys got to know us, too, and the bagel shop guys gave Daniel free cookies, just like in Brooklyn.

Shortly after we moved in, I placed a picture of a stone house on my bedroom mirror. I dreamed that one day, we would have a larger apartment and a country home, both big enough for Daniel to have his own bedroom. It would take time, that's all.

Daniel was managing to adjust. And despite disliking my department head, the job was good enough. It was a beginning. I was especially grateful for my close friends.

My journey now was a quest I could hardly articulate to myself. How would I explain to Daniel the unfairness of his parents' failed attempts to remain together? The process of our divorce was complicated. It was laced with irreconcilable differences that continued to make our legal separation difficult. Alan wanted revenge. He didn't want to put an end to the divorce process because he didn't actually want a divorce. I didn't want to go to court because it would be even more expensive than what we were already doing, and my legal bills were mounting. In my stronger moments, I trusted that my navigational system hadn't completely malfunctioned. Daniel and I would be okay. I would make sure of that. I had better things in mind for us.

Our bedtime talks were filled with stories about how our days had gone and dueling "I love you's" until one of us quit. I read to him until he finally gave in and fell asleep.

I put up a good front while mourning the broken promises of the life I had left. The hardest decision I made was whether to walk away or try harder. I had come to my marriage hoping to meet up with my best friend, but Alan was now my enemy. Daniel seemed sad and quieter than usual. His traveling between homes was hard on both of us. I missed him when I dropped him off in Brooklyn and feared for the day Alan wouldn't return him to me.

My medicine cabinet had a lot of prescription drugs in it. After Daniel fell asleep, I would sit on the couch and have a drink, or two, usually straight vodka on ice, and then I'd chase the cocktails with pills in order to sleep. When I woke up, I'd gobble antidepressants. I was functioning quite well; all of the sharp edges were gone. It was easy to seek comfort in their welcoming arms.

One day, a few months later, I dumped all the bottles. I'd stopped treading water for long enough to see through the fog. There would be a lighthouse leading me; I just had to cut out the pills and look for the light. I had faith it would be there. I believed in the life I'd create without any evidence of it.

When our nanny was sick or couldn't make it in, I had to bring Daniel to my office because I couldn't rely on Alan to take care of him. It was clear that Daniel's care was my responsibility. The corporate culture wasn't conducive to having my son at work, so I would whisk him into my office and close the door. I was self-conscious when Daniel's voice rose loudly, reaching above the quiet. My colleague Lisa was especially kind. She had a TV in her office and would let him sit with her and watch. There was another office decked out with toys, including stuffed-animal characters *The Cat in the Hat* and *The Grinch*. Having spied the goodies, Daniel once wandered in there. I tried to grab him before he could, but he was too far ahead of me. The attorney who represented the estate of Dr. Seuss wasn't overly outgoing and seemed a little confused as to who Daniel was, but he forced a smile. I breathed a sigh of relief. At least he wasn't mean about it.

My department head wasn't supportive. I made infrequent requests to leave early or make appointments for Daniel. His intolerance was evident in the faces he made and his disgusted attitude. Once, he pointed to his watch as if to remind me that it wasn't quite quitting time. It was his way of making it clear that he was the boss. I wanted to smack him. His earlier pitch to me, that he would be understanding about my obligations to my son, was filled with empty promises. He had no idea how many moving parts I was managing—special school, therapists, childcare, and a protracted divorce battle—but the details were none of his business. I wanted to appear confident and capable. I didn't want to leave room for him to suspect that I couldn't do my job and do it extremely well.

When I learned that a less experienced male coworker whom I had suggested we hire had been offered better compensation than mine, I was livid. Complaining wasn't going to get me the right deal, and it wasn't going to get me the next opportunity. Despite the fact that I was terrified of losing that job, I hired an attorney who suggested that we approach the firm seeking an equitable solution, not a lawsuit. I prevailed and was able to secure an appropriate raise.

I spent three years keeping my focus on our department's growth. Being competitive, I wanted to be "in the game." With one more year on my contract, my goal was to afford a bigger apartment. If things were still difficult at work at the end of the year, I'd make a move.

When friends came to visit us, Daniel would proudly show them around our 700-square-foot apartment. "This is our bed," he would say. I felt embarrassed about how little we had, but we finally had a proper dining table, couches, and a TV. Daniel was sleeping on a queen pullout couch and adjusting. He didn't like going to Brooklyn, but he was happy at school.

I joined a gym, rarely missed a morning workout, and went on small trips. Daniel and I went to museums and the theater, and we baked. When I left him in Brooklyn every other Sunday, I prepared homework folders, all the clothing he needed, and made sure he had money for lunch and school trips. I was sure Alan wouldn't pay attention to my well-intentioned notes. Any discussion would escalate into a contest of wills. Whatever I felt was best for Daniel, Alan would argue against just to argue. He also absolved himself of all financial support. My friends wanted me to fight. No. I was still adamant. I wasn't going to court. If I did, I feared Alan was so stubborn that the case would be dragged out for what could be years. He would make sure of it. Alan would face his own reckoning with the universe. I was sure of *that*. My values were grounded in staying out of victimhood. My love for my son and my faith would sustain me.

On my 41st birthday, I had no assets and $50,000 in legal and credit-card debt, which was rising by the month. Gone were the house, the car, and the bank accounts. They were all Alan's now. The monsters that stalked me in every quiet moment wore the faces of all of the unknowns. If I stayed present, I could handle it. I couldn't afford the trip to Paris I wanted to celebrate my birthday, but Scott convinced me to buy a secondhand Cartier watch. It wasn't Paris, but it was something French, and a symbol of something I would enjoy. Like a "starter home," it was my "starter watch."

THE BEST DEAL I EVER MADE

Freedom is nothing else but a chance to be better.
~Albert Camus~

As we neared the millennium, making a change at work was becoming a necessity. I had no idea where I'd go, but I was done with tolerating people who diminished me. In the three years I had been with this company, I had accomplished what I'd set out to do, and I was proud of that. I'd find another job. As soon as we returned from the holiday break, I would figure it out.

First, I was going to Las Vegas to see Barbra Streisand. I had been gifted the tickets for some charitable work I had done, and my friend and I were leaving that night.

I was in Lancôme on West 57th Street, buying mascara, when my cell phone rang. It was my former boss, Scott.

"There's a situation we need to discuss. Can you come to the office?"

I was clueless. *What's he talking about?* I couldn't go to his office. It was the day before New Year's Eve, and I was getting on a flight within a few hours.

"I can do it in about a week," I said. "Would that work?"

He said that there was a good opportunity for me. A number of talent agents had left to start their own company. My history with the company made me their first call. He urged me to meet with them right after I came back.

Where was this coming from? Luck, timing, divinity, Amy?

Maybe all four.

The meeting was brief, and we came to terms quickly. I would return to work there at the end of January.

It had been six years since I had left. When I walked into my former office, it was a homecoming. Familiar friends and people I had yet to meet all greeted me with a warm welcome. We had a lot of work to do. It would be challenging, helping to reorganize and restore stability, but it was an opportunity for leadership. More than anything, this was exciting to me.

Over the next two years, we established an even stronger and highly respected department within our company and within the business. We were diversifying and growing.

And then, without much discussion, both my mentors announced they were making changes. One was retiring, and Scott would be moving to Florida. I was promoted to executive vice-president and department head, a title held by few women in our industry.

As I began to do better financially, my shame about the debt I'd incurred, and the loss and failure of my marriage, began diminishing. Three years earlier, I'd initiated my separation from Alan, and despite his ongoing refusal to sign our settlement agreement, I wouldn't let him or anyone else interfere. I was now the captain of my ship.

Each morning, I started the day with an inspirational reading. I came across a quote that I tried to live by: "Do something that scares you, every day." (Eleanor Roosevelt)

I could afford a bigger apartment now—and required no extra security. My income and credit were on the rise. Daniel would have a bedroom with views of the East River.

When I'd been in my early twenties, I'd imagined I would one day live in a high-rise building with views of the river. *We did it!*

The doormen, George and Ray, would become our longtime guardians. We stayed in that apartment for twelve years.

One night, I was on my way home from a business trip to Los Angeles. A black town car with dark windows had delivered me to the Bob Hope Airport in Burbank. My driver opened my door. As I stepped out of the car into the heat, he took my hand to steady me and helped check my bags.

"Is there anything else, ma'am?"

"No thanks. Have a great day."

He left me at the check-in counter. My black sweater, black jeans, and black boots hinted that I was from New York. Women in L.A. don't usually wear all black. A man walked by and said softly, "You look beautiful." He might have seen my sense of humor in the wink I threw him, but he didn't see the complexity, the loss, or the depths from which I had risen.

The counter clerk said, "You probably hear that all the time."

I didn't reply, but I smiled and tipped him. My life wasn't exactly as put together as I looked, but in a few short years, I had come a long way from the underbelly of what had felt like an 18-wheeler rolling over me.

The gate was crowded. On the floor nearby, two young children were playing a game of baby tag, one crawling as fast he could away from the other, who was trying to catch him. Their laughter was the best thing I had heard all day. The parents of those babies didn't know what it felt like to wait long past the "normal" developmental age for their children's first steps. They might never know what it feels like to have a child whose speech is unintelligible, or who would wear hearing aids or might never handwrite or tie their shoes.

I sat with my laptop open and cell phone nearby. I typed with one hand while I held a cup of coffee in the other, and I watched along with the audience. The two toddlers were making their parents smile in delight at their competition.

My phone rang.

"Hi, honey."

"Hi, Mom."

"How's it going?"

"Good. When will you be home?"

"Around nine tonight."

"Why so late?"

"Because that's how long it takes to get there. What are you doing?"

"Nothing much. I love you."

"I love you, too, Daniel."

"I have a good idea for my game show."

"Okay, honey. When I get home, you can tell me about it, okay?

"I want to just tell you one thing now."

"Daniel, we are going to board the plane in a minute and it's hard for me to listen now, so can you please tell me when I see you? It will be so much better!"

"Okay, bye." I could hear his disappointment.

"Bye, honey. I love you." He had already hung up.

Like most 10-year-olds, he was in the moment. He probably didn't know how far away California was. I'm not sure he understood how hard I had worked for the upward trajectory our lives had taken. The most important thing was that he knew when I said something, I meant it. When I promised that the tooth fairy would come, she came. When I said we'd get furniture, eventually it appeared. Since the day Daniel had been born, beyond the reach of what I could hold was what I could create. I was strong, and yet I had yielded. I was willful, and I was afraid, too. These parts of me were forces I wrestled with; they inspired and informed me.

I had the emotional freedom to become whole and not just dream of what I could accomplish. A lot of will, a little luck, some timing, and the universal truth... Show your clarity, and clarity appears.

Show love and love surrounds you; show ambiguity, and you're in a spiraling tornado. I was not stopping—in fact, I had just begun.

I boarded the plane. I wanted to hear all about the game-show idea. There wasn't one word of what Daniel wanted to share that I didn't want to hear. I couldn't wait for the big hug my son would deliver. The "Welcome Home" sign that would be taped to our apartment door was better than any deal I could have made.

NO BUSINESS LIKE THIS BUSINESS

As human beings, our job in life is to help people
realize how rare and valuable each one of us really is...
something inside that is unique to all time. It's our job
to encourage each other to discover that uniqueness
and to provide ways of developing its expression.
~Fred Rogers~

It was my love of the theater that got me into the entertainment business. My eyes would well up with tears as the curtain rose at each Broadway show I saw, remembering that night when I was 18 sitting in the Shubert Theater, dreaming of a life in New York City. I would watch the Academy Awards with the same passion I had for movies when I was ten, went to the "cinema," and ate Jujyfruits, my favorite candy. They don't sell that candy now in the theaters, but I still love going to the movies. Later, I became a binge-watching TV junkie and lamented the long waits for the next seasons of each of my favorite series.

When my first job at a talent agency paid so little that I thought I'd need a second job just to eat, I stuck with it because I believed it wouldn't always be that way. It wasn't the pursuit of money that motivated me; at that time, I thought if I could just make 20,000, it would be a lot. I had a feeling early on that I wanted to be influential in people's lives. At a time when I was uncertain about my identity and what I would do, I was fortunate to discover this work that made good use of my nice clothes and the fact that I liked to talk. That I had once been bold enough to carry a knife didn't hurt, but mostly, I felt I would be good at it.

My first break came very unexpectedly when a man sitting behind me at a lecture liked my suit. My most important break came from the founder of the company where I would spend the longest part of my career. He taught me that each day is a blank canvas, and regardless of yesterday's successes, disappointments, or failures, you can start again. In the face of his own challenges, it was his unwillingness to lead from fear and his unwavering vision that led to his success. Leadership wasn't exactly what I had aspired to when I worried about how I'd afford my rent, but I learned that the less I worried about my rent, the better I got at my job. I paid attention to people much smarter than me. When I closed a deal, no matter how large or small, I didn't think about the ten percent we would earn for our services; I thought about whether I'd made the best deal for the client and moved on.

Being a good agent requires a complex skillset: identifying talent, curating a client list, and supporting people who, as powerful or famous as they may become, are human. Being a great agent is an act of unlimited devotion. Our clients choose bravely to live in the unknown, and the best agent marches into the unknown with them. I've had the privilege to represent both very famous and lesser-known performers who are exceptionally talented. I've been inspired by them and confounded by their ability to keep going against the odds.

The part of the job that can't be taught is the desire to identify and develop potential and to deliver for the performers we represented. The work is diplomacy at its best and frustration at its worst. I had to listen when I wanted to scream and scream when no one was listening. Sometimes, when things weren't going well, I had to keep going back, trying different approaches to resolve a conflict or a difficult negotiation.

One can lead from power or intellect, but when my turn came, I figured I'd lead the way I lived. I wasn't fearless; respect, humility, humor, advocacy, and love would show me the way. I worked shoulder to shoulder with my colleagues championing their losses and victories. I think the best leaders know they aren't heroes. I made mistakes. I learned from them.

I wanted to be known for how much I cared and what I'd achieved for others.

Most of the people who work in our industry are invisible and anonymously work long and thankless hours. Whether forward-facing or behind the scenes, they are there because they can't imagine or wouldn't even consider another profession. This was true for me.

Contrary to comments I've heard over the years about my "cool" profession, it wasn't always easy or fun or exciting. Coming to work on some days was like walking the deck on a choppy sea, but I held onto the rails and pulled myself along. When things were hard, and I thought "maybe I'll just quit," the morning came, I chose one of my signature suits or jackets, I did my hair, I put on my makeup, and I walked through the door, head up. When I sat at my desk, I knew why I was there.

It's a high-stakes business that's fueled by a unique combination of human and financial resources, and subject to extreme rises and falls. In the abundance of the 1980s, it was all about growth. Into the 1990s, the infrastructure shifted with faulty dot-com speculation. Hollywood titans were threatened by the unstable stock market and exiting Wall Street money. Those who fared the best adapted and merged, or created their own independent fiefdoms.

Eventually, technology was the most significant disrupter. It caused a tidal wave that swept across every media platform. Some of the biggest talent agencies took on investors or grew by consuming smaller businesses and diversified as the call for change resounded.

The early 2000s brought to life the vision of those who saw that there would be multiple screens—some of them very small—thus creating the need for content and the reality of competition for viewers' attention. The biggest winners would be those who owned the pipelines through which content would flow and their ownership of intellectual property. Technology helped to quickly create and therefore displace content, making the staying power shorter for new product, and changing the way both product and talent were valued. Broadcast and cable networks were no longer limited to a few empires. The digital age would radically alter every sector of entertainment and the habits of consumers, from terrestrial to satellite radio and viewing options that would quickly and deeply impact every corner of our business.

When I stumbled into the entertainment industry in the early Eighties, little attention was paid to the issue of underrepresentation of women or persons of color. I was conscious of the inequities, but idealistically or foolishly, I believed that enough time would pass to allow women, men, or people of any ethnicity to contribute equally. The movement of gender and non-gender identity was a long way off. For the business to change, minds needed to change. No one who wanted to succeed could do so by focusing on what would stop us.

From the beginning, I didn't identify myself as a woman working in a man's world. In the mirror, I saw a person who would get the job done. I believed that, no matter what, we were all people—and *people* would get the job done.

We got the job done. One day at a time.

SLOW DOWN

There is more to life than increasing its speed.
~Mohandas Gandhi~

I pulled back on the heavy glass door and stepped out of the July heat. I could feel a rush of cold air blow across my naked arms. My high heels clicked the rhythm of my fast walk. Cosmetics reps were lunging at me, trying to spray their perfumes. The sounds of hustling, scurrying, and consuming swirled up from the floor. Hundreds of scents blending together all wafted at me. I heard the dinging of the elevators and saw shoppers from all over the world moving quickly, all of them on a mission.

I could dress so that I looked like I belonged in Saks, but I didn't feel like I did. I felt I had little in common with everyone I saw, but my genetically well-engineered body moved gracefully and at my command. If success has a look, perhaps it began for me when, at age three, I insisted on choosing my own wardrobe. Since my twenties, dressing up has been a form of self-expression for me.

I generally walked the streets with focused determination. Daniel, now nine trailed behind me. Observing every detail of street life, he rattled off endless questions.

"Why are the sirens so loud? Why is this man in front of us walking so slow? Why is it so cold out? How much farther do we have to walk? Let's take a cab..."

I listened and answered: "I don't know why the sirens are so loud. I don't know why that man is so slow. Why are *you* so slow? We have to walk until we get where we are going. No, we're not taking a cab. I didn't notice that. Hmmm, why do you think it's so cold?"

I didn't suffer from that same need-to-know-everything-about-everything-every-second. In fact, I tried *not* to think of all the unknowns. I was just trying to look good while singlehandedly raising a complex child and growing a business. That's why we were in Saks—to get lipstick.

"What time are we going to be home?"

"Why?" I asked.

"Because there's a show I want to watch."

"Well, I'm not sure."

"Well, what time do you *estimate* we'll be home?"

"I don't know," I said.

"When I'm the president," he announced, "I will have a limousine."

He liked to talk about the "fact" that he would be the president.

"Why a limousine?" I turned and asked, and I realized that even with his hearing aids, all the noise made it impossible for him to hear me.

"Me, too," I said, loudly this time. "I always wanted a limousine—and a private plane, too."

He was still behind me.

"Why do you want a limousine so badly?" I asked.

"Because then I wouldn't have to walk anywhere," he said.

I had stopped wondering what it would be like to have a child who *could* be the president or who *would* walk faster. The fact that he walked was a gift. I once asked him if he could do anything besides being the president, what would it be?

His answer: "I would move the planets around."

"Move the planets around? And why would you move the planets around?"

"To get a better look at Pluto."

"Why a better look at Pluto?"

"I would know once and for all if it's a star or a planet."

I listened intently.

I didn't know there was any doubt as to whether Pluto was a star or a planet until years later when scientific evidence suggested that Pluto might not have been the planet we'd always thought it was. It is a star, but I have no idea why Daniel was questioning whether Pluto was a star and not a planet. He just seemed to know that maybe it was a star.

Daniel was overly confident of his future. He regularly talked about being president, a TV producer, or owning the Yankees. I, on the other hand, despite my relative resourcefulness, had no definitive sense of how the future would unfold. I just had to keep the faith that I would take care of us and that our life together would remain stable.

As we moved through the store, I noticed some women looking at us. One of Daniel's nannies got angry when people in public places stared at Daniel. I appreciated that she cared so much, but I usually didn't notice it. I looked back every so many steps. Daniel was still trailing behind me. This was how we had always walked. I moved past jewelry and handbags while Daniel dragged his feet. It would be a rare sight if he were walking by my side and if his pants weren't being shredded under his feet. His glasses were cloudy, as usual, and had slipped down to their usual resting place on his freckled nose. His thick dark hair was always messy; no matter who cut it, it always looked a little unkempt. He was a little chubby.

We got to the counter for the lipstick.

"Stay right here." I motioned him to stop, knowing there would be a lot of temptation to play with the samples that were out on the counter.

He stood there and fidgeted. I was trying to make it quick, knowing his attention span was short.

"There. What do you think?" I modeled the color I had picked.

"Let's go," he said. No patience. All the noises and smells were probably overwhelming.

We left the counter and made our way out of the store.

"Daniel, pick it up, c'mon, let's go." He was still dawdling behind me.

I turned back. And then I stopped. *How long had I waited for him to take those first steps?*

As we left the store, I stopped by a mirror. I scrutinized my face and checked out the new lipstick. Daniel didn't stop. Now, he was walking in front of me. That was a first! Usually, I was looking back to make sure he hadn't disappeared. He went out the door and took a right onto 49th Street and headed for Madison. From behind him, I watched his uneven gait. *Let's see how long before he looks back.*

He just kept walking.

"Hey!" I called to him loudly. "Wait for me!" But he didn't.

And then I thought, *Maybe today is the day I'll walk more slowly. Why rush?*

Daniel turned around and smiled back at me.

I smiled and waved.

Maybe, if I let him walk at his own pace, he wouldn't ask to take a cab.

9/11

If we learn nothing else from this tragedy,
we learn that life is short and there is no time for hate.
~Sandy Dahl, wife of Flight 93 pilot Jason Dahl~

On the Tuesday that would historically be known as 9/11, my assistant told me to put the TV on right away. It was 9 a.m. We watched a replay as the first plane tore through the World Trade Center. Then came the second and the explosion. *This doesn't look like an accident.* We were mesmerized as the edifice crumbled. There was a mess of rubble and twisted metal, broken glass, and the thick gray dust that hung in the air and covered everything. We could hear the muffled screams of people on the streets being picked up by TV cameras. The footage was played over and over again.

My coworkers were all stunned. I ran up a flight of stairs to let the founder of our company know that he should put the TV on. Then I ran back down to our conference room, where all of the agents were gathered for our morning meeting, to see if anyone had family members who worked in the World Trade Center. The circuits were busy, and none of our phones were working. I wanted everyone to know they could leave. There were eighteen of us in my department, working across two floors. Those of us watching in the conference room were crying and hugging each other. We had no idea whether there would be another hit or where. We were in midtown, about a mile away, but there were a lot of landmarks around us. The public library, Grand Central, Saint Patrick's Cathedral, the GM building,

Rockefeller Center...our *whole area* could be the next target. I ran into the offices for my department, looking for anyone who hadn't come to the conference room.

We needed to go.

I had to get to my son.

When I got downstairs, people were running around and looking up the block at the MetLife building towering above us. It was right above Grand Central Station. People were murmuring that it could be the next hit. I began running in the other direction, toward Fifth Avenue. As I ran, I just kept thinking that if there was another strike nearby, I might never see my son again. No one was talking—just running and looking back. It got harder to breathe. I had the wrong shoes on for running. I wanted to take them off. Names were flying through my head. I heard myself saying them out loud. All those people I loved and needed to see again. My boyfriend Peter, Ashley, Scott, Regina, Joyce, my parents, and my brother. *Why the hell didn't those three guys I left in the office leave right away? I TOLD THEM TO LEAVE. What were they thinking? Were they acting cool—like they didn't want to react? They weren't scared?*

Someone grabbed my arm. A stranger. "Everything is going to be okay," she said. I held her hand, tears falling from my cheeks. She must have heard me talking to myself. I was shaking. "Don't worry, we will be okay," she said softly. She walked with me silently for many blocks.

Daniel. I have to get to Daniel.

I told myself to slow down. My heart felt like it would explode. I didn't know where Alan was. We'd been divorced for two years. I wasn't sure if he was in the country. *Past Saint Patrick's Cathedral, past the GM building—one less target—past Central Park. No one would bomb us up here, right?*

I looked to the sky; to the north, it was blue, but to the south, it was black with smoke.

When I arrived home, I fell into Peter's arms. We had been dating for the past year. He had a plan—to get his car. If we couldn't get the car, we'd get to Queens. Rent a car. Take stuff. *How much stuff?* We might not be coming home. A change of clothes for Daniel, Kermit (his favorite Muppet), and water.

"Let's go," he said. *"NOW."* His voice was overly protective and demanding. We both wiped tears from our faces. We were okay. We were together. Daniel was fine. He was safe at school on Long Island. We walked out to York Avenue. I had already half-walked, half-run fifty or sixty blocks in my heels. My feet were blistered and bleeding, but I didn't care. I had to get to my son at school. He was an hour away. I was afraid that to secure the city, the bridges and tunnels would be shut down. There was no time to waste.

I finally reached the school on my cell phone. The children were told there was a bad accident and a lot of traffic. The parents who could make it were coming, and the children whose parents couldn't make it would sleep at the school. The cell phone kept cutting out. The circuits continued to remain busy, so I couldn't reach my family or friends.

We walked forty-five blocks back downtown to the garage, which was close to the U.N. I kept insisting on the way down, "They won't let us take the car; the whole area by the U.N. is shut down." According to the news, sections of the city were being closed off. The whole area by the U.N. was off-limits. I was sure all the blocks over there would be heavily guarded by security personnel. Nevertheless, though it seemed strange to me, we were able to get the car out.

They should have denied us entry and exit to the garage. They should have, but they didn't.

"That was strange," I said as we drove out onto First Avenue.

147

"You would have walked to get to your son; driving is way easier." He smiled and reached for my hand.

We drove around to the entrance to the Midtown Tunnel. A fortress of police cars was blocking its entrance. The tunnel was closed, and traffic was being rerouted to continue straight past the tunnel. There was no other way to get to Daniel's school. We pulled alongside one of the cops. I looked at the officer. He was wearing sunglasses. He locked into my eyes, the dark lenses reflecting my face. Did he see the desperate fear? Did he hear me say, "Please, please, let us get through the tunnel—I have to get to my son. He's only nine. He's a child with special needs, and he'll be afraid. Please." He didn't hear me because I thought all of that, but never said a word. He looked at me for a few seconds, and then, with a flick of his wrist, we were free to drive into the tunnel. There was no one in front of us, and as I turned to look back, I saw no one behind us. Why us? Why? Why had he let us go? No other cars were being allowed through the tunnel.

I had never seen the Midtown Tunnel empty. It was usually heavy with traffic. The long Island Expressway was empty, too. On the other side, the cars moving in the direction of the city were backed up for miles. The tunnel in both directions was closed.

On the ride out to Daniel's school, my mind raced back to when Daniel had been three.

On that day, he was in the backseat of the car. I was driving. I was taking him to his doctor in Manhattan. I could hear him gasping for air. It seemed like he was going to stop breathing any minute. His face was grayish-blue. There was so much traffic. We were downtown, and we had to make it uptown. He'd had a bad cough, and now it seemed his throat was closing up. I kept talking to him. I talked to him the way I had when I'd been only eight weeks pregnant and threatening to miscarry when Alan had been driving me to the doctor, speeding across the Brooklyn Bridge.

148

"It's okay. It's okay, baby. It's okay."

As I navigated the obstacles of New York City traffic, I thought he was going to die. I should have taken him to the local Brooklyn hospital, but I hated the idiots in the local hospital. I scanned every corner for a cop. Jesus. Where the hell were they when you needed one? I told myself to just keep driving. I thought about stopping at the Beth Israel emergency room, but I kept going. I wanted *our* doctor. She would know what to do. There were so many cars in front of me, and they weren't moving. I was shaking. I had only been a mother for a short time. My son was so little, and I felt helpless. I thought I was doing the right thing, but maybe not.

When we got to the doctor's office, strangely, there was no one there. I carried his limp body into the reception area, and I called out, "Hello... Hello..." There was no one. Finally, a nurse came from the back; she was wiping food from her face. I could barely speak. "I... I... he's not breathing..." We put him down on an examining table. She left for a minute, came back with an oxygen mask for him, and placed it over his face. It felt like it took hours, but maybe it was only minutes before one of the doctors came in and apologized for not being there sooner. A Park Avenue practice. One of the best in the city. There was always someone there. I didn't care why they hadn't been there that day. I didn't hear her. It was all just words. We talked about getting an ambulance. He was breathing a little better. I explained that I thought his throat was closing up. Another doctor came in. My shirt was soaked with sweat. I heard someone calling over to the emergency room at Mount Sinai. I heard them saying my name and that they were on the way. I scooped him up from the table and ran outside for a cab. No ambulance—I could get a cab faster. "Keep breathing, sweetie," I said. "Keep breathing."

X-rays, an emergency room, oxygen, and a nice young doctor. I've always liked those curtains that swish so fast, metal on metal.

149

Swishing open, swishing closed. I was lying on the bed with Daniel in my arms. They didn't have a reason for what had happened that day. Croup, maybe. But his throat was not closing. They gave him steroids through an inhalator. We rested. Hours later, I left with him. He was smiling and asking the doctors questions and more questions. When the questions started, I knew he would be fine.

I limped out of there with him. I was exhausted.

That was a long time ago.

As Peter and I approached the school in Glen Cove, I felt my heart start beating faster. I wanted to run from the car and grab Daniel. Outside his classroom, my knees buckled. I knelt on the floor and wept. His teacher came out and told me I had to pull myself together—my son couldn't see me this way. I wiped my nose and eyes, put my sunglasses back on, and walked into the room. He was in his favorite chair, reading. He looked peaceful and calm. He had no idea of what had happened. I stood behind him and watched him for a minute.

He looked up and smiled. "Oh, hi, Mommy."

"Hi, Peter." I took him in my arms and held him there as if I would never let go.

He wrenched away from me. "What happened? Why are you here?"

"Let's talk about it outside."

We went to a TGI Fridays. I tried to find a booth where I could shield him from the TV, but the screens were everywhere. CNN played and replayed the planes flying into the buildings.

"There was a plane crash?" he asked.

"Yes, darling. There was."

"Did people die?"

"Yes, they did."

"When are we going home?"

"I'm not sure. We have to find a place to stay."

"Why can't we go home?"

"Because the roads are closed."

"Who flew the planes?"

"We don't know."

We ordered food. We couldn't drive back to the city, so we would have to keep driving east. I found a Yellow Pages directory and searched for a hotel. No luck. Everything was booked because anyone who'd otherwise be trying to get back into the city needed a place to stay. It was already close to 6 p.m. I thought of everyone I knew who might have a place nearby. I was lucky enough to get through to a client who had a weekend home out east in the Hamptons. It was about an hour away. We had no idea how long we would be staying there, but he was generous to offer. We were safe, and we were together.

When we got to the house, it was hard to resist putting the TV on. I took Daniel upstairs to get ready for bed. His questions didn't stop.

"What happened? Why couldn't we go home? Why did a plane fly into a building? Who would do this? Why? Did people die? How many people died?"

"I don't know, honey. I wish I could tell you; I just don't know."

I tucked him in with Kermit, and he drifted off to sleep in my arms. I listened to his slow, even breathing. In the listening, there was peace. After that, I crawled into bed next to Peter. He was usually easygoing and calm. He held me tightly. It felt safe to be with him. When Daniel had first met him, we'd gone to an amusement park. They went on a Ferris wheel, and Daniel reached for his hand. He and Peter sat that way, holding hands, the whole ride. I took a picture of them.

I closed my eyes, but I kept seeing the crashing and people running, and the dust, and people falling in their last attempt to escape the inferno. *What thoughts crossed their minds as they fell from 100 stories? How many lives had been lost? How many survivors?*

Peter and I clung to each other and cried.

The next morning, we didn't say much. We were thinking it, but we never said it to each other. The question hung there: *"Is it over?"* Two weeks earlier, when Ashley was visiting, we all emerged from the Fulton Street subway stop. We'd turned and looked back. I'd pointed, and said to Ashley and Daniel, "Stop—look! There are the Twin Towers; look how tall they are. That is where some of the world's most powerful businesses are." We stood in that spot for a few seconds, just looking down the block at the buildings.

We found some food in the house for breakfast, and then we drove to a driving range. It was the most normal thing we could do. Peter played nine holes of golf. Daniel and I banged away at some golf balls. He missed most of them, but it was a good distraction. Peter went into the pro shop to check the news. By 5 p.m., one of the bridges and the Midtown Tunnel were reopened.

We packed up our things and left. As we drove toward the tunnel, I saw the black smoke rising and the hole in the skyline. Daniel was chattering away in the backseat. He had lost a tooth. There was a hole in his mouth where it had once been. A small loss. A new tooth would grow in its place. As we drove, we wrote a letter to the tooth fairy. But ahead of us, there was a hole in the sky, and nothing would ever be the same.

When we got home, I searched for an old picture.

Kathy and I were twenty. We skipped class that day. We went up to the top of the World Trade Center. We ate grapes and talked about all the things we were going to do with our lives.

There were no Twin Towers anymore. The sky was empty there. The world was fractured—in how many places, I couldn't imagine. I thought about the arrivals and departures, the knowns and the un-knowns, which had forever changed me since the day Kathy and I had taken that picture...marriage, birth, death, divorce, and the day that would come to be known as 9/11. I thought of the interminable letting go. How would we grieve this? How would we eventually accept this? Acceptance seemed impossible, but that is the only way peace comes.

Downtown, the air was thick with the smell of the fire that still burned in the sky. My heart cried in silence long after the tears left my face. Daniel asked if I would sing to him. I heard myself singing. The words just left my mouth, but I couldn't hear the tune. I closed my eyes. I was happy we were safe and home together. I told him the angels would come and bring him sweet dreams. I left when he was sleeping.

In my bed, I thought of the cop who had let us through the tunnel. Maybe he'd heard my sister whispering to him, saying that he should let us drive through. I closed my eyes and clung to my pillow. Then I remembered my promise. The tooth fairy would still come.

TODAY YOU ARE A MAN

For the length of days and years of life will they bestow on you;
let kindness and truth not leave you...
... Write them on the tablet of your
heart; so you will find grace...
~The Talmud~

When Daniel turned 12, we talked of how, according to Jewish law, a thirteen-year-old becomes a Bar Mitzvah (girls become a Bat Mitzvah). The original (biblical) rite of passage wasn't celebrated with a party. At the age of thirteen, a child was designated a responsible member of society, at which point they would be held accountable for their actions—no longer protected by their parents primarily because they could themselves bear children.

"Accountability" is a serious word for any 13-year-old, especially one like my son, whose independence hung precariously in the unknown, although it was a lofty goal—and a worthy one.

Daniel wasn't so sure he wanted to lead a religious service, a task that would require him to spend the better part of a year in preparation. Hebrew School didn't sound very appealing at all—especially to a kid who was already struggling with learning in English. My conservative Jewish upbringing had left me no choice when I'd turned 13, and yet, I felt my son should have a say. We agreed that he would meet a rabbi who could tutor him, and he could then decide if he wanted to follow through. The rabbi was a beautiful young woman who was barely 30, and I left them to sort it out.

When I got home, Daniel's smiling face tipped me off. He was in. As the year unfolded and he prepared for his Bar Mitzvah, I realized how my Jewish learning and values were not just the stuff of a past without choice but a meaningful part of my current identity.

Daniel's Bar Mitzvah day would take on a bigger meaning. For both of us, it would symbolize belonging. As I contemplated the service and the traditional celebration to come afterward, I was excited that we would be participating in a rite of passage that had been celebrated for thousands of years.

On that May day in 2005, it was unusually cold and gray, but the clouds made the day no less beautiful. Our guests had traveled from all over the country to be with us. Daniel sat on the bimah (like a stage) in a large chair that looked like a throne and made him look very small. He was wearing a navy-blue suit and a red tie he'd picked out. Looking out at the congregation, he nodded and smiled. Earlier, he had been nervous, but when I caught his eye, he offered up one of his quirky smiles and then looked away. I held up a tight fist to remind him of what I had said the night before: "Hold my heart right there in your hand. I'm right next to you, but this is your day!" He looked at me and then down at his prayer book.

I looked around the synagogue with gratitude for this gathering of our loving family and friends. Daniel stepped forward. The only sounds in the synagogue were the notes of the music and his chanting. We had made it.

I looked up at the stained-glass windows illuminating the biblical depiction of Abraham and Isaac on the mountain. God tested Abraham, asking him to sacrifice his son. At face value, it is just another story about a punishing God. But, digging deeper, the story is about love and faith. How could God demand this of a man who loved his son? If I imagine this literally, how could I have carried my son up a mountain and offered him as a sacrifice? My son fills my every second with life. *How could I do this?* What kind of God would challenge a man to choose obedience over his love of his son? The story confused me. And yet, Abraham didn't sacrifice his son. He heard the voice of an angel who urged him not to follow the command. Perhaps the voice of the angel was the voice of love, reminding Abraham of the leader within. Despite the unknown, Abraham was led by his faith to ascend that mountain in order to claim a part of his identity. He was wrestling with his inner voices. Was he dutiful? Yes, but in the Old Testament, even though he was designated by God as the "patriarch of the Jewish people," it is said that he never heard from God again.

I don't think God abandoned him. The test was not just about his commitment to God; it was about the way he defined himself in a time of turmoil and challenges. Without knowing the outcome, he had to believe there was a greater meaning to his life. He had to discover his faith in himself on his own. Abraham, always devout, proved himself extraordinary. In his willingness to step out, to do the unimaginable, he found the leader within himself.

Early on, when we received Daniel's Torah portion from the rabbi, I noted the words from Leviticus articulating the laws of who shall and shall not serve God. There were references to "defective, maimed, and imperfect" people being unfit to serve in the temple. When I first read the English translation of his assigned portion, I thought, *No way*. How could I let my son recite a Bar Mitzvah portion that directly stated that anyone with a physical disability couldn't serve God? But the Torah is read, beginning to end, with one passage for each day; those passages can't be chronologically rearranged or chosen to fit the "mood" of the given day. I had to let it go. I didn't discuss it with the rabbi or Daniel. Still, it seemed odd that the portion he would read was a direct reference to people who, in biblical times, were being discriminated against.

Alan and I stepped up on the Bimah together and wrapped Daniel in the tallis (traditional prayer shawl) that had been used as our wedding canopy. It was the first time we'd stood next to each other in six years. The tallis we wrapped around our son symbolized the union that had brought him into our lives and the possibility that, even if we were apart, we could love him together.

Daniel began to read from the Torah. Whatever we had encountered to get there, he belonged in the arms of that community, welcoming him and witnessing the climb he had made up his own mountain. Afterward, it was my turn to speak.

"I knew you long before I saw you. I knew I would one day have one son, and that you would make every sunrise and sunset more glorious, and though I didn't know your name, now that I know you, it is the only name I could ever imagine for you—Daniel, which means, 'with God as my judge.' I believe I was called into your life and you into mine. When we set out on this journey, there was so much about life and love and myself I had to learn. You have been my guide. The road has not always been easy, but we have traveled far from your first fragile moments to this amazing day. I dreamed you would be a very special child. I dream now that you will be a special person all your life—not because you were born special but because you choose to be special. I didn't realize how hard it would be that first time I left you after you were born. I can still see your hand leaving mine, that first time I let go when you crossed the street. I never could have known how I would feel the first time you spoke a word, took your first steps, or read a sentence from a book—those things were harder for you than other children, but your determination peeled my heart open like a flower, and for me, those moments will last forever.

It is easy for me to say 'I love you.' But I love who you have become. I love your inimitable and unique sense of humor. I love that your favorite two historical figures are Abraham Lincoln and Martin Luther King. I love that you are always the one who reaches out to help others, the one who offers an encouraging word, the one who tries to bridge a gap. You will look for the sunshine on the cloudiest day. You are always the one who will give of yourself so someone else can benefit. You will negotiate the 'yes' out of every 'no.'

I have longed for answers about the world I brought you into. I wish I could make it a more peaceful place for you, but I can only try to teach you how to find peace in your heart. I can only teach you that tolerance is not enough.

I pray the world you live in won't be threatened by differences and that you will be exemplary in embracing diversity. Know that your abilities are gifts, and every challenge is an opportunity. Never lose your curiosity, and keep an open mind. You are privileged to live as you do in this country, in these times, surrounded by your family and friends who love you.

The tallis you wear today is a symbol of courage. I don't know anyone braver than you. The yarmulke you have upon your head is a symbol that there is a great power in the universe to guide you. The flames of the Sabbath candles will shine so that you will know on the other side of darkness there is light, and greatness can be born of adversity. Whenever you need to steady yourself, remember that voice that tells you, 'I can do this,' because you can. And know that yours has been the voice I have heard when at times I didn't know how I would put one foot in front of the other. May you find your footing to dance your way through life, Daniel, and I will be dancing right there in your heart every step of the way."

Daniel threw his arms around my neck and held onto me as if he wouldn't let go. I looked through my tears at his head, buried in my chest.

Later that night, we were talking.

Daniel said, "By the way, about your speech today, it was very overwhelming."

"I know. It was overwhelming for me, too. Being overwhelmed is a good thing; it makes us know how alive we are. What about your Torah portion? What did you think of it?"

"Yeah, that was so unfair that people like me who have learning and other disabilities, and other problems, couldn't have been priests. That is really not right, but you know that was a long time ago, and we have to get over it. There are more important things to focus on nowadays."

"I know," I said.

He closed his eyes. "Maybe there are no miracles, only miraculous people."

"You are miraculous," I whispered. But I don't think he heard me.

CINNAMON SNAILS

It won't matter if they are all different; they
are all going to taste good anyway.
~Daniel Dubinsky~

Daniel had asked me the night before Mother's Day how to make coffee because he wanted to bring me my coffee in bed. I taught him, or rather, I tried. I went through the steps until the sound of the beans being pulverized made him put his hands over his ears. He was shifting his weight from one side to the other. Following instructions was never my forte, and making coffee is a process I took for granted. I didn't know what it would be like to try to make coffee if the steps had never been made clear to me, and I couldn't imagine it if my hands didn't work as mine do.

I could handwrite. I could tie my shoes. I could button buttons and tie knots and open jars and cut my food, and I could get the shampoo out of my hair. Daniel was fourteen, and he couldn't do any of those things.

When I finished the coffee lesson, he nodded. This didn't mean he totally got it. It could have been a sign of total boredom.

"Are you done learning how to make coffee?" I asked.

"Yes," he said.

"Should I just leave it on automatic? Will that be easier?"

He didn't answer. He walked into his room and put on the TV. Then he called from his bed, "Mom, do you want ice cream with your coffee in the morning?" I went into his room and hugged him, but he was too interested in whatever was on TV to hug me back.

The next morning, he approached my room walking slowly, carefully holding a cup with two hands so that the coffee wouldn't spill. He had waited a couple of hours for me to wake up.

I propped myself up and said, "Good morning, sweetie. Mmm-mmm...just the right amount of half-and-half. You figured it out."

"It was on automatic," he said.

I guess he'd paid attention to the important things.

He ambled back into my room. "I have a card for you." He was smiling; his big round glasses were already halfway down his small nose with his thick brown hair sticking up in the back. His hearing aids had likely been left on his night table. With his chin up, he was only four feet, ten inches. As he walked toward me, he looked more like ten than fourteen. His pajama bottoms were trailing on the floor. I thought he would trip, but I said nothing. He appeared with a heart-shaped card he had made out of red construction paper and cut crookedly with pinking shears. Inside, the sloping trail of words said:

Dear Mom, Happy Mother's Day.
My greatest memory is the day we
made the Cinnamon Snails,
And we said that they might need occupational therapy, too.
When I get married, I will never forget you.
Love, Daniel.

The part where he'd written "I will never forget you" was wet with my tears. I reached for him, but he had already slipped away. I heard the sound of the freezer door opening and the sound of the ice cream carton hitting the floor with a thud.

"I need some heeeelp!" he called.

"No, you don't!" I called back, sniffling. "If you want ice cream for breakfast, you'll have to figure it out."

I wasn't going to run in and help him. No. He could do it, even if I had to clean up the mess afterward. I used the back of my hand to wipe my face. I held onto the card.

His was the voice of reason when there was no reason and the one who could con the *yes* out of every *no*. He was the one who kept the stars up in the sky and the one who pointed out the harvest moons. He was the one who reminded me of our family traditions, like our bedtime talks and the way I blew on his hair to make sure all of the worries were gone from his head before he went to sleep. He was the one who reminded me we were "allowed" to watch TV, once a week, while we ate. He was the one who would try any flavor of ice cream at least once while I was the one who played it safe. He was the one I reminded to brush his teeth, wash his face, and brush his hair even when there was no one to remind me to do the same.

Daniel was also my baking partner. On cold winter mornings, he would be up at the crack of dawn. He'd flip through cookbooks on a mission to find outlandish recipes like chocolate-covered apricot meringue mushrooms and orange pecan fudge logs with Pernod. When I awakened, he'd bombard me with a shopping list of what I needed to buy. He refused to go with me to do the shopping. He would announce, "It's too cold out, and the store is too far; you go."

I would counter with, "Why should I have to go out in the cold alone?"

As a default, I usually insisted we make the chocolate chip cookies from the back of the Nestlé bag because we would already have all of the ingredients, and the cookies would come out great. One day, though, months earlier, just so I could see that freckle-faced, big-cheeked, squinty-eyed smile of his, I'd agreed to make the "Cinnamon Snails."

The snails required that we make dough. From the dough, we had to roll out strips. The dough was sticking to the rolling pin this time. I cursed the rolling pin and the flour all over the floor. The rolling of the dough wasn't easy for him, but I steadied his hands by placing mine over his, and together we rolled in a rhythm that would allow the dough to become flat. Then, the recipe required us to cut strips, massage the strips into coils, and shape the coils into something resembling snails. As we rolled the snails, some were fat, some were skinny, some were big, some were small, *and* we discovered we had forgotten to give eyes to some. It was a motley collection.

"Wow, look at these snails. What do you think?" I asked.

"Well, I guess the ones that didn't get eyes are not going to be able to see. And, the ones that have no ears are going to need hearing aids like mine." And then he asked, "Will any of them need OT?"

I stopped and realized what he was asking. Would any of them need occupational therapy? Would they? I didn't know. I asked him what he thought.

"Well, if they can't handwrite like me, they will."

"I guess they will then," I said. "And how do you think they will feel about it?"

"It won't matter if they are all different; they are all going to taste good anyway."

The midmorning winter sun was beating through the window. We sat at our little tile table. There was flour on the floor, sugar all over the counter, cinnamon that hadn't made it onto the snails, and chocolate chip eyes that had rolled onto a chair—and I realized that none of that mattered. Or, that is how I want to remember it. I didn't realize how, in the middle of that mess, I was happy.

Six months later, when he gave me his Mother's Day card, I didn't know Daniel remembered anything about the day we made the "Cinnamon snails." If it was his "greatest" memory, why? Did it make him happy because he loved baking, or because even though the cinnamon snails weren't perfect and looked nothing like the pictures in the recipe book, they tasted really good?

We ate every single one of them. They were delicious.

NO BETTER PAST

Forgiveness is giving up hope for a better past.
~Unknown~

It was late September of 2005. Six years had passed since I had been inside Alan's house. I was curious to go in, the same way drivers slow to observe a car crash. I entered the doorway hoping it would be better than I thought. Two Sundays a month, when I left Daniel for the weeks he spent there, I wouldn't look back after he closed the door. I was never invited in. This was Alan's way of making it clear that I was not welcome. I would walk to the car, and I'd go back to the comforts of my life in the city. I would worry about Daniel and then try not to think about it. I'd try to forget all of the reasons why I'd left Alan and that my son was living between two homes in a lifestyle which he neither wanted nor deserved. For an hour or two on those Sundays, I'd sit with a strong drink or two or three and fight my way out of the quicksand of guilt, and I'd resist the temptation, over and over again, to fight for full custody of my son. I didn't do it because Alan would make sure I'd lose.

I climbed the stairs to where we had once been a family. Alan and I had made a decade's worth of memories there, and yet nothing felt familiar. The floors were now worn. The walls needed paint. The washing machine door was open. There were clothes on the once-white floor. There was dirt in the sink basin. I peered into the doorway where Alan's office had been. I saw boxes and papers littering the floor; the dust crawled up into my nose and made me sneeze.

How long since he'd worked in there?

The door to the roof deck was open. I peeked outside. My rose-bushes that had once climbed their trellis were just dead stubs. There was no hint of the snapdragons and irises that had once reached for the sky. There was only a pile of gray, broken planks. As I walked through the space where I'd once been happy, the only thing famil-iar to me was the chasm that hung in the silence between us, the same as in those last years before I'd left.

Alan stood in the hallway and looked at me. Then, he looked down at the floor. He said the house wasn't as he'd hoped it would be. He seemed embarrassed.

I hadn't imagined it this way. I hadn't imagined that, on the day when I'd come back to visit this house, Alan would have cancer.

A couple of months earlier, Daniel and I were waiting for the bus to pick him up for sleep-away camp. After the bus pulled away, Alan and I were in the parking lot. Alan was about to ride off on his mo-torcycle, but before he put his helmet on, he blurted out that he was going to see an oncologist. They had found the cancer he'd insisted he had. He was agitated and mumbling. I asked him if he wanted to talk or if he wanted me to go with him. It just came out—I didn't even think about it. It seemed like the right thing to do. He declined my of-fer. And I heard the engine of his bike revving. I went home and just sat in my empty apartment for a while. Daniel would be gone for the summer. I took a deep breath. *Here we go*, I thought, remembering all those years Alan had insisted he was going to die of cancer.

I called Alan the next day. He was cold but willing to share some of the details. I learned it was stage 4 multiple myeloma. A blood cancer. He talked for a while. He was enrolled in an aggressive clin-ical treatment trial, and the effects of the chemo would be brutal. Within the next few months, he would also undergo a stem-cell trans-plant. I hung up the phone in a daze. I didn't imagine I would ever want to be involved in his life again or even act like his friend, but he had no one else. I had to help; I was too familiar with the devastation of late-stage cancer. I'd been so far away and helpless when, eleven years earlier, Amy had died, and at least she'd had her husband and good friends. Alan had only me and Daniel, and he was alone with this burden.

Daniel would stay with me when he returned from camp. But how would I tell him about his father?

I noticed a jar of tomato sauce open on the counter. The dried-up, pasty-looking rim was a hint that it had been there for a while. I stumbled on a roll of wire. The contents of Alan's toolbox were on the floor as if he had abandoned the search for something...how long ago? There was a hole in the cabinetry where the dishwasher had been. *Where's the dishwasher?* He said he was replacing it. There were bags of recycling items slumped like fat old men on the floor, waiting to be taken out. It looked like two years' worth. *Since when did he become a bag hoarder?* The walls had oddly colored patches of test paint. The shiny wood floors that had been finished by hand were scratched and dirty, and the dust was gently rolling around in the breeze. Piles of papers covered the table where we had eaten. Once, a long time ago, we three sat in the pristine home I kept, Daniel in his highchair looking out the window onto Sixth Avenue. Now, the couch had a fortress of folders around it. Some chairs looked like they'd been retrieved from the street.

So much had happened since I'd lived in this house. I'd fallen in and out of love. I'd re-built my career. I'd eaten more pizza and ice cream than I had ever dreamed I could. Daniel, now 14, had finished elementary school, gone to sleep-away camp, and was now in middle school. We had a dog and a piano. We lived in a high-rise on the Upper East Side with a view of the East River.

I looked at the shelves—now dusty—and remembered my small,

curly-haired, nymph-like son. His toys and books surrounded him as he sat on the floor and played. Raffi was singing, "He's got the whole world, in His hands..." Daniel's first words filled the whole upstairs as he serenaded us with "Mamamamama Dadada."

The white Berber that Alan didn't want to buy still carpeted the master bedroom. A large plasma TV sat propped on a chair, wires trailing from its backside, and hid the handmade glass doors that covered the fireplace. "Those doors are like jewelry; you can't just go out and buy these," Alan had said proudly on the day he'd mounted them.

The familiar art, hanging since I had lived there, was mostly gifted to him. Unlike Alan, the artists he had known had continued to work successfully in their chosen genres. The mess, mostly aesthetic, could be cleaned. The dust could be removed, and the place could be gutted, but we had done that before. In every corner, bursting out from behind all the stuff, the battles still raged. Grief hung everywhere like the cotton stuff you hang for Halloween. It was there in the mess, in the unraveling of my former husband's life, in the stillness of that afternoon, and in the bedroom that had been ours. I felt the chaos would consume me. I had to catch my breath.

Now almost fifteen, Daniel, standing in his room, looked so big.

How long had it taken for this place, with neat shelving for his books and toys, and its pristine surfaces, to become unrecognizable? I wanted to grab Daniel and run. This was the house where he'd been born, but not the home I'd dreamed of for him. I wanted to tell him about his first birthday party, the hundred colorful balloons that bobbed around and scared him when they popped, and the clown vanilla-cream birthday cake that he dug his fingers into, our family and friends surrounding us in celebration. I wondered if he remembered the fuzzy panda bears that had danced on strings above him as he'd slept. The small carousel and a collection of cows of differing shapes and sizes were still on his shelves. He had loved cows.

I heard the birds outside. Daniel reached for my hand.

"Mom. Mom, it's okay."

"Of course it is," I said, and I squeezed his hand, still in mine.

There was no clear sky for Alan and me anymore. Looking into his once bright blue eyes was like searching through a dense, thick fog—the kind that grounds planes. We hardly made eye contact.

I wiped my hands on my pants and swallowed. I didn't say a word. I could have stayed away. I could leave. I could turn the page again. I could take my son home to our bedtime talks, the furniture I had picked, the carefully chosen paint, the clean, soft linens, the white roses on our dining table, my piano, our dog Gracie, and the smell of the cookies we baked. Yes, we could go home and order pizza.

I'd made a promise on an April day fifteen years earlier when I'd said, "'Til death do us part." I would keep it.

If Alan never forgave me, I would still forgive him. I wasn't sure how, but I would do it. I would do it for my son. I would do it because I felt it was the right thing to do. I had no idea how I would be involved, but I couldn't conceive of Alan going to battle with this disease alone. His life expectancy wasn't long—a few years at best. I didn't know how I'd help, or what my role would be, but he would need support. I couldn't imagine how he would take care of the building where he lived and the tenants. He had a few friends, but he'd alienated a lot of people from his life. There would be specialists to see, healthcare needs to manage, housekeeping, and food shopping. Another pair of ears at doctor appointments. Like it or not, he knew I was a fierce advocate. And I would show up for him.

"Okay, let's go," I said softly to Daniel.

"Can we get ice cream on the way home?" he asked.

FOR EVERY POT, THERE IS A COVER

*You come to love not by finding the perfect person
but by seeing an imperfect person perfectly.*
~Sam Keen~

Daniel was waiting in front of "Leonard's of Great Neck." It was the same venue where his school held the junior and senior proms, as well as awards dinners. His shirt was untucked, his forehead sweaty, and his tie crooked, but his jacket was still on. It was the night of the junior prom.

"How was the prom?" I asked.

"Okay," he said.

"Doesn't sound very convincing. Everything *really* okay?"

"Well, I asked Danielle to dance with me, and I ruined her night."

"How did you ruin her night by dancing with her?"

"Well, we were on the dance floor, and I twirled her, and I was twirling her so hard, she tripped."

"Well, did you twirl her maliciously?" He wasn't capable of being malicious, and I knew it. He had asked her to the prom, but she had a boyfriend. This, along with the Valentine's Day card she had returned to him, had really hurt.

"No, I would never do that. I was just so happy that she was dancing with me."

"Okay, so then what?"

"I left."

"You left her alone on the dance floor?"

"Well, I was so upset with myself, I just walked away."

"What did she do?"

"She followed me out and asked me if I was okay."

"Well, if you had ruined her night, she wouldn't have asked you if you were okay."

He sat in the back, staring out the window in silence. "I am so stupid."

"No, you aren't. Being happy because you were dancing with a girl you like is never stupid."

"I am a kind, generous, good-hearted person. I am so nice. Why is it that she doesn't see this in me? What could she possibly want?"

I wish I knew. What did girls see when they looked at my son? I didn't know. I knew what I saw.

"I must be ugly," he said.

"No, you are not! And when you're older, you'll meet the right girl, and she'll see the beauty of your soul," I offered.

We drove home in silence. I wished my son knew how courageous it was for him to go to the prom alone. Danielle was only one of many girls who might be "the one." My fifteen-year-old son didn't want to hear it.

Single mother, teenage boy in love, and a rite of passage that was uncharted territory for us. Without evidence of a true and lasting love, I didn't think I had succeeded very well at "finding true love," either. I had generally made peace with the departure from the culture in which I'd been raised. Divorce wasn't the norm in our family. When I looked at my wedding pictures, hidden in our blissful smiles was the truth. I wasn't perfect, nor was Alan. In whatever ways we'd tried to make it, we'd missed. We'd made it nine years, some of them filled with adventure and love until we could no longer find our way, and then we'd become a statistic.

I had been unmarried for eight years. *The New York Times* wedding announcements and the "Modern Love" column in *The New York Times* intrigued me the way some people felt when reading the obituaries. I was a voyeur. In those engagement photos, I saw past the poses and the smiles. I saw the challenges of cultural diversity, same-sex unions, and older women marrying younger men. These strangers' nuptial snippets revealed a glimpse into the hidden frailties and faults that poised them for hopeful futures. I imagined what they'd overcome to get to those pages and what might lie ahead for them. I had traded in wedding anniversaries for divorce anniversaries. I felt excommunicated from anything marital.

In my Sunday searches, I noticed that more and more same-sex unions were making it into those once-coveted pages, but one photo was still missing—the photo of the couple that was "different." One day, if I found it, I would cut it out and put it in my drawer to remind me that my son would surely find his own true love—a special someone who would love him long after I was gone. For both of us, I wanted a guarantee that "for every pot, there is a cover."

One afternoon, I was in my bed reading the paper and feeling sorry for myself. Lying in bed in the daytime was not at all my "thing." I wouldn't even think of taking a nap. I'm not sure how long Daniel had been standing by my door when he spoke up.

"What's wrong?"

His voice had surprised me.

"I'm sad."

"Why?"

"I'm tired of being alone."

"You have Gracie."

"Yes. Yes, I have Gracie," I sniffled. "But she's a dog."

Gracie was as complicated as me and Daniel. A moody rescue dog known to bite, I'd been willing to take a chance on her. She'd been so lost and in need of love.

"You have me."

"Yes, honey, I have you. I am *so* grateful for you."

"Maybe you need to go out on some dates. I think you should get married again. It would make me happy."

I wondered if I would spend the rest of my life unmarried. It would be a very special man who would be the right one for us, but if he was out there, we would find him. The only way to him, I reckoned, was to wait for him. I wasn't only thinking of myself.

SOMEWHERE OUT THERE

When the night has been too lonely and
the road has been too long
And you think that love is only for the lucky and the strong
Just remember in the winter
far beneath the bitter snows
Lies the seed, that with the sun's love
in the spring becomes the rose.
~Amanda McBroom~

I needed to go on some dates. But how? Who?

I churned with the decision for a while. *You're an executive. Decisions are your forte, so just do it.* The singles ad I read on the internet sounded upscale enough. Whatever the matchmakers charged, it seemed like a small sum *if* they could present qualified candidates who would deliver on the non-negotiable stipulations for my life partner. Well-intentioned people were quick to give me the kind of advice no one needs: "Maybe you'll have to settle." Not if the matchmakers' ad had a shred of truth to it! The subtext of "settling" was twofold, though; I was in my late forties, and I had a child who was complex. But I knew something. Everything in life is uncertain, and the only way to get through it is to live it and to find out what happens.

There was no perfect man, and I was far from a perfect woman. I had not yet met the guy I wanted to make a life with, but I would.

My divorce had been finalized. I was paying off my debt. I had received a good bonus that year. *Why not? Something for me!* It was a rainy day. I could feel my hair frizzing up. I prayed the match-makers would see past it and focus on the dress I chose, the pearls I wore, my fishnet stockings and black stiletto shoes, my posture, and the graceful way in which I handled the interview. I assumed my impeccable manners, sense of style, and humor would mitigate their concerns about my age. At 48, if I was to be a trophy wife, the eligible bachelor would most certainly be 80.

When I got to the matchmaker's address, I realized the building was a condominium. Entering the lobby, I was a little skeptical, but I carried on. I was on a mission. This was one of those indulgences for which I wouldn't be asking permission. Not a soul knew I was doing this.

A lovely blonde who looked like a former model greeted me. She sized me up and down.

"I was a little worried about your age, but the good news is you are very attractive."

I cleared my throat. If I'd had any doubts about myself, they'd just gotten worse. I hadn't done any plastic surgery—all of my imper-fections, all of my parts, were all mine. I looked down at the shiny granite tiles and smiled a sheepish grin. My heels clicked across the floor, and I followed her into the chintz-covered living room.

Every element of the place was perfectly curated, including the striped satin pillows that sat plumped on the couch. Books on the shelves offered a homey touch, but no one would ever read them. I felt like I was on the set of a TV show, and the interview took an hour and a half. Questions covered my life, tastes, interests, and of course, the nitty-gritty details about the qualities of the man I would like to meet. I stated my answers as if I had studied for a test I really wanted to pass.

A series of questions revealed the right man for me would be 45 to 55, around six feet tall, and someone who worked in any busi-ness unrelated to the entertainment industry (I didn't want to live my work 24/7). The man would preferably be a widower (dealing with someone's divorce or ex-wife wasn't what I hoped for). I'd be fine if he had one or more children, and I guessed younger children would be better than older children—more accepting. The children's gender(s) didn't matter as long as they were school-aged and there was childcare in place. I loved being a mother and would have been happy to co-parent...as long as they were respectful, well mannered, and kind to my son. A tall order, for sure. The one non-negotiable was that, even if I was able, I would not give birth again. Ever.

I re-thought that last part, but it was the absolute truth.

I *preferred* a city man, but I would tolerate a commute up to an hour as long as he was doing the picking up and delivering. I wasn't driving an hour or taking a train for anyone. The most important things to me were that whoever he was, and wherever he lived, he was giving of heart and spirit, fun, intelligent, fiscally responsible, and most importantly, had the capacity to love and care about both me and Daniel.

I made my interviewer laugh a few times when I described the many men I had met throughout the past two years: the personal trainer who I'd really liked but was intimidated by me and the race-car driver from Nevada who I had met on a cruise—ruggedly handsome and sexy, but he lived too far away and had a girlfriend. The German Mensa member, ten years my junior, who could talk long into the night but was definitely not marriageable. The idea of the *N.Y. Times* bestselling author was brilliant, but the Southern gentleman interested me less than his dog. The promised friendship of numerous other men who were too young for me was enticing but iffy. All this, doled out in single servings, had not been very fulfilling. My emotional boundaries and sleep requirements were of high value. None of those guys had welcomed the morning with me. My relationship with Peter had been long and loving, and I was sorry when it ended. When that hadn't worked out, I'd decided to take some time for myself to write, to travel, and to think deeply about what I really wanted.

The matchmakers required their hefty sum in one immediate payment. Both the men and the women paid for the service. There would be no refunds no matter what. They made no guarantees but promised no fewer than six introductions, which would be based on the information I supplied. Based on the fact that I was 48, I suspected they were going to throw me into the pile meant for older men—men who could be decades older than me. They were thinking I would go on an average of one date a month. After they ran a background check on me, I would hear from them.

The rules were clear: No preview pictures, and when I went out on a date, the man would always pay. There would be a "feedback form" supplied afterward. It had to be filled out before another introduction would be offered. Conversations on first dates were to be kept light: no talk of ex-spouses or relationships, politics, religion, or children. With all those exclusions, what would people talk about?

As we parted ways, we shook hands, smiled, and hugged. I stepped into the rainy unknown realizing that monumental things had happened to me on rainy days. It had been raining when, eight years earlier, I had left my marital home.

The first arranged date came a couple of weeks later. He sounded nice enough. His voice was deep and friendly. He invited me to lunch at his "conservative" club. (I can dress conservatively, but I can't fake that I am conservative.) Okay, a warmup date! I went with an open mind but not very high hopes. The conversation wound its way through all the usual ins and outs of past lives, interests, likes, and dislikes, and yes, we did talk about all the "no-no's"—exes, politics, and religion. His references to how he "loved" how I ate, "loved" how I dressed, "loved" how I smelled, and "loved" everything about me within the first fifteen minutes were an indiscreet form of desperation. I excused myself to the ladies' room for a feigned business call, and I stayed as long as I could.

Not "the one."

I awaited call number two.

This one was, according to the description the matchmaker gave me on the phone, *all* I had asked for! A very charitable Wall Street mogul, no children, no ex-wife, 55, handsome, athletic—a New Yorker seeking a long-term relationship and definitely interested in settling down. Once again, he sounded nice enough on the phone. We agreed to meet at an upscale hotel bar. Because this was date two, I was a little more warmed up. I chose a short skirt, sexy tights, boots, and a low-cut top. As I approached the lobby, I saw a very tall, handsome man in a trench coat looking down at his Blackberry. Whatever was going on, he was voraciously typing. I knew it was him. I walked over and stood close until he finally looked up. He smiled a very broad, very white toothy grin, checked me out up and down, and said, "Wow, you are better than I expected," and then he looked back down at his Blackberry. I stood there wondering what he'd meant, but I assumed he was paying me a compliment. He showed me to his table. I sat down and offered a tight-lipped smile to a pretty redhead who wanted to know what I wanted to drink.

My date excused himself. "I have to make a quick business call."

I was unaccustomed to competing with a Blackberry. Being with a "date" who was so attached to his handheld technology made me consider leaving. What was the point of being there? I told myself that because he was a Wall Street type, his behavior was probably normal. This was new to me. In 2007, my own demanding business didn't yet necessitate 24/7 accessibility via technology.

I decided I should sit there, despite his obsession, and see where this competition with the Blackberry went. It got no better. Throughout drinks and dinner, the Blackberry won. Because we barely talk-ed, why had he insisted on the dinner?

He kept asking me questions, and as soon as I would start to an-swer, he'd look me in the eye, say how pretty and hot I was, and then he'd be looking again at the Blackberry. He emailed me the next day and wanted to know if I wanted to come over to his place to "watch a movie" in his "private screening room." I had a feeling it wouldn't be very much fun and politely declined. When I filled out the après-date questionnaire, I was hard-pressed to find the right adjectives for him without using the word 'asshole.'

Call three came right away. This time, it was one of the ladies sounding urgent. "We have a very important and special gentleman who is anxious to meet you. We aren't at liberty to give you any details about him. He's one of our exceptional clients." It sounded suspicious to me. *Why so anxious? Why the urgency?* He would be calling that night.

His voice was hushed. He explained he was in the midst of closing a big deal (as if this were any of my business) but that he would like to meet me. He suggested a little "casual" get-together at his home in Connecticut on the upcoming weekend. Some other friends of his would be attending. He would send his driver, who would then return me to the city. Maybe this wasn't so safe, but I assumed, just as they had me checked out, that my matchmakers had done a background check on him, too.

I felt like Cinderella staring into my closet. What to wear to a little Super Bowl "get-together" at the hilltop estate of a mysterious man I had never met? Who were these friends? Famous people? If he was such a "heavy hitter," they were probably press-worthy. I opted for tight, black designer jeans, a cashmere beaded sweater, black suede boots, and faux diamond jewelry. When I looked in the mirror, I thought I looked young enough, hot enough, and sophisticated enough. I grabbed my purse, and I also made sure I had my license in there just in case my body was found somewhere.

We pulled up to a circular driveway. The majestic stone house was lit up, and I could see the snowy backdrop of rolling lawns. The butler took my coat and offered me champagne. Then, he left me standing in the marbled foyer. I noticed a Degas and a Cezanne sketch hanging on the wall. *Are those originals? That sculpture is a Rodin, right?* I heard footsteps descending the stairs one at a time, and there he was on the sweeping spiral staircase. He was in his sixties. A slight man, tall and probably more handsome when he was younger. He wore jeans (whew, I'd called that one right!) and a plaid shirt. He walked over to me, barely made eye contact, and in a gesture of "hello," reached for my hand. His eyes tracked from my feet to my shins, to my knees, to my thighs, to my middle, to my chest, to my face, to my hair, and then back to my eyes. I felt like I was a dog being judged for "Best in Show." Finally, he smiled.

"Come in." He turned on his heels. I assumed I was supposed to follow.

The den was lovely. Beige-toned silks and satins adorned the room, which was appointed with some museum-quality antique Asian art. I was introduced to a "friend" whom I later learned worked with him in some aspect of his business. We were served hors d'oeuvres and made small talk. The friend did most of the talking, and he seemed more interested in me than my preoccupied host, who gave no explanation for his detachment. He left the room numerous times.

His friend whispered, "Want to leave at halftime?" He'd read my mind.

The butler ushered us to a table set for three and proceeded to serve us filet mignon. I don't eat anything that walks or flies, so I just pushed the meat around my plate. I excused myself to make a phone call to my son.

I was whispering from the powder room, "I'm fine... I'm on a date... I don't know where, somewhere in Connecticut... I'll be home by eleven. Yes, you can wait up..."

"Everything okay?" my host asked.

"Um, I just spoke with my son, and he's, um, he's having a problem at home?" I'd posed it as a question more than a statement. I was asking permission to leave. The friend picked up on the cue.

"I have to go get my daughter from a party back in the city. I can drive you."

"Thank you." I waited for him to push back from the table.

I looked at the butler, who was seeking approval to offer up our coats. Our host shrugged and gestured that it was fine. If he was offended, I didn't care. *Bye-bye, Rodin, Monet, and Picasso. See you in the museum.* The ride home was more entertaining than the dinner. The guy who was driving had noticed that I hadn't eaten and asked if I wanted to go out for a "nice" dinner.

"That was brutal," he said.

"How so?" I feigned.

"I got the feeling you don't eat meat."

"Nope. Not since I was fifteen."

"Well, sorry if he seemed rude. He's in the middle of a big deal. You'll be reading about it in *The Wall Street Journal.*"

An assumption that I read The Wall Street Journal.

"Well, it's okay. It happens," I said, feeling foolish. I looked over at him and thought he looked remarkably like Danny DeVito.

"I know a good place near where you live if you want?"

"No, thank you. I'll just get home to my son."

"Okay, well, if you want to get together sometime, I'll give you my card."

I shredded it upon entering my apartment. Not a chance. An overly talky man to whom I felt zero attraction? No.

Date four, whom I later nicknamed "Jack" (because he reminded me of Jack Nicholson), had the demeanor of a poker player and spoke in a near whisper. No broad strokes for this one, no outward displays of emotion, but there was something interesting about him. He liked art and music. I accepted a second and third date from him. With each date, though, his life seemed more like an episode of *Lifestyles of the Rich and Famous* and less like anything I could relate to. I learned that he had something to do with ownership of the Miss Universe Pageant and had once been married to "Miss Brazil"—and I just couldn't see myself undressing in front of a guy whose standards had been set by women who were Miss Universe candidates. I wasn't willing to get over that. All I could think of after our dates were the perfect rear end and breasts of his former wife. He never even discussed her, but there was something wrong with leaving dates with him and imagining his ex-wife's anatomy. Nope, he just wasn't "the one."

Three months passed, and no dates later, I told some friends about the matchmakers because it was comical. I had no faith that they were going to find "him," but oddly, I felt I was getting closer. Whomever "he" was, I was sure I was close to magically colliding with the man of my dreams. As I walked Gracie, I could feel him. I had a sense he was nearby.

IF YOU BELIEVE...

*When you realize that you want to spend
the rest of your life with somebody,
you want the rest of your life to start as soon as possible.*
~ Nora Ephron~

I was in my bedroom, writing. A storm pelted ice at our living-room windows. Then I heard a loud crash. *A bomb?* The atrium window above the couch had been hit by falling ice. Glass and wet snow sprayed the living room. I stood there in disbelief, staring at the big chunks of glass that had fallen and the ice melting on the rug. I ran downstairs to our doorman Ray and collapsed into his arms. More than a strong drink, I wanted a hug from my nonexistent boyfriend. The hug from Ray was the next best thing.

The super came up to help with the mess. "Oh, I hate to see a beautiful woman who is alone cry." *Oh, really?* I hated that he was calling me a damsel in distress, and I was exactly that. I later learned that he was fired for publicly berating his wife.

I had seen the white horse and the occasional white knight, but they weren't galloping toward me to rescue me from my life. I was supposed to go out with a friend to a benefit that night, but she canceled. The matchmakers hadn't produced anyone worth a Saturday night. I looked in the mirror. *"YOU, my dear, are going to have to go out ALONE!"*

Even though it was a Saturday night, I hoped my therapist would return the message I left her.

I was so tired of being alone. I was sick of it.

When she called me back, she listened for a while and tried to console me, but the truth was, I *was* very much alone. My relationship with my former boyfriend, Peter, had ended two years earlier. My parents weren't close by. I was trying to be helpful to Alan, and I managed the details of Daniel's life alone. I was having a full-blown pity party all by myself. Daniel was staying with Alan for the weekend. That was also stressing me out because Alan was not doing well, but Daniel had insisted on going. He was fifteen. I had to respect his decision.

I needed to get out. My dear friend Joyce, always my consigliere, shared with me that since her husband had died, she would sometimes pick a lively, upscale neighborhood restaurant with a bar where she would sit and enjoy a good meal by herself. I hadn't been in a bar alone on a Saturday night since I'd been in my twenties. I wasn't even sure where to go.

How would you wear your hair? What would you wear? You can do this. Keep it simple. Jeans and a nice top. Sit in a corner. Don't call too much attention to yourself. The closest good restaurant I could think of was two blocks away. I had eaten there a bunch of times but hadn't paid much attention to the bar.

It was early. I sat down on a corner stool where I could watch the action. I was deluding myself into thinking I wouldn't talk to anyone. I can talk to anyone about anything.

The bartender came over and asked what I wanted.

"Kettle One, olives, and rocks."

"Kettle One on the rocks with olives?"

I felt confused and quickly looked away. Maybe it was his eyes, or the way he stood, or the way he walked or talked, or his smile. Maybe I was just downright desperate. I hadn't experienced love at first sight since a long time ago when hormones had coursed through my veins without help.

I looked up into his blue eyes and said, "Okay."

I sat there drinking slowly and pretending to watch the baseball game. I was really watching my bartender. He had an easy way about him. He looked like he was in his early fifties, and he was in good shape like he worked out. If only it had been as simple as wanting to get into bed with him, I would have known what to do, but strangely, that was the last thing I wanted. I wasn't even thinking about sex.

"Something to eat?" he asked.

"Sure."

He handed me the menu. Then, when he saw I was holding it at arm's length, he pulled a pair of glasses out of his pocket.

"These help?"

Okay, this was good. We had reading glasses in common.

A meal, a book, a movie, or a man—I like to be captivated in the first five minutes. I'm not aggressive. I like to be entertained. I'm not patient. A man must quickly do the advancing. This was not what my bartender was doing. He was busy working. Hours became more hours with a rotation of patrons who came and went from his bar. I fought the urge to leave numerous times.

By my third drink and a salad, I learned his name: Jim. He'd known the owners of the restaurant since he'd been in his twenties and began bartending for them. He thought it was fun. He worked there on weekends, but he had a long-term career in the pharmaceutical industry. He lived about forty-five minutes away in Rockland County (New York). He had two daughters. We had some things in common—good work ethics and devotion to our children. His left hand was devoid of a ring. I was wise enough to know that meant nothing. By 1 a.m., I was ready to leave, and I was also no closer to finding out if he had a wife, a girlfriend, or both. Finally, I left.

During the week, I kept thinking about him. *What made him*

different than the dates supplied by the matchmakers? The natural, easy way he had with people as he worked the bar made him seem authentic and uncomplicated, and when he smiled, it was like a door opening to his heart. He was like Ted Danson's character, Sam Malone, in *Cheers*. Everyone really liked him.

The following Saturday, I thought about going to a movie. Then I thought about going back to the bar where I could find out more about my bartender. Then I thought twice about it. Two weekends in a row was excessive. *Life is short... Just do it.*

He smiled when I walked in. Plenty of single women came and went from the place, though, and a handsome bartender would know how to keep them coming back. That was his job. My corner stool was vacant.

"Kettle One, rocks, olives?" he asked.

"Very *good*." I smiled. "You remembered."

He came by with my drink. "Dining with me?" I wanted to believe the "with me" part wasn't just pro forma.

When I noticed a man walking toward the empty chair next to me, I became territorial. I didn't want my bartender to think I was interested in anyone else.

The stranger pulled out the stool. "I know you from the bus."

Stupid line. How am I getting rid of this guy?

My bartender came over to take the man's order. I looked up at him as if to say, "Help," but he was busy and didn't notice.

Of course, the intruder started talking nonstop, hitting on me. I wanted to make him go away.

"I don't mean to be rude, but the bartender is my boyfriend, and I like to sit here and eat with him."

It didn't occur to me that my bartender might hear me and have no interest in me or that my line about him being my boyfriend might be offensive to him. Nor did it occur to me that the intruder might not honor my request to be left alone. I fantasized that Jim would punch this guy, but he was at the other end of the bar. Finally, the intruder gave up and left.

When Jim came back, he gave me a curious look. "Everything okay?" he asked.

"Sure," I said, but I was thinking, *If you leaned over and kissed me right now, that would make everything better.* I laughed nervously. "The guy was a little annoying."

A week later, on Friday night, I was walking by the restaurant around 11 p.m. I had been out at the theater and noticed Jim through the window. *Hmmm.* I hesitated, and then I walked in. At the door, the owner, who had introduced himself the week before, greeted me with a smile.

"Hi there."

I smiled back.

"Good to see you again. I'm gonna buy you a drink from the loneliest bartender in New York."

Wow. *Someone* was paying attention.

The regulars were coming and going. It was a busy night. But I had a crush on this guy behind the bar, and I wanted to know more. I wasn't leaving.

Hours into the night, an older gentleman sat down and engaged me in a conversation about movies. At least he wasn't creepy. We were just having some fun, trying to remember actors' names in movies.

I was stumped by one of his questions. "I don't know, ask *him*." I gestured toward Jim at the other end of the bar.

Jim came back to us. "Everyone good here?"

My trivia buff was on to another drink and had forgotten the question he'd asked me.

"How 'bout you get her a drink on me?" The trivia buff, looking at Jim, insisted.

"Nope," I answered. "If I have another drink, someone has to walk me home."

"C'mon," he pushed.

Jim interceded. "How 'bout I buy you that drink, and *I* walk you home?"

I sat there waiting to see what would happen next. The trivia buff, dejected, left. The last patrons filed out. Jim started cleaning up behind the bar. I sat there nursing the drink he had poured me. I had no idea what time it was, and I didn't want to know. Eventually, he shut off the lights and locked the door behind us.

Outside, I was swaying. Fortunately, I only lived a couple of blocks away. A few feet from my building, Jim steadied me. I wanted to show him the view from the roof—37 stories above. Upstairs, he took me in his arms and began kissing me. I don't know how long we were there. It was the quietest I had been all night. Afterward, in the awkward silence, he asked me if he could take me out the following week. He said he would call that Sunday.

But Sunday came and went. No call. Maybe it would end there. It seemed strange; he just didn't seem like the kind of guy who would ask for my number and not call. The Monday morning conversation at work usually turned toward my weekend "luck"—everyone was rooting for me to find the elusive man whom I was sure I was destined to meet. That Monday, I was quiet and perplexed.

Three days later, there were a dozen roses and a note on my dining room table. I thought they were from our nanny, Elizabeth. *How sweet. She's so thoughtful.* I didn't open the card until later.

I would have called Sunday, but at 2:00 a.m.,
without my reading glasses, I was definitely challenged.
Your number never made it into my phone. I feel a little stupid,
so please accept my apology."
Jim

His phone number was under his name. Doors open, doors close. Both of us could have bolted. A lost phone number was an automatic out. I thought about the reading glasses I had borrowed and the kiss. I thought about how, for months, I'd insisted I felt someone close by, and the bar was only a couple of blocks away. Was he the one?

I called him. We talked for an hour.

Friday night, when I came down to the lobby for our first date, I felt hopeful, but I picked a place far across town. Just in case it didn't go so well, I didn't want to regularly walk past a bad memory. Jim, emancipated from the confines of the bar, was dressed in his typical daytime work attire. He looked handsome and businesslike in his suit. He seemed calm and confident. He reached for my hand.

I could hold another man's hand, and it would never feel this way.

The matchmakers were two dates and two months shy of fulfilling our contract. They came out ahead.

After we went out for a couple of months, Jim and Daniel had yet to meet. I hadn't shared much with Jim about Daniel—just that he was 15, I was divorced, and my son and I were very close. I didn't know how to describe Daniel because anything I could offer would seem like an injustice. I hadn't mentioned Jim to Daniel, either, because it seemed too early. I wasn't sure yet that Jim and I would have a long enough future to involve Daniel.

When Jim spoke about his daughters, it was usually about a cheerleading outing, an accomplishment at school or work, or a prom night. We went on long walks in Central Park and long weekends away, and we visited museums, went to movies, and shared good meals. In his presence, I felt that I didn't have to work hard to fill in the void of whatever had usually been missing with the men I'd met. The moments became days, and days became nights, and the goodbyes got harder.

When the time was right, I took a chance and trusted that Daniel and Jim would figure things out. I arranged a date to Yankee Stadium.

Jim was drafted by the Minnesota Twins in the early Eighties while he was in college, and Daniel had taught himself a good amount about baseball. I have no idea how he got into it; his father had no interest in watching team sports, and I didn't either.

I enlisted my friend Joyce who, like Jim and Daniel, was a big Yankees fan. I set it up with Daniel that a "friend of mine" was taking us to a game. He was excited. Daniel took the lead, teaching Jim how to navigate the crowded Number 4 train to the stadium. We settled into our seats, and Daniel immediately wanted to follow the "kiss cam" (a camera that scans the crowd, selects a couple, and their image appears on the jumbotron screen.)

"Is he okay alone?" Jim had quickly discerned that maybe Daniel's compass wasn't necessarily going to lead him back to us. "Should I follow him?"

Before I could answer, Jim had bolted from his seat and caught up with Daniel, heading for a walk around the perimeter of the stadium. Joyce and I looked at each other and nodded. *A good guy.* I also knew Daniel had been lost before, and it had been scary, but that was part of growing up. He would have found his way back even if it cost me a few heartbeats.

A half-hour later, the guys returned. They sat next to each other and chattered away about the game and the players. Joyce barely got a word in here and there.

Later, when we got home, Daniel asked Jim if he wanted to sleep over.

Jim declined. "Another time, buddy."

"When?" Daniel wanted to know.

"Soon."

Later, I asked Daniel what he thought of Jim. He put his two hands together as if to make a match. "I like the way you two are together."

On most Friday and Saturday nights, Jim worked at the bar where we'd met, and I would see him during those days Daniel was visiting Alan.

On Sunday nights when my son would return, we would order pizza and watch movies. I breathed better when he arrived home. The weeks were hectic. There were numerous specialist appointments related to the complications of Alan's late-stage cancer, and sudden hospitalizations, not to mention commitments related to my son's special-education school. My career was demanding, with long hours and many social and business obligations. Even our rescue dog Gracie had a "complex" personality. She bit Jim's foot the first time they met. Somehow, with all that going on, Jim and I made it work.

On the one-year anniversary of our first date, I overheard Daniel grilling Jim.

"How long have you been with my mother?" He knew the answer. This was typical of him. He was testing Jim.

"Why?"

"Are you taking her out for your anniversary?"

"Yes, I am."

"Are you going to ask my mother to marry you?"

"Daniel, I am sure I will spend the rest of my life with your mother."

"I know, but are you going to ask her to marry you?"

"When the time is right. First, I'll ask you, because you are the man of the house, and then we'll call your grandfather and ask him."

"When?"

I snuck away from the door. Knowing my son, the inquisition wouldn't end soon.

"When the time is right."
"When will the time be right?
"Someday.

GETTING PAST FIRST

The harder I practice, the luckier I get.
~Unknown~

Throughout high school, Daniel wanted to make the softball team, but he couldn't qualify. Now, in his final year, the year his father was battling cancer, Daniel had his own battles. His social life had been beaten to a pulp by girls he liked who never reciprocated, and his father was very sick. It didn't seem fair that Coach P, a tough guy, would be so tough that he couldn't find *something* for Daniel to do as part of the team. There was no way Coach was going to play a kid that would either get hurt on the field or allow precious runs to score, but Jim and I encouraged Daniel to advocate for himself.

"What do you think you can do for the team?"

"I know a lot about baseball. I can keep the stats."

Daniel couldn't handwrite, so I wasn't so sure about this.

"What else can you do?"

"I can carry equipment."

"Yup. You can definitely carry equipment. Talk to the coach. See what he says."

"Mom, the guy hates me."

"He can't hate you. He doesn't even know you."

"He knows me. I am the slowest kid in gym, and I always get yelled at or hit with the ball when we are playing catch."

"Well, if you want to be on the team, you have to convince him you can do something."

The next day, Daniel came home with a release I had to sign. He had made the team. Well, he had been made the head schlepper—a.k.a. equipment manager. I thought we should celebrate and took out a bottle of champagne.

I would leave work early and take the subway to places I'd never been, walking onto the dirt in my high heels and sitting on dirty benches in the heat and the rain to watch the team. Daniel watched from behind the fence. Jim and I went to fields in parts of the city we'd never visited just to watch games our son would likely never play in, but he was part of the team and, like the other parents, we supported him.

One day, when the team was losing miserably, we heard Coach P call out: "Dubinsky! Get on deck!"

Daniel jumped when he heard his name.

He's not playing him, is he?

Daniel, who had never had an "at bat" in his life, ran to the plate. The pitches came at him fast, and he swung at two bad balls.

The umpire leaned in and said softly, "Only the good ones, buddy, only the good ones." And then, ball three. WHACK! He'd made contact. I heard myself yelling, "Run, Daniel, RUN!"

He had never heard those words leave my mouth. I had never cheered my son at a game. Jim and I watched and called out to him as he ran for first base. The ball beat him.

As he walked back to the fence, I looked at his feet. He wasn't even wearing sneakers! He hadn't believed they'd ever play him.

That summer, when I approached Jim about playing on my company's softball team, it was Daniel who welcomed the idea. He saw an opportunity. He would accompany Jim to Central Park for the games, cheer for the team, and try to get a shot at getting on the field. We all knew (including Daniel) that an "at-bat" with the players of the Broadway Show League might mean a broken nose, a black eye, or worse. They were serious about playing even if they weren't the best athletes. Still, Daniel went to every game he could and hoped that one day he would swing the bat.

That day came when the team manager put him in at the end of a lost game, and predictably, he grounded out, never making it to first.

Later, when Daniel moved to Cambridge, the change in scenery didn't deter his commitment to his softball team back in New York. He would get on the Green Line to South Station, board a 7:30 a.m. bus, travel five hours, walk to the fields at Central Park, watch the games, and then leave at 7:00 the next morning.

"Are you coming to the game today?" he'd ask me.

"We'll see," I would answer. Sometimes I would get there and other times not.

When I did go to the games, I saw more than a bunch of men and women playing softball—I watched my son grow from an uncoordinated, lost, late, and unprepared kid to a committed champion of a team he loved. Before every game, he was the one who gathered everyone to offer the game invocation. All hands in, heads bowed, and Daniel offering words of inspiration. He admired them, felt their triumphs, shared their frustrations, and laughed and cried with them; even when he sat out most of the time, he showed up. When they were losing miserably and got pissy, he would remind them, "Hey, it's just underhand softball; it's supposed to be fun."

One day as he stood watching from behind the fence, I heard, "Get in there, Daniel." I could see the beads of sweat on his forehead. He stepped up to the plate, took a breath, and swung at the first ball. I heard the hard smack of the bat.

I jumped up. "GO, DANIEL, GO! GOOO!" I called to him.

The ball was heading for first, but he made it safely to the plate. One of the guys on our team ran over and offered to pinch-run for him. All I could see was a brush of Daniel's hand. *No thanks, I can do this.*

The next batter came up and, THWACK, the ball sailed into the outfield. Suddenly, everything was going very fast. Daniel ran for second. I watched as the second baseman went for the ball and then I closed my eyes. When I reopened them, Daniel was rounding third.

The crowd on both sides stood and cheered for him as he made it home.

No matter what uniform they wore, just for that day, winning meant more than who had the higher score. A bunch of men and women who didn't say "no" just because Daniel wasn't the typical guy on a softball team were all willing to make it possible for him to accomplish what had taken ten years of watching. His first home run.

The opposing team offered up the team ball. On a bad day or when the score wasn't in their favor, I hoped they'd remember Daniel's smiling face as he crossed the plate and what life had taught him: "The only failure is giving up."

'TIL DEATH DO US PART

Why think separately of this life and the next
when one is born from the last?
~Rumi~

A week after Alan died, I stood on the corner in Brooklyn in front of his building. Its peeling paint and crumbling facade reminded me that both he and the building had deteriorated together. For thirty years, they had been inseparable.

Long before Daniel and I were part of his life, the building was the cornerstone for Alan's identity. I looked for the place on the sidewalk where the year we were married, he carved his initials and neglected to carve mine. They were gone.

I hardly recognized the woman waving to me. She was just a little girl when I moved to Brooklyn. She was Alan's neighbor. I guessed she was probably 30 now. There was a boy holding her hand. Her son? I waved back. I had been gone ten years. Even after all this time, she remembered who I was. I wasn't a stranger. It felt good in an odd way.

I sat in Alan's bedroom sifting through boxes and piles of paper. It was where we had made love and dreamed of the life we'd have. This was where we'd brought our newborn baby home. A siren screeched outside. I was excavating the important from the unimportant mail. Two dump trucks had barely made a dent in the fuselage of the valuable and invaluable, the useful and the useless. There were still boxes containing forty years of photography. The ceiling fan I had watched spinning on sleepless nights still whirred overhead. I'd bare-ly scratched the surface of bills that hadn't been paid, checks that hadn't been cashed, and offers for everything from memberships to credit cards, as well as personal letters and cards. I began making piles: "Keep" and "Toss."

Jim and I began to clear the building out so that we could reno-vate. Alan's sister lived in Virginia, and they hadn't been very close. Both of his parents had been deceased for quite a while. As the executrix of the estate, I was responsible for deciding its fate. The building would miss Alan.

Alan's office, once a functional space, was now impenetrable. It had been home to a growing business where he had supported us through the early years of Daniel's life. Dust covered his art studio, where years ago he would get lost in his projects. It would need to be emptied of an old table saw, obsolete computer equipment, boxes of tools, thousands of nails and screws, and broken cameras. He had not worked in a long time.

Over the past two years, we had hired numerous aides and house-keepers. None of them had lasted long.

Before he left each weekend, I asked Daniel, "Are you sure you want to go?"

"It's okay, mom, he's my father. He's sick; he needs me."

The difficulties that defined his father were, according to Daniel, still worthy of our love. I regularly visited and checked in on the house to make sure it was reasonably neat and clean. As soon as I would organize things, he would intentionally mess them up again. One of the aides asked me why I did it.

I did it so I would know I had done it. That's the only reason I could give.

When our marriage was disintegrating, I was reluctant to label his behavior. Later, it was easier to call it a "breakdown." The words that described Alan's demons were easy to come by, but living on the other side of them wasn't easy. Any number of psychiatric terms could be used to describe him, but in the end, I was left alone to salvage the truth from the mess. Early on in our relationship, I'd rationalized that his "dark side" was the fuel for his artistic soul. A psychiatrist suggested he was "manic-depressive," and later, the words "borderline personality disorder" and "narcissistic injury" surfaced. I had the diseases to blame, and now the cancer and its treatment. It was impossible to know where they'd all met up with each other, eventually ravaging his mind.

Ten years after I'd left Alan, while sitting in the aftermath of his life equipped with my "coping mechanisms" and my so-called explanations, I was unprepared for the remains of his life staring back at me. My attempts at partnering with him through the end had been as futile as the lack of partnership in our marriage. I wiped my sweaty face. I took a deep breath. I had accompanied him to his appointments, advocated for him, sometimes despised him, and sometimes hated his doctors with their lethal-weapon IVs and false hope.

He didn't easily say "I love you" even to his son, but his deep love for Daniel was evident in his fight to live through the most humiliating and debilitating of times.

During his last years, he would rage at me and ramble, and sometimes I raged back, and then at other times, we laughed. We argued over his safety, and I combed his hair, shaved his head, held his hand, and cut his nails. I held him while he cried. I accompanied him to the hospital; I made excuses to the nurses for his tirades and brought them cookies and flowers. I assured them that his bark was meaner than his bite. I listened to oncologists doling out data and numbers and stood by him suited up in space gear as he marched bravely though two stem-cell transplants. I watched the years and the disease take him, bit by bit.

Whatever I had endured by way of Alan's anger, cancer and mental complexity it wasn't the past that I was protecting. By supporting Alan, I was preparing Daniel for a future without him.

One of the last things we all did together was to go to a movie. As Alan approached the theater, he moved slowly, as if he could barely walk. He was only 61. When the movie was over, even if he was still angry with me for leaving him, I didn't want to send him home alone.

Later, as I sat there on the floor in the bedroom surrounded by a sea of paper, I felt the anger and sadness consume me...all that unfinished business like flames lapping at my hands. How unfair for my son to have witnessed the distorted end and loss of his father. It should have been a joyful year; he was graduating from high school. I held my head in my hands and curled up on the floor. The papers next to my face were soaked with tears. *Why, why, why?*

On that Monday, when Jim and I had gone to see how Alan was doing, we hadn't known what we'd find. Neither Daniel nor I had heard from him in days. We'd taken the train to Brooklyn. I was armed with my prayer book, a list of funeral homes, and swirling fantasies of what we would discover. We found Alan in his bed. He sounded like he was taking his last breaths. I called an ambulance.

The next day, I was sitting on Alan's hospital bed holding his hand. He had been drifting in and out of consciousness. The only sound in the room was the steady inhale and exhale of the respirator breathing for him. I asked the doctor to remove it so he could speak with Daniel, who was on his way.

"We can't assure you that he will survive it. He could stop breathing."

I was willing to take that chance so that Daniel might speak with his father.

When Daniel got to the hospital, I left them in the room alone. A few minutes later, Daniel emerged, head down. I wanted to hold him. He knew what I didn't have the words to tell him. We walked to the street in silence. There were no taxis. We waited for the bus. I watched as it pulled away. Jim would be waiting for him when he got home. I wept all the way back to Alan's room. I sat down next to him. He looked at me.

"Thank you," he whispered.

I just nodded and reached for his hand.

When I left, an older Italian woman whose husband was sharing the ICU suite looked over at me. "You are an angel."

"Oh, no. I am no angel."

"Yes, yes, I see how good you are. You come. You sit. You care. Your husband?"

"Not anymore. But once, yes."

"Good luck to you. You are a nice lady."

"Thank you. Good luck to you, too."

The next day, we were leaving for hospice. I rode with Alan in the back of the ambulance. We were weaving through traffic on the FDR Drive, heading to Calvary Hospital.

When we arrived, he asked, "Is this my room?"

It surprised me because I hadn't been sure he would wake up again. Those were his last words.

I had brought pictures of Daniel, and I placed them on the windowsill. I sat on the crisp white sheets that smelled like bleach. I pulled the covers over him. As he drifted into sleep, with each labored breath that he took, the lines blurred between who we had been together and who we had become apart.

LOVE

Love recognizes no barriers. It jumps hurdles, leaps fences,
penetrates walls to arrive at its destination full of hope.
~Maya Angelou~

Jim and I ensured "the Brooklyn building," as we all affectionately called it, would be a productive investment property. We'd gotten to know the existing tenants and learned all we could about the building. We'd renovated the top floor, which took the better part of a year, and we were planning on transforming the second floor into rentable space. Being landlords was a demanding and sometimes exhausting job. With an old building depending on us, we had a lot to learn. For me, it was a story of completion, bringing this place where I had once lived back to where it would have a vibrant new beginning.

I hoped the next chapter would start with a young couple living there, getting married, and having a baby—a creative couple. And just as I imagined it, they appeared. They were lovely. He was a literary agent and she was a writer, and they did get married and have a baby.

Jim and I had been together for four years. It was time for us to begin a new chapter, too. We didn't have to get married; there was no practical reason for it. But, there is a Jewish belief that if you create a family, you birth a new world. I wanted to put the pieces back together, to be a wife, and to find a big house where we could share a home with our children—where we would launch family traditions, gather for holidays and celebrations, and create memories.

We had been together long enough for me to know that Jim and I had differences. Jim is a born athlete. I'm not. His long line of genetics has produced a family that lives well into their nineties and hundreds. They've played professional sports, and their accomplishments have been housed in halls of fame. Jim was gifted with the capacity to play baseball and football. He was all-star varsity and offered sports scholarships at more than a few universities. My genealogy suggested our family talents were for the most part academic.

My idea of a good day in high school was when I could get out of gym class. My idea of a horrible day was knowing no one would pick me for the field hockey team. I was a "theater freak" and always got A's in English and literature. Jim was a handsome "jock." He majored in baseball. He was a sophomore in college when he was the eleventh-round pick for the Minnesota Twins, at which point he moved to the Midwest and played professional baseball. He was a catcher. When he was released because of an injury, his dream of becoming a great baseball player was taken from him. We both knew what life-altering wins and losses felt like, in significant and different ways.

His kind of luck was different than mine. He won contests and football pools, bets and awards. He has "President's Club" on his resumé and proof of his achievements in boxes filled with his trophies. I've never won anything, really. I don't think of myself as outwardly competitive with others. I am internally competitive. My biggest wins have been intangible, invisible; they are the personal victories that aren't recognized by mementos or public recognition. My greatest triumphs are those I have shared with my son.

Jim was raised Protestant, and I, conservatively Jewish. Growing up, he ate things that came in boxes and cans that I was forbidden from consuming—I was raised kosher. A tasting menu of Chef Boyardee with meatballs or Dinty Moore is not likely to happen now. We celebrated both Chanukah and Christmas. I learned to cook my family recipes for our Passover Seders, and macaroni-and-cheese and honey-glazed ham for Easter. I don't eat meat, and Jim is a carnivore. His favorite meal is a good steak dinner. I try to be gluten-free, soy-free, meat- and poultry-free, and dairy-free. I carefully pick around what most people eat; it's not easy. Jim eats everything. He believes ice cream cures all ills. Even though I won't usually eat it, if I'm sick, I do swear by homemade chicken soup.

Jim's long-held career in the pharmaceutical industry could not have been more different than mine in the entertainment industry. People always thought my job was interesting. Big Pharma changes lives but doesn't win any prizes for most popular dinner conversation.

By the time I was 30, I had traveled out of the country extensively. Jim had traveled extensively too, but domestically. He'll watch a baseball or football game and drink good bourbon or gin. I love writing, reading, watching foreign films, and shows about love affairs and mysteries. I like movies that are slow-moving, provocative, and challenging. I watch them once and forget them. He likes revenge movies and watches them numerous times. But, I knew I would marry him after we watched *P.S. I Love You.* I looked over at him sitting next to me. Tears were rolling down his cheeks. It was a sign. We belonged together.

I surprised him one birthday with ballroom dance lessons. It was my fantasy to become a good dancer. He was a former baseball catcher; Jim is built more like a fighter than a dancer, but he was really good at it. Of course he was; it required balance and coordination. I, on the other hand, was no Ginger Rogers. I was more like Lucille Ball in expensive dancing shoes. We laughed and sometimes I cried out of frustration. Eventually, we were good enough to look like we knew what we were doing—as long as I didn't try to lead.

When we got to the conversation about what kind of ring I wanted, he made one request. Because shopping was my only sport, and I had a high threshold for exhaustion, he asked that I pick a ring and then let him know where to fetch it. He couldn't endure the hunt with me. I understood. We decided to be married someplace neither of us had visited—the Greek island of Santorini. We would cruise there in June of the following year.

He still had to propose.

WITH THIS RING, I THEE WED

*On the difficult days, when the world is on your shoulders,
remember that diamonds are made under
the weight of the mountains.*
~Beau Taplin~

Jim said, "Go find the ring."

My office was two blocks from New York's famed Diamond District. A whole sparkling block of rings. *Here I come.* I found it in a window. The minute I saw it, I knew it was mine. I went inside and discovered it was my size. It was like me—very sparkly, a little different, a little traditional—and the setting had barely perceptible intertwined hearts on the sides of the center stones. I asked the jeweler how much it would cost to get it out of the window. I gave him a hundred dollars. I scribbled Jim's first and last name and phone number. I explained that I wasn't sure when but that he would come soon. I took a business card. That night, I handed it to Jim.

We were leaving soon for Italy. Since my divorce, my colleagues had focused their Monday morning conversation on my dating activity. Now the stakes were high. Where and how would Jim propose?

On the plane to Italy, my heart was filled with yearning and curiosity. We meandered and wandered the old streets of Rome, the Trevi Fountain at night, the Spanish Steps, and the Colosseum. I gasped at the breathtaking Pieta in the Vatican. We watched long, glorious sunsets and gazed upon landscapes in Tuscany. We drove hours to the seashore and back. We made our way up and down the hills until one dusk when the daylight faded and we got so lost, we thought we'd never find our way back to where we were staying.

We drank Brunellos in Montalcino, and we stuffed ourselves with homemade pastas, sauces, and gobs of bread soaked in olive oil—like nothing we ate in the states. We licked gelato with Nutella from our lips. We gasped at the details of the Santa Maria Del Fiore and learned the historical context of the centuries-old art in the Uffizi. I posed on the Bridge of Sighs, wandered the canals of Venice, and drank coffee or wine at one romantic café after the next. With each day that passed, the best places (both private and public) for Jim to go down on his knee passed, too.

On the last day of our trip, the sun was cresting over the city. It hung large and luminous. It was clear to me that the ring I had left back in the shop hadn't made the trip with us.

On the flight home, when the first-class attendant asked what "Mrs. Weiss" would like for dinner, the "not-Mrs. Weiss" answered, "Nothing." I rolled over and put the blanket over my head. I was dreading the ring-less walk of shame that would come when I returned to work.

Once we got home, I was tired. We unpacked in silence. It had been the most romantic trip of my life, and I should have been grateful. *Focus on the good.* I just couldn't shake the sadness—I had been with enough men and knew this was it. Jim was the one. He loved Daniel, and I was sure he loved me. The chasm was widening between what I had expected to be his seamless and romantic proposal and the harsh reality that, since the day I had handed the jeweler that hundred dollars, I was no closer to that ring.

Maybe Jim just didn't want to marry me.

On the Monday I returned to work, I went straight into my office and closed my door. My empty finger would have to tell the story. At lunchtime, I went to the jewelry store to check on my ring only to discover what I already knew. The ring had not been fetched.

"When do you think he will come?" the jeweler asked.

"I don't know." My lip was quivering. I had to wipe my eyes before I got back to the office. I felt like I was 23, not 53.

My friend, Scotty K, called to see how the trip had gone. When I answered, he could hear something was wrong.

"What's up?" he asked.

"Nothing."

He knew better. "Wanna go out for a drink?"

"No, silly, not in the afternoon. But, I need to get out of here. I'll meet you downstairs."

Scotty K and I walked the four blocks to my favorite place to forget about life: Lord & Taylor. The second floor smelled like shoes, hundreds and hundreds of shoes, their scent drawing me to them and awaiting my indulgence.

I pointed to a couch. "Wait here."

I walked along the tables of shoes and boots, picking up one at a time and inspecting them. Having collected a dozen, I gave them to dutiful Scotty, who sat waiting.

"If someone comes, tell them size seven and a half. I'll be back." I went hunting for more shoes.

After an hour, twenty-four pairs of shoes came and went. I bought two pairs.

On the street, Scotty K asked, "Do you often do this?"

"Only when I'm really happy or really sad."

"Oh."

"Why would a man tell a woman to go pick a ring, and a month later, take her on the most romantic trip to Italy ever, and not propose? Do you think he doesn't want to marry me?" I chattered on. It escalated into a rant. He couldn't get a word in. Finally, I stopped for air.

"Uh, no, I, uh, don't know." Scotty was dumbfounded. "Jim is a good guy. He loves you and Daniel."

"Well, I just don't understand. What does this man want?"

"Do you want me to talk to him?"

"FOR GOD'S SAKE, NO!"

"Okay. Just trying to help."

"I appreciate it. You can't help."

A week went by. I remained quiet and confused. I suggested Jim and I go out for drinks at the place where we'd gone for our first date. If he was going to back out, the place we started was a good place for it to end.

We ordered martinis.

He broke the silence. "You've been really off lately."

"Oh, you *think?*" I offered.

"What's going on?"

"We were all over Italy. We were in the most romantic places on earth. I just thought you'd...um...you'd...um...you'd have asked me. To marry you."

He looked at me quizzically. The pause was too long. Deadly. "Why is this marriage thing so important to you? Do we really have to get married?"

I had three options. Break my martini glass and stab him, throw the drink at him, or walk out. I opted for the latter.

I grabbed my coat and began walking. I crossed Broadway, and Amsterdam, and turned onto Central Park West. It was late. Later than I had ever entered the park. I was determined to walk all the way home. The "Central Park Jogger" and other stories were good reasons not to do this. Jim was now running to catch up with me.

"Stop. Stop now. You can't do this."

I wouldn't answer. I kept going.

"This is dangerous. You need to cut it out. I'm going to pick you up and carry you. You need to stop now."

I kept walking.

He was beside me now. "You can't do this."

"Watch me." I huffed on, going as fast as I could.

At home, I went into the bedroom, got undressed, and threw myself onto the bed and cried until I couldn't breathe. Jim attempted to come in.

"Stay away from me. Stay out."

I didn't sleep. When the morning came, I had a splitting headache and felt nauseous. I looked like hell. I couldn't go to work. I stumbled into the kitchen to make coffee. Jim intercepted me. I pushed him away. The crying started again.

"Why would you do this to me? What did I ever do to you? What about Daniel? He will be heartbroken! Why, Why, Why?"

"You need to stop."

"NO. I am not going to stop. You need to tell me why you would be so mean to me!"

He grabbed me by the arms. "Robyn. Listen. You need to look at me, NOW."

I turned away.

"I wanted to surprise you."

I grabbed a paper towel and blew my nose. I started into the bedroom. He followed me. I was sitting on the bed. He was suddenly kneeling on the floor. He took my hands in his.

"I wanted to surprise you. I had it all planned...with Daniel. I promised your son I would ask him first and then your father, and then you. Daniel wanted to be there."

We just stared at each other for what felt like a very long time. I sniffled.

"Robyn...Robyn...can you hear me? Crazy woman. I just can't surprise you. Will you marry me?"

Just Who We Are

I answered, "What about the ring?"

"We can go get that ring right now. Are you sure it's the ring you want?"

"Yes."

"Okay, let's go get it."

I splashed water on my face. I waited in the car. Jim went in. Then he handed me the box. "Are you sure this is right?"

We got home and he took the box from me. "You'll have to wait."

A few weeks later, Jim and I were coming back from seeing a show on Broadway. We stopped into the bar where he and I had met. The place was packed, but my stool, the one in the corner where I'd sat on the night we met, was empty. Within minutes, Daniel came in. The neighborhood regulars and the owners started circling around. We all exchanged the usual hugs and "How are you's?"

Jim whispered something to Daniel. Before I could put it all together, he went down on one knee, took my hand in his, and asked, "Will you marry me?"

Cheers all around...champagne flowed...glasses were raised.

There in that dark corner where I'd contemplated being alone the rest of my life, my bartender proposed to me.

***

Nine years later, I was feeling antsy while answering an insurance adjuster's questions. I had come into work after having an MRI. I'd sat down at my desk. I'd started up my computer. And I'd looked at my hands. The ring—not the other rings, MY DIAMOND RING—was missing from my finger. What the hell?

Before I'd entered the magnetic monster, I had put all of my jewelry in a black velvet pouch. Now, I sat at my desk and closed my eyes, reimagining putting the jewelry back on my hands. First, my watch, then the ring I wore on my right hand, and then my wedding band. WHERE WAS MY ENGAGEMENT RING? It wasn't in the pouch. It wasn't in my purse. I checked the floor. *WHY DID YOU PUT YOUR JEWELRY ON IN THE CAB? WHY ARE YOU SO IMPULSIVE?*

I didn't want to confess this, but I had to. I walked out of my office. "I can't find my engagement ring." I'd said it quietly and slowly. Matter-of-factly because I was hiding the panic I was feeling. Like the Rockettes, Victoria and Stephanie, whom I worked with, as if rehearsed, said in sync, "Oh no!" Silence shrouded the room.

I had to mobilize.

The compassionate, slow-speaking woman at the insurance company suggested I try to locate the taxi. I didn't have a receipt. I didn't know that, with an address and a timeframe, the Taxi and Limousine Commission could locate the taxis that would have been in the vicinity. They gave me three phone numbers. Not one of the cabbies had found my ring. *OF COURSE THEY DIDN'T FIND THE RING! ANYONE WHO FOUND THAT RING WASN'T COPPING TO IT!*

The ring had its own story to tell, and no matter who found it, that story was a secret. No one knew about my tantrum or the late-night walk through Central Park. But the ring's history was steeped in even more—in years of wanting something, something that I hadn't had in my first marriage. Something that was more important than carbon and precious metal. To vow to be married is a divine act. It isn't really about consecrating love, which most people commit to when they start out. I wanted to be married again so that I could do it right. I married Jim twelve years after I'd gotten divorced. I'd never thought I'd be unmarried for so long. I guess I had some things to learn. Love changes, and my love for Jim had definitely changed since that day when I'd picked the ring, but what it symbolized then, and now, was that together we would make a life. We had been there for our children and for Ashley; we had ushered our loved ones through the ends of their lives; and we had commemorated every celebration and graduation, dorm move, and Daniel's many triumphs and challenges. We had lifted each other up and challenged each other to the edges of our sanity. Even on the days when I didn't know what I was doing in this marriage, I believed in it. When I wanted to give up, I discovered that, for me, marriage was about how two people can stand together in the world. I didn't get to do that the first time. That ring was my reminder that maybe if we kept finding the way, we could do it. Every day, I woke up and I chose this man again and again.

I walked over to the jeweler where I had originally found the ring. He was sorry to hear it, but he could no longer get the same one. I Googled the manufacturer. The rings were made to order through authorized jewelers. I found a lovely woman in a shop in Ohio who said she could help. It would take six weeks to make the ring. Okay. I breathed. At least I had found it.

I wore a variety of rings on that hand. They were visitors, but they didn't belong. In nine years, no other ring had adorned that finger. I counted the days until the ring, bearing a new chapter in its storied history, would arrive.

When it came, I placed it on my finger and remembered that fabled walk through the park, shoe shopping with Scotty, and the way I have never been good at surprises. I forgave myself for that and for losing it. I forgave whoever had found it. I hoped it was someone who wanted to ask the love of their life to marry them and who might just learn what I knew—that there is no perfect marriage, but maybe there is the perfect ring.

NO PLAN B

*Every blade of grass has an angel that bends
over it and whispers, "Grow, grow."*
~Hillel~

In Daniel's final year of high school, Jim and I cheered for him at track meets and softball games. We stood by for the emotional fall-out of more than one bully and more than one broken heart, and we thought of what possibilities were ahead. Daniel wanted to live away from home, find a community, make friends, and eventually discover a career path. We looked at many programs and schools. We had been to Florida, New Jersey, and Cape Cod; we'd even considered Napa, California. None of the places we saw were perfect; just *one* had to be right.

We were amazed at Daniel's resilience. Life had not been fair—so many obstacles were put in his path—and yet, he was determined to do well in school and to excel in life. He was only 18, yet composed of self-confidence, grace, and dignity, and he was really funny. I was excited about the possibility of his next chapter away from home, and if anyone was deserving, my son had won the right to go on, to pursue his interests beyond what we could provide for him by living with us, and I was sure he would.

Eventually, we found our way to Cambridge, Massachusetts. We were sitting in an informational orientation for families considering the Threshold Program at Lesley University. Daniel, Jim, and I sat in a room with robin's-egg-blue paint on the walls. The wainscoting, brass chandelier, and portrait of the founder made it official. This was college. It didn't have that cozy feel of his high school, which was a small special-education school. Daniel was next to me dozing off. Before this, we'd toured all over, mostly by foot. Not an easy feat for a guy who tired easily and had a tough time walking long distances.

We were in the first row. I nudged Daniel every once in a while, hoping he was listening to the Dean of Students giving her overview of the program. Jim was sitting on Daniel's other side nudging him, too. College was a given for Jim's daughters. Just two years earlier, as Daniel had neared the beginning of his junior year, I hadn't been so sure I would ever be sitting in a room like this with my son.

Threshold is a micro-unit of Lesley University, established to meet the needs of neuro-diverse young people who are capable of a modified college experience, with both vocational and educational aspects to the program. The young people they accept must demonstrate the ability to live away from home and have the goal of eventually living independently. At the time of our visit, Threshold would receive roughly one-thousand applications each year, and twenty students would be accepted.

Cambridge is right outside of Boston. I grew up nearby and loved leaving the suburbs and coming into the city. Like an old sweater, it wrapped me in a comfortable nostalgia. It was easy for me to feel safe there. My father had worked in Boston for forty years. Daniel leaving for Cambridge would be like coming full circle. The bar was high—he would be living four hours away from us—but I believed he could handle it.

As the student ambassadors of the program entered the room, I was scanning, looking for someone who could be a friend for Daniel. I saw past their awkwardness. Making eye contact could be hard for them. Through their fidgeting and silence, I saw their courage.

220

After the meeting, Daniel was excited. He insisted that we fill out the online application on the train home. There would be volumes of reports and testing to follow. Unbeknownst to him, the rejection letter from a school we had visited in western Massachusetts had come the day before we'd left for Cambridge. The letter stated that he wasn't "ready," not "independent enough." I didn't cry that time. I hadn't cried when we'd received rejection letters before, even when I wanted to. Many schools we had applied to along the way hadn't accepted him. I didn't confuse my sadness with failure. I had always found the right schools. The admissions committee at that school in Massachusetts had no clue who they had rejected. What I had learned so far was that angels are hard workers—but they like to be met halfway.

During those years when my son's intelligence was challenged by a court of nonbelievers, an educational consultant condemned my son to have "great difficulty learning to read." I was sure that any child who loved books as much as Daniel did was going to read. Being "taught to read" wasn't what he needed. We spent more time in Barnes & Noble than any other store. He "experienced" books of his choosing, and of course, he read—he taught himself. Later, he became an avid reader. We were told our son wouldn't handwrite. No, he doesn't handwrite much. Who does? But he types very fast. In 1994, I foresaw that computers would be far more useful to him than a pen or pencil. We gave him a computer when he was three and spared him the frustration of trying to manage a task that would be obsolete in his lifetime.

When he was ten, we discovered Daniel had significant hearing loss. We had continuously been to audiologists only to hear our son had "attentional issues." We later discovered that there was a malformation of the tiny bones in his middle ear that enable hearing. He would need hearing aids. At first, he wanted nothing to do with them.

They weren't comfortable even though we picked the type that were usually used by adults that would be less visible. Sounds that were familiar to me, like traffic or sirens, were suddenly way too loud for him. We discovered many sounds he had not been hearing at all. In the first few weeks, he would keep asking, "What's that?" Birds chirping, the rustle of leaves, the creaking of a floorboard, the sound of our doorbell, butter sizzling in a pan—all new to him. There was some relief that we had made the discovery, but guilt, too, that we hadn't known this earlier. Eventually, like his glasses, those hearing aids became a natural part of his getting dressed.

We waited anxiously for the letter from Threshold. Four months later, we were invited for an interview.

The admissions office was in an old house. Daniel was upstairs for a long time. I was sitting downstairs in the living room, waiting and praying. He's a good storyteller. God only knew what he was saying.

Finally, Jim Wilbur, the Director of Threshold, came downstairs and asked to speak with me.

I braced myself.

"After you," he offered as he gestured toward the stairs.

"Your son is an interesting guy." I had heard that before, and it wasn't always good. From every school we had applied to since nursery school, comments had begun with the words, "We just don't feel it's a good fit."

"Daniel shared with me that he works at a bar, and he doesn't like doing the olive-spearing." *Oh no. He told him he works at a bar? He'll think Jim and I are totally irresponsible. Did he mention the small detail that longtime family friends own that bar? And that it's not just a bar—it's part of an upscale restaurant?*

Mr. Wilbur continued, "I've never met a professional olive-spearer, but I have bar-tended. So, we have something in common. When I

222

asked your son what the biggest challenge of Threshold would be for him, he said, 'None, but I don't do laundry.'"

I prayed Mr. Wilbur thought that was funny—because I did. Even if he had read the reams of paper we'd had to produce to get to this interview, he never could have known the whole story of the past eighteen years. He didn't know this beautiful boy of mine had just lost his father less than a year earlier. But Daniel would prevail. I was sure of that.

"We have wash and fold," Mr. Wilbur said confidently, "so we solved the laundry problem. He is just the kind of guy we are looking for here at Threshold."

I wanted to lunge across this man's desk and grab him and kiss him. I refrained.

We went back downstairs.

Daniel jumped up from the couch.

"So? Am I accepted?"

"You are just the kind of guy we are looking for here at Threshold, David."

He reached out to shake Daniel's hand... Daniel, bypassing the offer, threw his arms around Mr. Wilbur and gave him a big hug.

My son rarely hugged strangers.

Thank you. Thank you. Thank you. I didn't want to seem as desperate as I felt.

Later, Daniel said, "It's okay he called me David. I forgive him."

That was a good thing. There was no Plan B.

THE ROCKING CHAIR

I guess this old chair encouraged me
to become more than I was.
~Doren Millstead~

"Daniel, can you tell me what's wrong?"

There was a long silence and sniffling.

"Honey, did something happen?"

"No." He choked out the words, "No, I just have to come home."

It was mid-September. We had left him at his dorm in Cambridge not even two weeks earlier. At the time, he'd seemed happy and excited to be there.

"Can you tell me what's going on?"

"No. I just have to come home."

"Okay, it's probably better if I come there. I'll come this weekend."

"Can you come now?"

"Daniel, sweetheart, I have to work. I can come this weekend."

I hung up the phone and told myself that every kid who leaves for college—even a special program at a college—has a hard time at first. But I didn't convince myself. I fought hard. I wanted to leave right away.

I looked out the window of my train, feeling like I was back on that tightrope of faith—balancing my old friends, hope and fear. I had been practicing this long enough now. Most of the time, I didn't think about it. The scenery blurred past me like the years of advocating, therapies, specialists, and finding the right communities. It was just

225

the deep end of the pool. That's all. He wouldn't drown.

I started to write:

"I'm not sure anything I can say will make you feel better. I know these past ten days have been challenging. I know you have been far away from all the things that make you feel comfortable—your home, your dog, your friends, Jim, and me. You've been adventuresome and curious to have many great experiences away from home—you've had to be self-reliant—no one could have taught you how to do that. You had to figure it out by making mistakes and getting back on track. When you lacked the physical capacity to compete, you didn't settle for no—even if you couldn't play softball, or run, you showed up, willing to champion the team, assist the coach, and if you were lucky, wait for an 'at-bat' in the last inning of the game. That is stamina. That is excellence. And although you might have wanted to quit—you didn't. I know you to want to belong, to fit in, to be like everyone else..."

Being like everyone else wasn't an option. Daniel wasn't like everyone else.

When I arrived in Cambridge, I called him.

"Can we buy a rocking chair?" he asked.

"*A rocking chair?*"

"A rocking chair I found in a furniture store on Mass. Ave."

"You went furniture shopping?"

My son has a sudden interest in furniture?

"Okay. When I get there, let's take a look."

I walked through Harvard Yard toward Oxford Street. I stopped for a minute to admire the venerable brick buildings and the statue of John Harvard. The students, starting their school year, walked in every direction. Their backpacks in tow, they were the chosen few—gifted with an intelligence reserved for only 0.2 percent of the population. Do they get scared, too? What would it be like to have a child attend Harvard? I already knew. Daniel attending school in Cambridge was our Harvard. He had far exceeded the "meets expectations" part of his still young life. What would I do if he insisted that he couldn't stay?

I'd tell him that no one would force him to stay and that of course he could come home. And I wouldn't tell him that, if he did, my heart would break.

As he entered high school, the idea of my son navigating from classroom to classroom was a stretch. Watching him cross a street was a gut-wrenching experience. He hardly ever looked up. Even with sunglasses, the sun blinded him. The principal once grounded him because he didn't pay attention when he headed across a busy street to get to his favorite pizza place. A little breeze felt like a turbine engine; a slight bump in the sidewalk could send him falling. All of these things were navigational hazards caused by differences in sensory integration.

Daniel will find his way—his favorite foods are on the other side of Harvard: Pizzeria Uno and Good Licks Ice Cream. Do I want too much for him—living in a dorm like me and my sister? What if he can't do it? What if his "executive functioning" (the part of the brain that makes complex tasks simple for someone like me) doesn't activate? He'll lose things. He'll get lost. His mind will wander. He'll fall down, get hurt—and who'll be there? If he gets sick, who'll help? If he gets lonely, who will he reach out to? If he gets scared, what then?

The thoughts cascading through my mind that only he could silence, and they were pummeling me. People were looking at me. I must have been talking out loud.

When I arrived at his dorm, I expected his room to be neater. There was stuff everywhere. Clean clothes mixed with dirty, papers on the floor, a full garbage pail with evidence that my son had discovered Starbucks.

"Let's make your bed," I offered.

"Mom, please. NO!"

"C'mon, it's nice to have a clean room; let's get it all picked up. I'll help you." *Did I come all this way to clean his room, really?*

Chaos mattered less to him than it mattered to me. I would clean his room for me, not for him.

"Can we get the rocking chair?"

"Where is it?"

"A few blocks away."

"Okay, show me. Let's walk. What's making you so sad?"

"I don't know."

"Can I tell you what I think?"

"Yeah..."

"You were at Lowell nine years and now you are starting over—what's harder than being a rookie?"

"I know."

"I heard you played basketball—how was that?"

"Good."

"Okay. Well, if you bring your sneakers next time, I bet someone can help you tie them!"

"How did you know I didn't have my sneakers?"

"Jim Wilbur told me you were a very enthusiastic player, but you didn't wear sneakers."

I wondered what being unable to tie my own sneakers would feel like. Daniel couldn't tie his sneakers. Someday, he might.

"How 'bout you get some friends together and we'll go for dinner."

"I don't have any friends."

"Well, I bet there are some kids in your dorm who might appreciate a good meal.

We can go into Boston. See if you can get anyone interested.

Yes?"

We entered the furniture store. A man came out to greet us. It was a small place with a lot of used furniture. Daniel made a beeline toward the back. I was surprised the rocker wasn't in the window. What had drawn him into this store?

"My son likes a certain rocking chair."

"Here it is!" Daniel pointed.

It was a simple wooden rocker. The first thing I noticed was the broken foot on it.

I wanted to say, "No, it's broken." I didn't say that.

"Can you make sure the bottom is fixed?" I asked the guy who worked in the store.

"Sure."

"Okay, and can you deliver it?"

"Sure."

Daniel chimed in, "When?"

"Later this afternoon."

Done. I handed Daniel my credit card.

We walked back to his dorm.

"When do you think my chair will arrive?"

"Soon, I'm sure."

He called me around an hour later. "The chair came. How many kids can I invite?"

"How many do you want to invite?"

"I think there are four."

"Okay. Where do you want to go?

"Cheesecake Factory."

"At the Prudential Center?" It had been a while since I had been on the T. That would be a real excursion from Cambridge into downtown Boston, but I liked the idea of taking them on an adventure. "Sounds good. See you at six."

"Okay, bye."

When I got back to his dorm, the rocking chair had been delivered. That rocking chair meant something: something personal, something comforting. To me, it was a small investment in a big commitment.

When we got downstairs, five smiling faces greeted us. Five was better than none.

"Do you guys know your way to the Prudential Center?"

Five sets of shoulders shrugged.

"Okay, we'll figure it out."

Daniel walked ahead of me. Everyone was chattering and laughing along the way.

A new rocking chair and new friends. Mission accomplished. I would go back to New York City in the morning.

ALL I EVER WANTED

I don't have much money, but boy if I did,
I'd build a big house where we both could live.
~Elton John~

The picture of the stone house I had taped to my mirror moved with Daniel and me from our first one-bedroom apartment to our bigger apartment. It was my constant reminder: one day, I would walk into a bank, get a mortgage, and buy a house.

Jim was content living in our apartment, but he understood my dream. He had bought his first home at 28 and paid it off, and then bought another home he'd paid off. I had never been house shopping. I believed we would put our family together in a place with a lot of bedrooms and space, surrounded by nature.

When I was asked repeatedly, "How are you going to deal with Daniel being away?" I answered, "I'll be fine." But the truth was, having a second home was not just a longtime dream; I needed a new project—something I could bring to life.

Eventually, after a lot of looking, we landed in the northwest corner of Connecticut in Litchfield County. I'm from New England. The farms and cows grazing nearby felt familiar. The house we purchased had a stone façade and an old stone wall on the property... the stones were like the stone house in my picture. I wondered when our wall was built and by whom? Probably by a farmer in the late 1700s or early 1800s.

We discovered the swallows' nest the morning after we moved in.

The light flooding into our bedroom woke me. The sun won a good fight over the clouds, and I wondered if the birds really sang louder in Connecticut or if it just seemed so. Outside the window, I could see the foothills of the Berkshires veiled in their mist, regal and knowing.

Weeks later, the nest was crowded with baby birds. "Bambino," a white-spotted fawn, appeared on the grass. A baby turkey hurried by, so animated as it ran to keep up with its mom and dad. They strutted along the back fence with their careful glances warning us to keep away as they looked for dinner.

The weekends came one by one, and our house was becoming a home. This was where I would share my love of feeding people and cook in a kitchen bigger than a closet. Our children would come. We would watch things grow and grow together. At least that was the plan. I could do things I had never done like hang birdfeeders, fight with the garden hose, and learn that moles can destroy a lawn. I learned to catch ladybugs that got into the house in bowls of soapy water. I would walk up the driveway in my slippers to fetch my beloved Sunday paper. I'd look back at this beautiful home, a reminder of how far I'd come since those days when I hadn't even been able to rent an apartment.

The leaves turned, and for those precious months, the mountains became a changing palette.

One day, when Daniel was visiting, we parked by the side of the road in Kent. We pushed past the rough and found the trailhead. The climb got hard fast.

"I have to stop."

I could hear Daniel behind me. I turned around and gave him a look that said he didn't have to stop; he just had to stop thinking he had to stop.

"It will be worth it when we reach the top," I said. "Then you'll know you did it."

I'm not sure it mattered to him if he made it to the top. But it mattered to me.

"One step at a time, buddy. Go slow. Keep your weight forward." I heard Jim behind me as I ran ahead to see how far the summit was.

I would go back and report, "Not too much further. You can do it, Daniel, just go slow." His breathing was heavy, and his hair was soaked. Mosquitoes feasted on our sweaty skin.

"It's so close now." I reached for Daniel's hand. "Soon, we can rest."

The view at the top was really good. Another memory we made together.

That night, in the quiet before sleep, I rolled over to be near Jim. I kept still while he slept, alone in my head with the complexities of the world... I wanted to live out my days going on our long walks... thinking up ways to make our home better... How long would we have here? I didn't know.

We only have the present. We've come this far, like Daniel on his own mountain, so who knows what's next?

In the still of those nights, I counted backward from 100, searching the numbers for how I could show the universe my gratitude. I would check in on Daniel, sleeping in his big room—my promise kept from long ago.

The hawks were circling. I looked up at the swallows' nest. Two hatchlings were down on the driveway. It was searing, and surely they would fry or be eaten. Later, three of them were down on the grass. I watched their mother frantically flying up and down, to and fro, as if to show them what they had to do, and to signal to us—stay away.

The sunsets would lure us to the deck. Drinks in hand, we would sit for hours watching the changing sky, fireflies sparkling, and all those stars. I could see constellations I had never seen. When we'd first met, I had written in a letter to Jim, "...perhaps if you look to the night sky, and believe as I do, we will put some stars up there, together."

I'LL BE THE BOW, AND YOU BE THE ARROW

You are the bows from which your children
as living arrows are sent forth.
~Khalil Gibran~

The rocking chair followed Daniel to each of his three dorm rooms. When he left Threshold, he assured me, "Don't worry about leaving it. Someone will appreciate it. We'll have to buy new furniture for my apartment anyway."

That was positive thinking: *"My apartment..."*

On graduation day, Daniel stood before a few hundred people. He described dragging his suitcases (which were empty) down the rickety dorm stairs only to haul them back up to his top-floor room. Time after time, a resident assistant would report this to Jim and me. Usually, we'd have "the talk," which always went the same way: "Life can feel crappy, but if you run away, the same problems you're trying to escape will be there to greet you." He always stayed.

In his speech, he shared a few things he had learned:

1. "I'm a different guy today than the one who packed my bags and threatened to leave."

2. "If you stick it out through the hard times, things get better."

3. "I lost less stuff than I used to."

4. "I surprised even myself that I could get up on time."

5. "I have my friends to thank for my success. You are the first real friends I've ever had."

We laughed about the first day of classes when Daniel called me from the street, convinced he had gone to the wrong building. He didn't know what to do. He walked half a mile back to the office only to discover that he had arrived at class so early that no one was there. He'd been in the right place all along.

He had learned to navigate his way into Boston, succeeded at his jobs, and earned good grades. On a visit home, when he announced to us that he had defected and become a Red Sox fan, our doorman Jimmy wouldn't let up on him. One day, Jim asked, "Hey, Jimmy, did you ever do anything stupid for a girl?" And that was the end of that. We guessed a girl did have something to do with it, but Daniel wouldn't confess.

Daniel insisted, "You have to root for the home team, and Cambridge is my home now."

I've been told I was brave. But I wasn't. I think I was stubborn and determined. I was willing to trade my terror for my faith that things could work out. I couldn't protect Daniel from life away from home. That wasn't the deal. I was the bow. He was the arrow. And we were partners.

When the "Boston Marathon Bombers" were being hunted, Daniel was locked in his dorm room. He didn't ask to come home, and I didn't ask if he wanted to leave. It wasn't my first instinct to go to Cambridge. We could be afraid and apart. I just hoped that whatever was going on would get resolved quickly. I called to check in.

"I'm worried about eating. What if I can't leave my room for a long time?" he asked.

You could go a few days without food, and you'd live, I thought.

"Yup," I said. "Let's hope you're out of there soon."

After graduation, Daniel returned to New York, but we had agreed that he would go back up to Cambridge the following September. The Threshold Program had provided community, and it felt right for him to want to try to establish his "post-college" life there. This would require resources to secure a job and find an apartment. I wasn't entirely convinced he was ready for the challenge, but he had been in Cambridge for three years. This quest for an independent life was everything we had all hoped for. I reached out to the director of the daycare center where Daniel had volunteered for two years. She agreed that he could stay on as a full-time volunteer assisting in a classroom.

In early July, Daniel and I left on a three-day trip to secure housing. With each apartment we saw, I remembered that, just a few years earlier, I imagined that this would have seemed like a nice idea but not reality. There's a lot to be said for imagination and readiness. Daniel was going to live by himself in an apartment in Cambridge. He was going to do what millions of young people do when they move away from home. His co-signature scrawled in black ink on the lease made me think, *This is the craziest thing I have ever done.* Yes, this was crazy, but crazy good. We had journeyed twenty-three years for this day. It was no different than any other time when we'd walked into the unknown. We would do it one step at a time.

The apartment was close to the Lesley University campus. Nestled between Porter and Harvard squares, its prewar bricks and tiles reminded me of the building where I had lived in Greenwich Village in the 1980s. Unlike that apartment, this one seemed to be free of cockroaches. The hallway smelled like someone was cooking. The apartment was a fourth-floor walkup. I rationalized all those steps would be good for him.

On the day Jim and I moved him in—even with each piece of furniture that arrived, the trips to Bed Bath & Beyond, the hardware store visit, and waiting for the cable guy—this was still hard for me to believe. Jim was putting the finishing touches on the air conditioners, and soon it would be time to go.

Exhausted, we headed down the stairs. When we got outside, Daniel turned and started to walk away. We got into the car. I was very quiet. I could see Daniel through the side mirror. He was walking in his slow, uneven gait. He didn't look back.

"What's wrong?" Jim asked.

This was my dream come true. What *was* wrong?

"I didn't even get him food."

"If your son couldn't put food in his refrigerator, you wouldn't be leaving him."

Right. I wouldn't be leaving him. He could forage for food; that was for sure.

When he returned from the A&P, the nearby market, he wouldn't be coming home to the place where he and I had made a life. He'd return to a place where he'd make his own life.

"We have to go." Jim was trying to encourage me.

I heard the same voice that had always come when I didn't know how I'd put one foot in front of the other. It was Daniel's voice. It was the voice that said, "I'll be fine, Mom."

As we drove, I stared out the window.

"Are you okay?" Jim asked.

I don't know, I thought. But no sound came out of my mouth. Jim had come into Daniel's life when he was 15. From the day they'd met, they were connected by me, by baseball, and mostly by the love they had for each other. Jim didn't have a son, and since Alan had passed away, Daniel didn't have a father, so they completed something in each other. This rite of passage was each of theirs to share, too, in their own way. Jim's eyes were teary.

I called Daniel when we arrived home.

"Is it hard to let go of me?" Daniel asked.

"Yes, it is hard to let go of you."

I sent you far away on the school bus when you were only six and waited for your call when you came home. I left for business trips and counted the days until I'd return to you. I ran beside the first city bus you rode to the next stop, where I waited for you. I held my breath waiting for you to come up from your first subway ride. You went away to sleep-away camp, teen tours, and traveled to other countries. I waited for your emails and pictures. When we left you in your dorm room, I prayed you'd be happy. Now what?

SURRENDER

Choose to trust that there is a greater plan for you
and...
it will unfold in time.
~Debbie Ford~

Everything seemed so right after Daniel moved, but at the same time, there was so much uncertainty. I would look at his baby pictures. In him, I saw only joy. In myself, I saw a protective, strong, funny, and playful young woman. I didn't see the pain I had been in. I had moved on from those years, but they were part of me. The fragile and scared parts of me hid behind the prestige and confidence of my life as an executive. My warrior exterior masked the humility of being a "special" mother.

It was no surprise, in the weeks after we moved him into his apartment, that my son was talking about dyeing his hair pink. At least he wasn't talking about tongue piercing. I went with the flow, offering my fashion advice that he would be better off blond than pink. His refrigerator probably wasn't stocked with the healthy foods he ate when we lived together; maybe there wasn't even any food in it. It was time for a little rebellion.

We had agreed that the local nail salon could take over with nail cutting, and the barber would be his 'go-to' for shaves. His handling of something with a sharp blade near his face wouldn't produce a very good result.

Let go, let go, let go, let go. He is 23 now.

Eighteen years: special education. Thirteen years: speech therapy, occupational therapy, and physical therapy. Ten years: plastic braces on his feet. Six years: seizure medications and growth hormone shots. Ten years: hearing aids. Look at what's possible, Robyn, and see what you've always seen.

There were days when was I proud and peaceful, and other times when I worried. *There are lousy people who might take advantage; there are mean people who might not be kind; there's the possibility someone will rob him or hurt him, or he could become sick and no one will be there to help. What will happen when his glasses get broken or his hearing aids don't work?*

Don't rehearse every tragedy that could befall him. Let him thrive. Celebrate all that's going well.

A couple of months after he had moved into his apartment, I awoke at 5 a.m. and then again at six. I'd missed his call the day before and hadn't heard back. We usually spoke at least twice a day. No text message went ignored for a whole day. I called his work. He wasn't there. I called his organizational helper, who had been visiting twice a week. She was the only one with a key. I called her multiple times and finally got her. "Please, please, go over there."

Silence. She didn't know if I was overreacting.

"Please, go. I think something is wrong with Daniel."

I told Jim I was getting on a flight. He wanted to know how I could be so sure that Daniel was in some kind of danger. I just knew. I couldn't explain.

When his helper arrived, Daniel could hardly breathe. Fortunately, they got to the hospital. Daniel's oxygen levels were dangerously low. His fever was 104, and his heart was racing. The ER attending told me they were admitting him to the ICU. Daniel got me on the phone to say, "Don't come, Mom, I'll be fine."

It had been just twelve hours from the time I had missed his call the day before until I boarded the plane. It felt way too long. When I arrived at the ICU, his breathing was labored, and the oxygen tubes were annoying him. He had an IV and O2 monitor attached to him, and a bedpan beneath him. The attending doctor explained that he was severely dehydrated, septic, and his lungs were heavily infiltrated with an unidentified pneumonia. I asked if she had checked him for Ebola (at the rate he was using the bedpan, it seemed possible). She said it wasn't a concern.

"I told you not to come," he squeezed out in a soft, hoarse voice.

"I'm not here just for you. I'm here for me," I countered.

The doctor came with an entourage of Harvard medical students.

"You are a lucky man," he said.

"Mmmm-hmmm, I know," Daniel replied.

The beeps of the monitors and his occasional cough were the only sounds in the room. I couldn't take my eyes off of the green lines and numbers.

I had recently been walking through Grand Central at rush hour. People were hurrying in every direction. I noticed a young woman motoring past me in a high-tech wheelchair. Her head was listless and tilting to the side. One finger was controlling the vehicle. A young man walked next to her with a palsied, left-leaning limp, his hand on her shoulder. He was keeping up with her as she slowly made her way through the crowd. It was pouring outside.

Did they know where they were heading? Was it even my business? I walked close enough behind them so that I could ask.

"Excuse me." I moved closer to them. "Do you know your way around here?"

"We want to get to Times Square," the young man said in a thick accent that sounded German.

"Okay, well, if you just..." I stopped. There were stairs. There was no way they could make it out.

"Okay, you just go..." I stopped again. The subway had stairs, too. I looked outside at the pouring rain.

"You've been to Times Square before, or is this your first time?" I was stalling. I couldn't imagine sending them out into the pouring rain.

"Our hotel is there."

"Where are you from?"

"Switzerland."

"Switzerland," I repeated. "First time in New York?"

"Ya." Big crooked smile.

"You like it?"

"Ya. We came yesterday."

"Sorry about the weather." I shrugged. They just stared at me.

I imagined their parents at the airport. I saw them saying goodbye. Were they scared? This young couple had motored onto a plane. They'd left their home. They'd left their country. I wondered how this young woman got dressed. No part of her—limbs, feet, hands—except one finger seemed to work. I wondered if he helped her. I didn't even know them, and I was happy they had each other. *What does their kind of bravery feel like?*

"Okay, well, here's the best way to Times Square." I described the rights and lefts. It sounded like a lot, but he nodded. She nodded, too, and he smiled. I watched them motor out into the pouring rain. Neither one of them could hold an umbrella. By the time they would reach the

hotel, they'd be soaked. I thought about how annoyed I'd be if I didn't have an umbrella. I felt ashamed.

"I don't want to die. Jim Henson died from this." Daniel's voice brought me back to the hospital room.

"No, honey, this is not where you'll die."

That night, I slept in Daniel's apartment. I listened while the pipes banged. I noticed how steep and tiring the stairs were. *How perse-verant he was when he went to work the day he called me. How sick he must've been as he walked a mile home. How did he make it up those flights and into his bed when he could barely breathe?* This was the price for the life we dreamed of.

I brought his laundry to the laundromat. I walked past the elementary school on the corner and watched the parents drop off their children. I noted how far the stores were, where he went for his coffee, and the mile-long walk to work. How many times had I taken those steps for granted? They required more stamina from him than me even when he wasn't sick.

Each day, I sat by his side. He didn't eat, and he slept a lot. The doctors would address Daniel. If I tried to interject, they would look at me and continue speaking. He was an emancipated adult now. This was very different from the years we had been visiting doctors, and I was making all the decisions about his care and treatments. My instincts were to challenge tests and ask questions. This team of doctors had no idea of the history Daniel and I shared, nor would they. I wasn't prepared for this rite of passage. My son's medical care was no longer based on my consent. I had to respectfully give him an impromptu education so that he would understand why I was taking issue with certain interventions.

When Rosie came each day, she waved me out of the way so that she could draw blood, change his gown and sheets, and help with bathing. It had been a long time since anyone had cared for my son in this way. It wasn't easy to just watch.

I asked if she had children.

"Four," she said.

I asked her where she lived.

"Roxbury."

"My grandma lived in Roxbury," I told her.

"Really? No way." She seemed surprised. I knew why. Not too many whites were there. Her scruffy, wiry hair looked the same every day, and her missing teeth made her smile no less beautiful. We had enough in common. She was a mother. She understood. I knew her twelve-hour workdays were harder than any I would know.

Daniel's new friends Ana and Brandon, came to visit him in the hospital. They had figured out how to get there on the bus and a train. They brought balloons and a handmade card. They stayed for hours. Even though he was so sick, their visit reminded me of the unexpected blessings that appear when we least expect them.

Ten days later, the team of doctors who had rescued my son from his near-death cautioned him that it would take a long time for him to fully recover. Maybe he should go to rehab or have an aide.

"I'll be fine on my own, Mom."

"I know," I said. "But I'm not leaving you alone."

I handed Rosie a little brown bag. In it was a small, ceramic angel I'd bought in the gift shop. I hugged her. It was the smallest way I could show my thanks to her.

"Good luck, Danny." She shook his hand.

Jim came up from New York to get us, and then we drove home. We joked once that Jim is like a Saint Bernard, but it's true. He was our true-blue rescuer.

A month later, when he was strong enough to leave, Daniel insisted on walking to his bus alone. It was time to let go again. I imagined an angel walking by his side.

LEAVE OF ABSENCE

If you surrender completely to the moments as they pass,
you live more richly those moments.
~Anne Morrow Lindbergh~

"Mom, why would you want to live in Connecticut full-time? What were you thinking?"

Sometimes, you hear something, and it sticks like a dead bug on a sticky trap. Daniel lived 200 miles away now, and I had only my work to tether me to the city. Jim traveled a lot, and it seemed fair for me to want to try something new. If we found a tenant for our apartment, I could imagine, for the first time in 38 years, living outside of New York City.

There were slow-moving school buses, roadkill, bobcats, tree frogs, lightning bugs, bats, and paper delivery people who crossed the rural routes to throw newspapers out of their cars onto driveways. The birds called to each other in the morning. There were sunsets and moonrises and scenery and so many shooting stars. There were neighbors whom we might never know, but they waved. I drank my morning coffee and yelled about things I read in the local paper. *What were these people thinking?* Jim would say, "Run for office." Never. The New Englander in me wanted to fight for old things like stone walls, old homes, and bridges that the stupid town council would argue weren't worth saving.

"Mom, why would you commute if you don't have to? You've lived in New York City for almost forty years."

Correct. I didn't have to. I chose to. It was a conscious choice.

"Mom, you aren't supposed to be doing this at your age; you should be slowing down. This is too much for you, commuting to work in the city."

"A lot of people do this commute."

"Mom, how much is your commuter ticket and your new car and the gas and the parking? It must be more than a cab fare every morning."

Yes. It is a lot more money than a taxi every morning—especially after coming from an apartment close enough to walk to work. My relationship with the city was like a long marriage. I knew a thing or two about hard relationships, though, and hard doesn't have to mean bad. Something about the city had made me. When I had nothing, I had my love of the city. My boyfriends had come and gone; my friends had moved away. I still had my city. Perseverance coursed through me like blood, and when I'd felt sorry for myself for lacking financial resources, in a city of such riches, the fear of returning to my past in Massachusetts was the only reminder I'd needed to keep my faith in myself.

My city was my partner. That didn't mean I couldn't try something different. Our beautiful home sat empty all week long, and I wanted to be there. Maybe one day, this would be our life. We could get a tenant for just a short-term lease, and I'd find out.

I explained to skeptical friends that I wanted to experience the country...*really* experience it. I wanted a break. I thought maybe this was a beginning. I looked at it on paper, and it all seemed like it was going to work out just fine. I'd be coming home to glorious sunsets and space. But I am quintessentially a New Yorker. They were shocked by my decision.

I bought a second car. I paid for a commuter parking spot and a commuter ticket, and I did what I'd never done: I drove to the train station to get to work. It would take two and a half hours each way, door to door. I was committed.

"I've never had a bad time in New York City," came from a loud young woman a number of rows in front of me. *Who are these people? It's 8 a.m. How can they be so wide awake? They are so loud in a public, enclosed place. It's an hour and 20 minutes down to Grand Central. I just drove 40 minutes to the train, and I am tired. I want to write or nap.*

Next to me, "tapping lady" was texting, and she hadn't silenced her phone. I put my headphones on, but the pecking persisted. She was putting on makeup now—her elbows were as sharp and long as a fireplace poker. She was invading my space. Beginner's luck.

The leopard-print coat making its way down the aisle signaled, "Something wicked this way comes." The smell of her perfume made my eyes water and my nose run, and I coughed the whole way to Grand Central. It might not have been so bad had "perfume lady" not sat nearly on top of me. Lesson learned: Never sit in the middle seat. Always sit in the "quiet car" by the window. I now understood how commuters could be moved to acts that are punishable by law.

Before I'd left that day, our dog Bailey had wandered into the guestroom and peed right in the middle of the white carpet. She had NEVER done that. *WHY? WHY? WHY?* Did she know I would be gone for longer than usual? I was sure she was mad at me, and like my son, I was sure she thought I had lost my mind.

In the morning, I would be awake at 5 a.m., sit for an hour with Bailey by my side, and drink my coffee. As I got into my car and drove past the cows and green grass, and got stuck behind school buses, I suddenly missed walking out to First Avenue—stepping onto the recently hosed-down sidewalks and the faint smell of dog poop and pee. I would assess weather and traffic in seconds, and then raise my hand and fork over ten bucks to a cabbie for a smelly few blocks. That would be unnatural to most Americans, but for almost four decades, it had been my normal. I tried to convince myself that I was adaptable.

When my son was born, my parents were sure I wouldn't hear my own baby crying, and yet, I learned not to sleep for the eight years he shared my bed. I am quite sure we discover who we are in places of great discomfort.

The first night, when I got back to the house, it was quiet. Jim was away. I did a calculation and realized I hadn't spent this much time alone...ever. Five hours each day in the silence of the car and the train, and then coming home to a silent, empty house. I sat on the deck and looked out at the mountains. The lawn was so green in the light of the late sky. "Make sure you alarm the house," I heard my best friend say. *Whatever. I'm not alarming the house.*

I poured a glass of wine and slipped down into my chair. The fire-flies would soon be sparkling out in the rough near the woods. My bats would soon be circling.

One morning when I was walking Bailey before work, I rounded the corner by our home, and I saw something very large and black. It was the backside of a black-and-white cow. I couldn't believe it. There was another cow grazing by our front yard. *What the hell?* I suddenly got frightened. *What if they charge?* I ran with Bailey back into the house. I yelled out to Daniel, who was staying with me, "Call the police! There are wild cows outside!"

I got into the shower. Within twenty minutes, I heard the doorbell. I grabbed a towel and went to the door.

Two cops were standing there. "Hello ma'am, we got a call you have a cow problem?"

"Did you see them?"

"Yes ma'am, they are grazing in your backyard down in your meadow."

"Okay, well, what do we do?"

"Do you know whose they are?"

"No sir." I wanted to say, "Do I look like I know *anything* about cows? I might as well be Eva Gabor from *Green Acres*." But they probably wouldn't get the reference.

"Well, we will just stay parked on your driveway and keep an eye on them."

I thought that was an interesting way for law enforcement to spend their time—sitting at the end of our driveway, taking in the views, and making sure the cows didn't do anything illegal.

When I got to work, I called my neighbor Pauline, who had not only seen the cows but figured out who owned them. I don't know the first thing about how you get cows back to a location at least a mile away, but they must have busted through their fence and come through the woods.

The next morning, the sunrise woke me. I could hear the robins and barn swallows darting around outside. It was 5 a.m. I rubbed my eyes and looked out. The time-tested foothills of the Berkshires and the old stone wall in our backyard reminded me of the endurance of nature and things that are meant to last a long time. I wondered if the cows were still out there. What would I learn by being there? How long would I stay? I walked through the house, its walls only the container for the life we had filled it with. I lit a fire.

What if I discovered that, here in Connecticut, cows and all, I wouldn't find all I'd ever wanted?

CRAWL OUT THROUGH THE CRACKS OF YOUR BROKEN HEART

Those mountains you are carrying, you
were only meant to climb.
~Najwa Zebian~

Two months after the pneumonia that nearly claimed his life, Daniel returned to work at the daycare center in Cambridge.

After school, he called me to report how his day had gone.

"Kiko welcomed me back by saying, 'Hi, motherfucker!' Who talks like that?"

"I don't know. Why do you think he does it?"

"I think he hears it from somewhere."

"Okay then. What can you do?"

"I can speak to him about it, and then ignore him if he does it again. I think he needs to nap, but he doesn't like to."

"Sounds like a challenge."

"Well, I try to read to him at naptime."

"Good strategy!"

A record 105 inches of snow had fallen in Boston, and that winter, the temperature didn't rise above 20 degrees. Daniel, the child who once could barely walk a few blocks, walked to and from work, more than a mile in each direction. Despite my stalking him with texts about the severity of the Boston weather and my insistence that I

253

would pay for taxis, he wouldn't accept my offer.

In January, he enrolled in a small college in Boston to take a course so that he could become certified in early-childhood classroom assisting. After two years of volunteering full time, he was hoping he could get a promotion from volunteer to paid staff member. He took it upon himself to meet the registrar and figure out what course he needed. He arrived at work every day a half-hour early. He left work at 4 p.m., took a train to the class he needed for his certification, and at 9:30 p.m., headed home on the T. He didn't miss a class. When I asked if he wanted a tutor, he said, "No, I'll be fine." He got an 85.

I would get blow-by-blow reports of how things were going at work, which included block throwing, kicking, the occasional bite, and other workplace hazards associated with preschooler behavior.

As the year came to an end, we were reflecting.

"How do you think school went this year?"

"Well, at first it was hard; those kids were tough. They have no attention span. But I'm a lot more confident now. The kids respect me more."

"What do you think changed?"

"I just had to trust that I knew what I was doing and show them that I'm an authority figure. Also, I get criticized a lot less by the staff now because I had to learn what to do and how to be helpful."

"Little kids are very smart and can be very challenging."

"Kiko is graduating."

"Nice."

"Yeah, I'm going to go to graduation."

"That's very sweet of you. What was the best part about this past year?"

"I got Kiko to take a nap."

"That's amazing. How did you do that?"

"I never gave up."

Over the summer, the preschool was undergoing changes in management. Daniel's boss and mentor had mentioned a new opportunity. It was an hour away, and the program was set up differently. She cautioned Daniel that there might not be as much support for him, but if he wanted to try it, she would advocate for him. She had regularly invited interns from the Threshold Program who came from special-education settings. The school where he wanted to work didn't provide the same support for their interns as his former school. Daniel insisted on being considered for the position. After two years of volunteering in the same location, he reasoned that it would be good to work with new people.

On the first day, he had trouble finding the school, but things seemed to go well. He observed that it was different. The teachers seemed more "orderly." The kids were calmer and polite. He was trying to learn how to fit in.

After a couple of weeks there, Daniel called me. His voice was shaky.

"Daniel... Are you okay? Are you hurt?"

"No. I...just...I am..." Long pause.

"I, I...got fired. I got fired."

"Okay. Where are you?"

"I am outside my school."

"Okay, can you tell me what happened?"

"I...uh...I'm... Never mind."

"I want to know what is going on, but it's hard to understand. Can you take some deep breaths?"

Sobbing. "Yes."

"Can you get yourself home safely?" It would take an hour.

"Yes."

"Call me as soon as you get home, and we'll sort this out."

There was a misunderstanding. The teachers lacked experience with "complex" young assistants, and my guess, based on what he was able to share, was that they didn't know how to handle an error in judgment he had made. Daniel thought that taking this job was the best thing for his personal development. Instead, he'd been met with the consequence of getting fired.

Those fucking idiots was my first thought. I listened as he struggled with telling me the story. His beloved job was gone, his mentor and boss unable to intervene. His self-esteem was leveled, and his friends couldn't quite understand.

After days of hearing out his grief, I urged him not to assume that his employers had hurt him intentionally. Even if I wanted to call them and scream at them, I was smart enough not to. His heart was broken. He believed he had failed. Being his witness was hell. The Threshold alumni job center was unable to help him, and we both felt betrayed and let down.

It was time for a family discussion. We had a problem to solve, and making a villain out of everyone involved wasn't going to help Daniel get to where he wanted to go.

"What is your dream?"

"I don't know."

"Okay, well, think about it for a minute."

"Well, I want to be a history teacher in a special-ed classroom."

"If you want to be a teacher, what do you think you have to do?"

"I think I would need a lot more school."

"You definitely need a lot more school. Where could you go to school?

"I don't know."

"Didn't you just finish a course at Urban College?"

Urban college was somewhere in downtown Boston. I didn't even know where. Jim and I encouraged him to see that the rest of his life couldn't be defined by a single negative experience; his job now was to find the next right step for himself.

The following week, Daniel called me from Urban College. He had figured out that he could enroll for an associate degree, and together we made a plan for the first three classes he would take. It might take a few years, but that was okay. He would find his way.

He was sitting with Nancy Daniel, Vice President of Academic Affairs. "Your son is a stubborn guy. He's determined to do this without help. He doesn't want a tutor."

"That's okay," I said. "He's not the guy who wants to fail, either, so let's see."

That semester and each one afterward, Daniel kept his grades at mostly A's and B's.

He was 24. It was his first "mainstream" school experience. He went to class dutifully, usually arrived early, and seemed to be enjoying it. Once, there was an issue with a grade, and the need for a tutor did arise. And on another occasion, a professor was overly critical of his writing and seemed to have little understanding of how far he had come from his years in a special-education setting to this mainstream school. But that's life. I had unfair and critical professors, too. The grades he was receiving were admirable, and I encouraged Daniel to advocate for himself. But I also knew only he could decide for himself how to handle issues as they arose. He was on his own now (until it was time to pay).

It had been a long time since he'd needed me to help him with homework. The last time that happened, he was in eighth grade. After a few tests, the teacher suggested a tutor. The tutor called me into his office, grilling me about what our homework habits were. Yes, we did homework together. No, we did not watch TV while we were doing it. Yes, it was quiet. Yes, it was early enough in the evening. Yes, I was helping.

"Well, Ms. Stecher, I have observed that Daniel has no problem with the math when he is with me. Maybe you have a math problem, but your son does not." Daniel and I still laugh about it. I was always lousy at math.

In my last phone call with the registrar at Urban, I was trying to get a fix on how far he had come, and she told me that he would be graduating at the end of the year.

"We love Daniel. He's an inspiration to us."

Later, I asked him, "How does that feel?"

"Pretty good. Not everyone could pick themselves up and just do this."

"Yup. Very true. And you're not just everyone."

In June of 2018, six years after he had moved into his dorm room in Cambridge, we sat in the Colonial Theater in Boston. Daniel was graduating. He was standing at the podium and delivering an acceptance speech for the Tony Williams Award, which is given to a student who, despite a "disabling condition," has achieved excellence. As my son began to speak, his words barely made it past his lips. Tears filled his eyes. The president of the college put his hand on Daniel's shoulder. At first gasping for breath, he forged ahead.

"Urban College has done a lot for me over the years, such as the following: I did far better than I thought I would do. I only needed two tutors, and I thought I would need a lot more. I started classes with Carole Hilliard and was extremely apprehensive because I was not sure how well I would perform. This was my first educational experience outside of special education. Among my many teachers at Urban, each contributed to the man I am today. The most important thing I accomplished at Urban College was accountability.

"Through all my years in Urban, I learned a lot of things—but the most important thing is that no one is 'normal.' Everyone is different than one another. Lastly, everyone has something to give. It's up to you to find what your gift is and put it to good use... I would like to thank a couple of people here. First off, Mrs. Nancy Daniels for all you've done for me and your support. Secondly, Mr. Jim Weiss, my stepfather, for teaching me about integrity. The biggest thank you goes out to my mom, Robyn, for being there for me since day one. I also want to thank my Cambridge family for all the support you have given me. Also, to my stepsisters Samantha and Kim, and Samantha's boyfriend Matt, for your support in this. Thank you to the Urban College community for being part of this important chapter of my life. Everyone needs someone to believe in them; I have mine. Thank you, and congratulations to my fellow graduates."

I'm not sure what receiving a standing ovation feels like, but Daniel had earned it.

Before we left Cambridge, he said, "Now I can start talking about my bachelor's."

The following year, he enrolled in Lesley University to complete his B.A.

NOT QUITE MOTHER,
NOT QUITE DAUGHTER

A stepmother knows that some days she's a stagehand,
some days she's the leading lady,
some days she's the audience...and always
learning to play each role with grace.
~Unknown~

After Daniel was born, I was done with having more children. My reasons were clear and practical. I was unwilling to divide my heart into too many pieces. My one son would be the beneficiary of all the mothering I had to offer. I was sure of it.

When Alan and I separated, I had the romantic notion that I would soon remarry. I was a "certain kind" of single. I didn't have a lot of time for dates. I imagined I would meet a man who also had a demanding career, and if there were young children, I conceded, we would raise them together. Magically, like a Hallmark movie, we would become a new, loving family. Daniel might just get those siblings he had hoped for. It was self-deception at its best. It never happened. Further, I had very little experience with other people's children. Ashley and I had grown close, but my sister Amy was her only true mother.

What made me think I would slide so easily into some man's life and into his children's hearts? Exactly. That, too, never happened.

When I was 48, after nine years of being single, I fell in love with Jim. On our first date, he showed me a picture of his 12-year-old daughter, Kim, wearing a cheerleading uniform. He told me that he didn't have a picture of his other daughter, Samantha, who was 17, and she was also into cheerleading. It wasn't something I knew much about, but I imagined that if he was showing me pictures and telling me about them, he truly loved them, and they must be good cheerleaders. I later learned they were excellent cheerleaders. He lived in a suburb where most people's children participated in team sports. I didn't have much experience going places to watch my son compete, but this seemed to be a highlight of his daughters' lives.

By the time I met Kim, it was almost a year after Jim and I first went out, and she was turning thirteen. She lived with her mother, and she bravely agreed to a weekend in Montauk with us. Sam, who was also invited, didn't come. I assumed she had other plans. Meeting Jim's 13-year-old daughter was scary for me. Our first hours together were spent in the car. She was in the backseat with her headphones in her ears, sleeping. I was in the front, afraid to speak because I might wake her.

Two and a half hours later, we arrived at the house. I wished Kim a happy birthday and offered up a book on makeup, guessing from things I had heard and pictures I had seen that she would like it. It was a start. We sat on the porch and talked in vagaries. I could tell she was on a reconnaissance mission. Later, I thought I heard her refer to me as "mad pretty." I assumed it was a compliment and that she was talking to either her mother or her sister.

As much as possible, I tried to make sure she was in the middle between Jim and me. "Awkward" was an understatement.

Neither of his children was prepared when, six months after our first date, their father moved in with Daniel and me. I imagined they were confused, angry, and sad. There was nothing I could say or immediately do to prove I wasn't the queen of an evil empire or that my unusual son had the biggest heart they might ever know. I wanted to take his daughters into my arms and promise that they weren't being left behind by their father, but that story would unfold with time between the man I loved and the daughters he would never have abandoned.

Throughout Kim's high school years, she lived with her mother and older sister an hour away. I didn't see either of the girls much. Occasionally, they would join us for a dinner or a trip to the mall. They tolerated me and Daniel. I just hoped they would know what I knew—that their father had talked about them on our first date, always thought about them, only wanted the best for them, and would do anything for them. He loved and missed them. He wouldn't let the most important moments in their lives slip by, even if it meant waiting in a diner to get a picture after a college graduation.

There were long periods when planned get-togethers didn't materialize. Executive functioning is one of my great strengths, but it served me better at work than in micromanaging outings with teenage girls who weren't reliable for various reasons and who weren't my own.

Daniel, having been an only child, was so happy to have the prospect of two stepsisters; regardless of how little he saw them, he just hoped that one day we could all share Jim and be happy. He was in the middle. The way he saw it, it was a unique opportunity to have an older and a younger "sister." It would be a long wait until our family blended to the point where we seemed to belong together. He eventually became the birthday ambassador, accounting for every celebration and keeping the ice cream cake tradition from Jim's childhood, alive for all future generations.

Jim shared stories about how, since her teens, Samantha had managed a pizza shop. He spoke of her keen ability with managing money. The few times we had been together, I'd seen things in her that reminded me of myself. At work, she was ambitious, resourceful, and identified opportunities to take charge and offer solutions to complex problems. She also took responsibility at home, helping her mother and sister navigate the challenges of living in their house on their own—a monumental task for a first-year college student with her own pressures. Her first post-college internship helped her land two impressive positions that would enable her to travel to many countries she probably thought she'd never see. She later got her MBA. I imagined her becoming a CFO for a large multinational company, and if that's what she aspired to, I was confident she would get there.

Jim's younger daughter, Kim, attended college in Florida. After one of her breaks, we offered to escort her back to school. When we got to the airport, we discovered Jim had forgotten his ID. She had to get down there, so I offered to fly with her. The plan was that Jim would meet us the next day. After we got lunch, she and I, two strangers, sat in silence. Halfway through the flight, she started asking me questions. My answers indicated that I was no pushover. With my own son, I had set the bar very high. At one point, she looked at me and said, "I am so happy you aren't my mother."

Knowing she had a python that ate mice and crickets, and a hamster and a lizard, I was thinking, *I am so happy you aren't my daughter!* She probably couldn't imagine that, in high school, I didn't wear a bra, carried a knife, hitchhiked, shoplifted, smoked pot, and did drugs. I opted not to share all that immediately, but I'm sure that if she'd tried to picture this from the seemingly "put together" woman sitting next to her, it would have both shocked her and made her laugh.

My rebellion gave me the strength to endure my most difficult times. I recognize the bold beauty in acts of individuation. Her father's stories of her college dorm escapades and nonconformity were familiar to me. She might have tried to hide behind her self-pro-claimed contrarian persona, but she had to be her own kind of special if she had such an interest in the not-so-average pets most people feared.

One holiday at a time, over shared meals, family gatherings, shopping trips that commemorated new jobs, boyfriends coming and going, birthdays, moves, and woman-to-woman moments, we inched our way into each other's lives. It didn't happen fast. I waited for the late-night conversations about career changes and thoughts of how I could help with a job offer or big decision. Whatever fantasies I had about it, I wasn't prepared for the experience of someone else's children, and I'm confident they never dreamed they'd have a stepmother. I was never comfortable with that word, and despite my creativity, I have yet to come up with anything better.

When Daniel and I lived in our small apartment, we wondered what it would be like to be part of a bigger family. When we all stumbled into this unforeseen and imperfect merger, it was sometimes messy. Lines were crossed. At times, I got frustrated. I was silenced and halted into wondering, *How will I fit into these young women's lives? What's my place?* But their different values and different pasts didn't keep me from seeing in them the cherished parts of my younger self—the dutiful and hard-working me, and the rebel who did things my own way.

I have learned to accept that our immediate family is cobbled from how we are the same and different. If I could give each of these women a gift, it would not be my ambition. It would be my faith in them. I'm inspired by how determined they are to succeed. We have all come a long way from those turbulent years when I wondered if I'd ever know them or if they would ever really want to know me or Daniel. Both Jim and I left the door open so that both daughters could enter and leave. We may not be related by blood, but we are connected by the love Daniel and I have for their father, and the choice Jim made to love all of us unconditionally.

The love I have for my "not quite daughters" wasn't always there. It is a special love, a love that has been cultivated over the years we've known each other. This love waited quietly to meet up with the women they became; it waited for the laughter and the hair colorist we now share and it waited for all of the times we've hunted down good finds at sales together and for their rites of passage—and now mine, too.

On the day Kim got a big promotion, it reminded me of the day Daniel said, "Mom, Kim thinks she's a dark person, but she's not. She's a shining star and doesn't know it yet."

When Samantha got engaged, that question surfaced again: How will I fit in? When she asked if I'd go dress shopping with her and I took pictures of her trying on bridal gowns, I imagined her wedding day and realized I had found my unique place—sometimes in the audience, sometimes the stagehand, sometimes hanging back as they lead, and sometimes walking by my "not quite" daughters' sides, celebrating life and who we are.

ASHLEY

We do not need magic to change the world.
We carry all the power we need inside ourselves already.
We have the power to imagine better.
                                    ~J.K. Rowling~

That summer of 2005, when we visited Ashley at Circus Camp in Vermont, she came into the big top on stilts. She was so strong and yet graceful up there. I remembered her at two, before Amy was gone, running around in a dress with her deliciously chunky thighs exposed. The next time she appeared in the show, she was hanging from the trapeze with a big smile. I wondered, *Will I always do these inventories, looking for my sister in her face, in her eyes, in the shape of her body, in her voice? Is that unfair of me?*

The show lasted a couple of hours. Afterward, the applause went on for a long time. Ashley disappeared into the crowd to say good-bye to her new friends. Suddenly, I felt a pair of hands over my eyes. I whirled around and hugged her. We left the hay-filled tent and walked across the grassy field toward her room to gather her things. A young counselor came over and introduced himself.

"Ashley is very special."

My sunglasses did their job; my eyes were tearing up, and I didn't want him to see. I looked away and then back at him. I nodded. "Yes, she is very special."

I helped her with her bags. We walked to the car. The conversation turned toward the Ben & Jerry's factory. We were in Vermont, so we had to go—everyone in our family is genetically engineered, lactose intolerance and all, to love ice cream. My mother, in the front seat, commented to my father, "No one in their right mind eats ice cream before dinner." *Since when is anyone in this family in their right mind?*

Now 13, Ashley wasn't the little girl whose hand I'd held on walks that were very short but took a very long time because she stopped to inspect pebbles. What did she see in them? Small universes? When I wasn't holding her hand, I was on the other side of the country, holding her in my heart.

When I turned 40, I was in the middle of my divorce. I didn't have a big party. The only two people I wanted to be with were Ashley and Daniel. We shared annual summer visits at Barbara and Bernie's home on Cape Cod. I visited her in Santa Barbara as much as I could. When I missed her, I would collect pictures I'd taken on trips we'd made: the zoo, the beach, the Santa Barbara parks, hikes, walks, talks, and picnics. I would make slideshows for her.

After my divorce, when I could afford it, I took Ashley and Daniel to Disneyland and Universal Studios. We got VIP tickets so that we didn't have to wait in line. Ashley wanted to know why we were "cutting." I explained that, for Daniel, standing a long time would be hard. She looked at me in confusion. "There's nothing wrong with Daniel. Why can't he stand?" I just smiled.

Knowing she loved roller coasters, I was willing to try Magic Mountain. It was my first and last time. I thought I was going to get an aneurysm. Once, we went to the Empire State Building. I had never been up to the observatory, and she really wanted to go. After we were done looking at the views, the crowd had grown large, and the line for the elevator was overwhelming. I insisted to the guard that we had to leave right away because I was claustrophobic. We had to get on the first elevator going down; it was urgent. Ashley shook her

268

head in disbelief and whispered, "Aunt Robyn, *really? You aren't claustrophobic!"*

We both love Broadway shows, and I still have all of my playbills from the shows we've seen. When she moved to the East Village, I showed her all the places where Kathy and I used to hang out. We visited Ellis Island and the Statue of Liberty. When I got a good bonus one year, Ashley, Daniel, and I went on a cruise to Alaska.

It was hotter than hell the day Ashley and I wandered around New York visiting colleges. She was interested in NYU, Sarah Lawrence, Columbia, and Barnard. We stopped at Tom's Diner on Broadway for lunch. I kicked my shoes off under the table. My feet were so swollen, I didn't think I would get them back on. Barnard was last. My heels landed loudly against the stone steps we climbed to the reception area. I sat outside while Ashley went in for her admissions interview. Afterward, we went to the visitor's orientation. I looked up at the ceiling. *This is it. This is the place.* She belonged there. I just felt it.

Later, she shared with me that a college consultant had discouraged her from applying. I was incredulous. I knew her grades were excellent. She shared with me that her SAT scores were lower than what the counselor had thought she'd need to get accepted to Barnard. I countered that I was a lousy test-taker, and maybe it was genetic. I encouraged her to take the test again and to disregard what this counselor said; a second round would probably produce a better result. She possessed every characteristic of a viable Barnard candidate. She had always been a strong student. Grades were not an issue. She was curious and a risk-taker. She surfed, bungee jumped, and had learned to mountain unicycle (there is such a sport, and it's insanely hard). There was nothing she was afraid of or wouldn't try. When she was still in high school, we figured out a way she could raise the necessary funds for a trip to Rwanda. Her college essay described how she connected with women there who had suffered generational loss from genocide, but she learned the universal truth that even such incomprehensible grief can lead to happiness and even the joy inherent in their culture. At 16, she felt she wanted to advocate for the rights of others.

Her first day at Barnard was just the beginning.

Ashley would become an advocate for social and climate justice. Her endeavors centered around recognizing and protecting the importance of diversity. She joined a sorority, learned to cook, traveled to South Africa, and studied apartheid and solutions for clean water and sanitation. She won awards, made friends, ran for student government, served on committees, and had papers published.

Ashley participated in marches, calling for an end to racism and police brutality. She organized demonstrations at Rikers Island, New York City's most notorious and criticized jail complex, calling for it to be closed. Debating with me that she wasn't quite an activist, I challenged her. If she met up with Angela Davis, they would have much to talk about.

A few months before Ashley graduated college, we were riding on a train to Philadelphia for her first job interview. I thought of how we'd traveled together, most recently to Italy, Turkey, and Greece when Jim and I had been married. I asked what the best thing about being at Barnard had been. She said she'd appreciated being surrounded by brilliant women and exceptional educators. Barnard had pushed her to think critically and become politically engaged. She felt she might not have had the confidence to step out or stand out before, but now she was more self-assured. I still see in her that little girl who was fascinated with the pebbles that collected by the curbs where we took our walks. That college consultant back in Santa Barbara was very lucky never to meet with me.

On the train back, we agreed that we were fortunate to have parents (although from two different generations) who were liberal and conscientious enough to allow us to find ourselves. They let go even when it meant watching us struggle and when our choices differed greatly from theirs. After finishing school, Ashley stayed in New York and worked as the assistant director of the Fund for NYC Health + Hospitals Corporation. She helped manage the "Guns Down, Life Up" gun violence prevention program as well as the "Music and Memory" program, which brings music to patients afflicted with Alzheimer's.

She left New York to attend U.C. Berkeley's School of Public Health, where she received master's degrees in public health and urban planning. She traveled to Bihar, India, to research women's hygiene and health issues in rural India. Her work has been published in a scholarly article about environmental research and public health. When she was a U.C. Berkeley teaching assistant, many of her students acknowledged her for inspiring them.

Ashley has traveled to numerous continents, stepping off the beaten path and inspiring me to keep searching, to keep finding my own relevance. Whenever the challenges seem overwhelming or when there isn't enough time to get everything done, or when her heart breaks, there is an angel—clapping at her circus camp, whispering in the ear of the Barnard admissions committee, watching over her in dark caves and in far-off countries and places where her perspective and ideas might be challenging for some and will one day make a difference for others. I am just the messenger, knowing the angel is there. The angel asks nothing more than Ashley's pursuit of all that fills her with purpose and joy. She is a teacher, a seeker, a leader.

My prayers for Ashley are not the same now as when she was two and her mother was dying. She won't need the angel's wings to lift her. She has her own wings with which to journey to the worlds she wants to influence. She has taught me to look past what we are told or taught, to dig deeper, and to find truths in the hidden corners of our human story. I hope I have taught her to do the same.

Ashley is the young woman Amy birthed, but I am lucky to have been there as she paves her own trail. Even if Barbara said all those years ago at the Ben & Jerry's factory, "No one in their right mind eats ice cream before dinner!" I hope we stay out of our "right minds" and stick with each other...always.

THE ASHES KEEPER

*In one of the stars I shall be living. In
one of them I shall be laughing.
When you look at the sky at night...only
you will have stars that can laugh.*
~Antoine de Saint-Exupéry~

Amy died in 1994. We didn't have iPhones, droids, or anything we could hold in our hands and call "smart." We still used landlines, and phones rang busy or we had call waiting. And we waited. We used "answering machines." Only a few people had clunky desktop computers. The internet was a vast, coveted thing that no one understood. It was called the "information highway." It was mysterious, too—something only universities and hospitals could access.

Amy and I were teenagers when civil rights rioting, the anti-Vietnam War uprisings, the Watergate hearings, and the eventual demise of Richard Nixon were televised. We saw the world through a single screen. A person of color or a woman coming close to winning a presidential campaign was a long way off. We couldn't imagine a reality TV star becoming president. We didn't even have reality TV.

When we lived thousands of miles apart and hardly saw each other, we had long talks on the phone. I have boxes of the letters and cards we sent each other. When we were pregnant, we didn't have Google to ask about what to expect; we just asked each other and guessed at what we didn't know. When the country had just entered the war called Desert Storm, I remember feeling that, somehow, everything would be forever changed, but I don't remember us talking about it. Our children were born three months apart. We talked about the things you talk about when you have babies. When we occasionally visited, we went to playgrounds. We had picnics. We went for rides to nowhere. We ate gluten and dairy and lived with the bloat and the gas. We giggled at farts and other stupid things. We made each other laugh so hard that we peed in our pants.

After Ashley was accepted to Barnard, her dream had come true, but mine had, too. She was no longer going to be 2,500 miles away. She had grown from a curious two-year-old into one of my favorite people. After we helped her settle into her dorm room, she handed me a bag. Her face was emotionless, but tears were welling up in her eyes. At first, I didn't know what was in the bag. There was a box in it. Amy's ashes.

It had been sixteen years. I was tempted to open it and look inside. I didn't. I put it in my closet. From time to time, I thought maybe I should get an urn or something, but that felt too permanent, and the ashes had a destination...we just didn't know where exactly. Sometimes, I would take the box out of the bag, and I'd think of opening it. When I visited with the ashes, I coveted my job as their "keeper."

On the first Thanksgiving that she was in New York, Ashley and I were cooking.

"I think we should decide what to do with Amy's ashes."

She just looked at me. There was a long silence. We hadn't discussed what was in the bag since she'd handed it to me. Ashley and I started to cry. It felt good to have someone to cry with about Amy. Usually, I cried alone.

"What do *you* think?" she asked steadily—the same way Amy would have asked that question.

"Well, Grandma and Papa have strong feelings about the ashes being here on the East Coast, but they haven't made it clear what they want to do with them. You are her daughter; you should decide."

We talked about the ashes' return to California, and that felt right.

Ashley suggested, "Maybe we could go to Santa Barbara. We could bury them under her memorial bench at Shoreline Park."

Burying cremated ashes in a public park is illegal but fitting for my sister—who wore bright red tights under her Smith College graduation gown.

It would be six years until we could all be in Santa Barbara at the same time.

The ceremony would take place on my birthday. I called my father to share the news of our plan. He and my mother wouldn't be able to come. I could hear the sadness in his voice. Amy was leaving the East Coast for the last time.

"Say Kaddish" was all he could say.

"I promise I will."

Before Jim and I left for the airport, I opened the box. The ashes were gray and had small fragments in them. I lifted two handfuls and placed them in a Ziploc bag. I would bury some with each of my parents.

I was prepared for the TSA. Jim went ahead of me and quietly said, "We are carrying ashes." I was armed with Amy's death certificate. The officer just nodded. I watched them travel through the x-ray equipment and observed the manual inspection that followed. When the ashes were given back to me, I carried them proudly, the way an officer accompanies the casket of a deceased soldier.

Ashley's family, Jim, and I all gathered at the Wilcox property where, twenty-one years earlier, we had Amy's memorial service. Several bluffs overlook the ocean where you can see whales and dolphins. Hang gliders were launching, floating like big seabirds from the cliff. Each of us offered some words, and then we said goodbye to the ashes. Ashley and I threw the last handfuls over the side of

275

the cliff. Up, up, up they went, and then the wind brought them back and they showered us.

I was born at 2:19 a.m. Amy was born on 2/19. I don't believe that was a coincidence. I miss her in moments that sneak up on me and surprise me. I wish she could have watched Ashley and Daniel become the special people they are. I wish she and Ashley hadn't have been robbed of sharing how alike they are. What would she look like now? Would we still laugh until we peed in our pants? I was sure we would grow old together.

When the house where we grew up was being sold, my father was stripping the flowered wallpaper on Amy's childhood bedroom. On her wall, he discovered a small heart she had drawn with a black crayon. Inside of it, she had written: "Amy and Robyn true love forever."

TAKE A DRIVE

Grant me the serenity to change the things I can,
to accept the things I cannot change,
and the courage to know the difference between the two.
If this is not possible, take a drive.
~Adapted from the "Twelve Steps"~

One day, I felt like I wanted to leave my life. I don't remember what provoked me. I wasn't raised to walk out. I had been known to throw a few plates, slam a few doors, but now, I had graduated. This time, I went out to the car and pulled out of the driveway, wishing Jim was the kind of man who would come after me, but I knew he wouldn't.

This is one of the advantages of living in a house in the country and owning a car. I could drive away. I left in an emotional dust storm, hoping not to be blinded by it. I drove too fast winding down the familiar turns in the road. I wanted to call Lexus Assist and ask them to find my "happy place." But I knew I'd have to get there on my own.

I wanted to distract myself from my rage. So, I started thinking of the men I had slept with, and it made me laugh. Was it a lot? Since I hadn't compared myself with anyone else on this subject, I wasn't sure. Could I remember them all? I can't even remember old friends who reach out with claims that, in the 1980s, they slept on the couch in our apartment. I started thinking of some of the guys' names. I have no idea if that was "good," meaning I wasn't a slut, or "bad," meaning I was too loose and should have thought more about who each of these guys was. As I played this alphabet game with myself, just like the ones we played on long car rides with our parents, I thought, "This is a good trick. If you want to go to bed with someone, try to think ahead and ask yourself, *Will I even remember this later, and if I do, will I be annoyed with myself?*"

After about a half-hour, I looked in the rearview to check my lipstick. *Can't go home until my mouth goes back to being kissable, and a good roll in bed is not a preposterous thought.* Even if it didn't happen, I wanted to know when I walked in that door that it *could* happen.

I don't stay mad for long. Too many people close to me have died young. I hold onto the good—the first time Jim kissed me, how sweet and warm and tasty it was, and the feeling of holding him tight and so close that nothing could come between us.

True love comes in stages. First, I liked his smile and the way his hand felt in mine. And then, I liked how he made me feel. I remembered licking the nasty battle scars of our first fight—the first test. Even if it wasn't "good" fighting and he didn't say "sorry," and we went to sleep angry, which I was raised never to do, I kept my faith that neither of us would give up. We went through very hard things together. We had been through divorce, ends of life, and Daniel's unique Pandora's box. We had celebrated seven wedding anniversaries. This was a different kind of love than what I'd felt the first time I'd said, "I love you."

An hour into the ride, I thought, *The only way to stop fighting is to stop fighting.* If I kept driving, maybe I would just keep going. Anger would not just be a singular loss; it would be our loss.

Jim calls me the "accountant." But it's not only the inequities I remember. He saved my precious, old '45-rpm vinyl records from one of my "dump the junk" rants. Jim, the collector, had more of my memories in our basement than I did. *I should go buy a record player and say, "thank you."* Jim would fetch me from a nail salon, umbrella in hand, when an unexpected rainstorm came through. I would take a train all the way from New York City to Connecticut when he forgot his keys.

I pulled into the driveway. I imagined he'd get up and say, *"You're home! Thank God."* Nope. He would be sitting in silence, watching *Taken* for the hundredth time. He wouldn't look up. Instead, Bailey would run to me, tail wagging like a metronome on speed, and lather my face with her kisses. Jim's lack of reception wasn't an indication that he didn't love me; it was just his way.

I started to cook for us.

No one really knows how things will go. We took a chance on each other. The cracks either let the light in or swallow us. We are imperfect, struggling with our differences in order to belong to something and each other. Choosing who we are with is the closest we can get to choosing our destiny. We comforted all the children when they were sick and helped them when they had problems. We celebrated every holiday in the homes we had made. We laid our beloved dog Gracie to rest. We welcomed our rescue girl, Bailey, when she arrived in the middle of the night from a North Carolina shelter. As Bernie and Barbara had for 64 years, I wondered if we, too, would keep finding the gains even when the losses were devastating. I wanted to believe that we could get better at being together. It took me a long time to learn that neither of us was changing, but maybe we were growing closer even when it felt we were drifting apart.

I thought about the chapel in Greece where we were married, under the bluest sky I have ever seen, with an endless sea of possibility beneath us. The rings we exchanged were symbolic of the connection we'd earned after life had taken everything we'd thought mattered and then showed us what we'd found in each other. I think that if two people are really lucky, they see each other's broken parts, and together, they get them working better. I searched for the love that, like faith, would prevail without evidence. So few loves are meant to be enduring.

I walked out onto the deck. I looked out onto those foothills. I remembered a hike we took in the Berkshires. We had been dating for a few months. As we rounded a bend in the path, a waterfall appeared. I was ahead of him. I turned around, and in the silence of the woods, sweaty and with conviction, I called out, "I LOVE YOU." He was the only one who could hear me. It was the first time I said those words to him.

I wondered if I'd be sitting alone for long.

LOST AND FOUND

You were the one I wanted to sit next to
when we watched The Wizard of Oz.
It took a long time for me to understand
why. It was because there, I felt safe.
~from a letter to my mother~

I have a picture of my mother holding my newborn son. She was 58 when the photo was taken. I am older than that now. I know things about her, but I don't really know her.

Before my mother's personality began changing, she was repeating herself and forgetting conversations. For Barbara, there would be no more book club, mahjong, sisterhood, lunches, or driving her cancer patients. I couldn't imagine the day my mother gave up her car keys.

She was a crossword puzzle whiz. She was a fierce mahjong player. I once asked her to teach me how to play. We got through the basics, but she forgot some of the rules. The next day, I asked for another lesson, but she didn't remember the first one. I was sorry I didn't ask her to teach me before it was too late. Once, she could beat all of us at Scrabble. There used to be books piled up on her night table and in the car, waiting for their return to the library. She could no longer read. Could she still play the piano? When I was little, I wanted to learn to play "Moonlight Sonata" because she could play it. Some part of her became unclenched when the music came through her.

When I was 14, I got very sick. I liked how it felt to lean on her as she carried me to the doctor. It was rare that our bodies touched. Staying home with her was special. Watching her soap operas was like being invited into her private world, where the slow-moving love stories, and the indiscretions and problems of the fictional and beautiful, trumped whatever our problems were. She still watches soaps. When I visit, I sit with her, and we watch them together.

She used to say, "When life gives you lemons, make lemonade."

She never made lemonade. She drank Tab. She smoked cigarettes until my father threatened to leave her if she ever got lung cancer. She did eventually quit smoking. I'm not sure who quit first, me or her. I smoked because she did. And I quit because, like her, my husband hated it. Bernie never left her—not even when the rages enveloped her like swarming hornets, or later when the dementia robbed her of remembering the last things she'd said or did.

When we were growing up, she cooked supper every weeknight. She hosted many Thanksgivings. She would make a dip with sour cream and onion soup mix. It went with Ritz crackers. We loved to lick the bowl. There was nothing better than her sacred "hello dollies." Sticky-sweet condensed milk, coconut, graham cracker crumbs, butter, and semisweet chocolate chips combined to make the best dessert I've ever eaten. We wanted just one each, but we had to wait until after the guests were gone to see if any were left over.

My mother made special cakes for our birthday parties. My sixth birthday was a good one. We had just moved, and I had a lot of new friends. The bright lights from Bernie's movie camera blinded us; all the kids covered their eyes. Then it appeared: a sunflower cake with candy corn for the petals and licorice for the stalk. It was my favorite cake of all time. I liked black licorice because my mother liked black licorice. I imagine her smiling while she made the cake, even if in the movies she didn't look so happy.

But she had tirades that would come like tornadoes swirling up unexpectedly and leveling all in their path. They were terrifying and weren't talked about. Maybe whatever brought on all that rage could have been "diagnosed" and "managed."

When I was 15, I took a bunch of pills. Because I was supposed to be sleeping, I'm not sure what caused my mother to come into my room. I heard her voice speaking to me, but when I answered, my speech was slurred. I was scared and confessed to the act. Off to the hospital we went. Tube up the nose—I threw up. The pediatrician was stern. I was kept in the hospital for "observation." My mother might have saved my life, although I'm not sure if what I took would have killed me. It seemed unfair that I was the one who was "diagnosed" and "managed."A social worker told me I would benefit from "talking to someone."

For everyone who didn't know what I knew about her, she was funny and nice and helpful to strangers. In those days, she would have company. Her friends would come over, and I would overhear her telling stories in a sweet and lilting voice.

I thought she was much sadder than any of her friends knew. Her mother died suddenly when she was 21. Her father died when she was 35. Her best friend died when she was 40. Her son went to prison. My sister died when she was 61. We never talked about any of that.

When I finally conceded that I would go to college, we went together to visit schools. I remember driving to Long Island and Connecticut and staying in hotels. It was the first time we were alone together and doing something that centered around me and my future. I remember that one day we were eating lunch, and she said she was sorry. I didn't exactly want to hear it, but I knew what she was talking about. It was her way of letting me know that she wished things could have been different for us.

After I left for school, I carved out a new normal. No longer a self-defeating teenager, I became ambitious, started a career, and worked hard, but I would meet people who felt like her. They weren't always what I asked for, but they showed up—those who could sniff out my faulty wiring. I'd thought I could hide it. The blows came, but I felt nothing. Abuse was all around me. There in the men I dated, there in the men I worked for in my early twenties, and there in the man I first married. Even when my insides were shredding like the coconut on the "hello dollies," my brand of loyalty to those who hurt me was a finely-honed survival skill. I kept quiet. I endured until I fought back by proving I didn't need them.

Barbara was in her early eighties when, after years of saying "no," my father agreed to adopt Maggie, an abandoned Maltese who would become my mother's best friend and comforter; they remain inseparable. It was smart of him. Her friends retreated not because they didn't care but because they didn't know how to manage the fractured parts of her. Her memory was like trying to hold onto water, her judgment was compromised, and her vision was fading. From the day she came home with them, Maggie was always by her side.

Bernie was Barbara's primary link to life. He kept everything going. He held her hand and sat next to her while she watched the Hallmark Channel. He made her meals and served her favorite ice cream, chocolate almond chip, every night. He didn't leave her for long—just to run an errand or go to the gym. Still, her tirades were macerating. Randomly they came, fired from fragments of old wrongdoings and old arguments. Bernie, like a sturdy beach house in a brutal storm, let her be the way she was. He defended her. He protected her. He had been doing this for as long as I could remember. When I was young, I thought I'd never forgive him for it, but I got better at understanding. He could fix anything, but he didn't know how to put her back together, so he just kept trying.

As her "symptoms" progressed, he took her only once to a neurologist. After that, there was no reason to return as there wouldn't be any news they would want to hear. Bernie's unrelenting devotion to her has kept her on his side of the chasm. The valentines, birthdays, and anniversary cards he buys for her always appear on time, displayed in the usual spot on the desk in their living room. The cards for him stopped years ago. One day, I noticed a card signed in her handwriting: *"Dear Bernie, Happy Birthday, Barbara."* I don't know how she got the card, who put it there, or who reminded her it was his birthday. Maybe it was the housekeeper. It was beautiful and mysterious.

I live from the scars, not from the open wounds. My hurtful memories of her are now less menacing. I have good memories, even if we can't share them now: how she made those unique birthday cakes, passed on her favorite books to me and the talks we would have about them, the visits to bridal shops where I modeled the wedding dresses she bought for me, the gifts she would bring me from trips or clothes she thought I would like. Once, she came with Amy to New York City, and we went to Sardi's (a famous Theater District restaurant) and ate Friendly's chocolate almond chip ice cream, her favorite flavor.

I was saved when Daddy would come home from work at the same time every night; supper was at seven. He didn't work on Sundays and played with us. When I lost a tooth, the tooth fairy always came. Lying on the grass in our backyard, I looked off into the clouds and daydreamed about somewhere far away, a man I would marry, and the family I would have.

I would travel the world, and I'd have one son.

My mother welded me into someone who did that and more. I have learned how to navigate the treacherous. I became independent. She is there in my hands as I slice lemons. She is there as I

285

walk past my piano and wish I could play as well as she did. She is there in my every unshared secret, and in my sense of humor, and in all of the times I quit because I thought I wasn't good enough. She is there when I start over again.

When I think she is silent, she will appear, urging me on. If I have unfinished business with myself, it's those piano lessons I quit. Maybe I could still learn "The Moonlight Sonata." She is there reminding me that on a hot July day in 1958, I was born, strangling in my umbilical cord. Made from that elixir of her best and her worst, she and I began that way, and whatever we have lost and found along the way, it's all there in who I am. Up, up, up. I surface. I hold my breath and emerge, still coughing from the bottom of all that is unforgettable.

When we speak, I end the call with "I love you," and I hear her voice saying in return, "I love you, too." Even if it is me imagining it or her forgetting it.

GO FORTH

*If you knew who walked beside you on the path
you have chosen, fear would not be possible.*
~A Course in Miracles~

"You're *Jewish?*" I hear this a lot. I'm not sure what that means.

My Hebrew name, Shoshana (which means Rose), is not special—it's a very common name, but I like it. I was named for my mother's mother, whom I know little about. She died before I was born.

When I was 12 and preparing for my Bat Mitzvah, I began questioning my kosher upbringing. Keeping kosher made good sense as a sanitary practice in 500 BC, at a time when dairy and meat were eaten from separate dishes in order to limit the potential for illnesses caused by spoiled mixed foods, but in the early 1970s, this practice made no sense to me. We had a dishwasher that did a decent job of cleaning dishes and a refrigerator which, for the most part, protected our food from deadly spoilage. Keeping six sets of dishes and silverware would seem strange without the context. Milk and meat dishes and silverware were kept separately. There was a set of everyday dishes, a set of "good china," and two sets of dishes for Passover. I think we kept kosher because my grandmother was religious, and she wouldn't be able to eat in our home if we weren't kosher.

Where we grew up, there was a rumbling of anti-Semitism. We would be criticized by some kids for taking off school for the high holidays, and we also walked in a group to Hebrew School so no one would hassle us. I was aware that we were in the minority, and we stuck together. Until high school, it seemed like the "Jewish kids" were more likely to be friends with each other.

I went to a lot of my friends' Bar and Bat Mitzvah parties, and there was way more Bar than Mitzvah—the religious ceremonies demanded our seriousness, but the celebrations were all about a bunch of 12-year-olds sneaking liquor and finding out what it was like to "be with" a boy or girl. At my own party, I was under a table... with my boyfriend. My mother was calling for me. I just remember the tablecloth hiding us as we kissed and giggled.

By the time I was 13, a year after my Bat Mitzvah, the women's movement was getting louder. I was suspicious of the rabbis and cantors who were older men. *Where are the women?* God was described as a male entity to be feared and exalted. This seemed contradictory. I was curious. I read about Buddhism, but the idea of meditation that included long periods of silence and stillness felt like a form of torment. Protestantism seemed confusing with its many gospels and denominations, but maybe no more so than Judaism with its range of sects from orthodox to reform. Catholic dogma was so strict that it remained far adrift in my sea of religious ponderance. It was especially hard to process the idea of a human son of God because I had been raised to believe that humans could not be deified. Everyone I knew was one of the big three: Jewish, Protestant, or Catholic. I was probably in my thirties before I met a person of Muslim or Hindu faith. After all that thinking, I decided I was Jewish for a reason and left it at that.

Jews from New England seemed very low-key compared to the New York Jews I met. In the town where I grew up, we weren't in the majority. We kept a low profile. We weren't animated, and we didn't kiss, hug, or try to out-talk each other. I wasn't led to believe that I was entitled to a Chanel pocketbook. No one I knew owned one, and at that age, it never occurred to me to want one. I didn't even know what a Chanel pocketbook looked like, but it seemed to be the badge of honor for a certain group of Jewish girls I met from New York.

My best friend Kathy, raised in a wealthy suburb and schooled by Catholic nuns, didn't have a Chanel pocketbook. She, too, was questioning her religious upbringing. Together, we put up a Christmas tree, but we rationalized that it was a pagan custom. We couldn't afford fancy decorations, so we adorned it with strings of popcorn. There was nothing spiritually uplifting about the idea of us going to church, but decorating the tree, forbidden in my childhood Jewish home, was our fun yearly ritual.

When Alan proposed to me, even though I had not been actively religious, I wanted to be married by a rabbi. Although he was born Jewish, Alan knew little about Judaism. I had basically become a "High Holy Days" Jew. I went to temple alone. I didn't work on Rosh Hashanah or Yom Kippur, and I fasted. I had a couple of close Jewish friends who invited me to join them. Mostly, I had no one to be Jewish with until after Daniel's Bar Mitzvah, when he and I attended High Holy Days services together. When I stood next to my son, his prayer shawl draped around his shoulders, I no longer felt so alone.

When Alan died, Daniel recited Kaddish. He stopped and started, barely making it through the words. He insisted on finishing the Jewish ritual prayer of mourning. My heart ached for his loss. If we had no other words, we had that one prayer.

When Jim and I planned to be married in Greece, I knew the Chapel Santorini in Fira, named for the 13th century's Saint Irene, was not exactly a Jewish setting. There was a large cross under which we would be married. Yet, the whitewashed buildings against the bluest ocean I had ever seen was the perfect place for us to exchange vows. Daniel, Ashley, and Kathy (who had changed her name to Kathleena by then) were our witnesses. Our officiant was the equivalent of a Greek justice of the peace. He barely spoke English. We didn't even know what we were agreeing to. A second ceremony in our home was officiated by Rabbi Rubin (Daniel's beautiful Bar Mitzvah tutor), whose grace delivered Jim and me from separate faiths to the words of our ketubah—the written vows that Jewish people sign in contract to each other. Surrounded by friends, Jim and I broke the traditional glass to symbolize the last thing we would intentionally break without trying our very hardest to put it back together.

Jews are taught that life comes first, but it can be hard. We are taught not to give up. I've been accused of liking a good fight. I do, but I think Jews argue by nature not only because we fled and fought to defend ourselves, but because creating possibility means we must question the status quo. Even when the Torah ends, the story that takes a whole year to tell of our creation and our journey from enslavement to the Promised Land is never fulfilled. The Jewish people approach the Land of Milk and Honey, but they don't enter. We are left to imagine their beginning there.

I am made of the DNA of immigrants—those grandparents and relatives of mine who left everything to begin again not because they dreamed of it but because it was a mandate for their survival. The generational narrative that lives in me is laced with the threads of loss and hardship, discovery and determination. Studying and learning are at the heart of a Jewish life. I don't think that, even if I tried, I could lose those aspects of who I am. I wish I could say "thank you" to those who made the journey and "I'm sorry" for all those family members whose names we do not even know who perished at the hands of the Nazis. I only knew two of my grandparents, and my mother's aunt and uncle who traveled here from Eastern Europe. Few relatives from the "old country" made it out. The ones who came here contributed and gave me everything I need to know about how privileged I am.

I have crafted a well-spun understanding of the God I embrace. I no longer imagine the old bearded man, whom I prayed would spare me punishment for taking a shortcut through the synagogue because I was late for Hebrew school. I imagine a universal spirit, a power that lies in the collective good we can allow to guide us. I imagine there is godliness in every random act of kindness—in birthing a baby, in helping someone less fortunate, in teaching, in expressing our creativity, in holding a hand, in being a friend, in cooking a meal, in sharing resources, in bearing witness to pain, in being present at the end of a life, in giving and asking for nothing in return.

I'm grateful for the upbringing I challenged and the rituals I dismissed as a burden not worth shouldering. I chose to be Jewish not because I was born that way but because my Judaism taught me to put education first, to embrace tolerance and diversity, and to look for how I could fulfill the tradition of Tikkun olam, the healing of the world.

The issues we face at home, at work, in our communities, in our country, and in places near and far can feel overwhelming and disastrous. One hour of reading to a child who is homeless or at risk, one pair of tickets to a Broadway show for someone who might not have been able to go, one day of service delivering meals to homebound people, gifting to those who are just shy of a financial goal, mentoring a young person, listening to a problem, donating to organizations that resonate with me, surprising a friend, making a memory with someone I love, helping a terminally ill person realize a dream...this way of life is not exclusive to being a Jew, but it is at the heart of being Jewish.

The branding of my people during the Holocaust was to deny them their individuality. Their shaven heads and standard-issue uniforms stripped them of their uniqueness, and instead of using their names, they were assigned numbers. It seemed offensive that I would want a tattoo. I thought about it. Maybe I could adorn myself and mean no disrespect. What words or picture would be so meaningful to me that I could imagine my pristine skin becoming distorted with aging permanent ink? Where would I put it? Not somewhere sexy. I wanted it where I could see my own reminders of my people, so few and rare, made more glorious by those who know this and remember.

The Hebrew words from the Bible, Genesis 12, wherein God commanded Abraham to leave all that he knew—"Lech L'cha," which means "go forth"—are tattooed on my forearm. I also have a tattoo on my hand, the single word "faith," and the two Hebrew letters that spell the word for life—"chai"—on my left wrist.

Together, we will grow old and fade.

ALL I EVER WANTED CODA

Peace in my heart. Peace in my soul. Wherever
I'm going, I'm already home
~Buddha~

Six years to the day after we had moved into our Connecticut home, we would be leaving. Our closing was scheduled for the end of April. I had boxed the china, glassware, and clothing we were keeping. Rolls of bubble wrap, tape, boxes, and moving paper covered the living room. Most of the contents of the house would be sold. Tables of housewares, art, clothing, and furniture had been arranged by the women who would oversee our "estate sale." No one had died, but it's called that anyway.

The dreams I'd filled this large, once lifeless house with would soon be another piece of my past. The "practical" story was that Jim and I had concluded that this home came with a long-term commitment and price tag that didn't feel like our future. Its upkeep, the personnel it demanded, and its constant need for our energy and caring weighed on us. The privilege of owning it meant we couldn't leave it for long, and so we decided to leave it forever.

The house sat perched on an exposed, western-facing ridge. In harsh New England storms, its good bones, mahogany deck, and strong structure never let us down. One of our favorite things about it was how safe and warm we felt when we were sitting by a fire and gazing out through the tall glass windows as thunderstorms and blizzards came through. The snowfalls made a magical, private winter wonderland as we waited to be plowed out. After her first snow, without hesitation, Bailey ran outside and jumped around in the white stuff until she sank to her chest.

One night during a snowstorm, Jim came up from the basement with his Flexible Flyer sled. "C'mon," he said, "we're going sledding!"

"What?" I was curled up under a blanket.

He walked over and took my hand. "Come on..."

We went outside, fighting the wind and the cold to the top of the driveway. I sat on the old wood slats, and he got behind me. Whoosh! Down we went until we stopped just short of a snowbank.

The next time, I dragged the sled up and got on my belly. "Push!" Off I went.

"Steer!" he was calling, but I was heading for the snow-covered grass. I crashed.

He took a video. It was hilarious.

The spring would bring the blooms of our garden. Torches lit, we'd gather on the deck, talking long into the starry, summer nights. Ashley and I once saw a large, lime-green Luna moth, rarely sighted by humans. It was so big that in the dark, it looked like a bat. I was very lucky to see two of them; one was even rarer—an albino I found dead on the front step. It's in my jewelry drawer now.

In just a few weeks, we would have less of everything. We would reside full-time in our New York City apartment, which was a quarter of the size of our home in Connecticut. We would have a simpler life. The picture of the stone house I had taped to my mirror years ago had done its job. I didn't know what happened to it.

What would I miss? The smell of the carpet-like freshly-cut grass, the bunnies that came in spring, the deer, the cows that got loose and grazed on our land, the smell of leaves burning, and the color of fall. I would miss our neighbors, the only two people we knew on our road. The expanse of the house had allowed me to reclaim my creative self. The "Robyn's Nest," my beloved writing room, would become someone else's imagination space. The kitchen where I fearlessly cooked the brisket generations of women in my family were known to make. I'd made my grandma's kugel and latkes, and my mother's "hello dollies." I'd made Kathleena's mother Gloria's eggplant parmigiana. I had a collection of cookbooks, old and new—even with stains and spills, my favorite recipes were not ruined, and there was always something I was willing to try. My coveted yearly tradition, the Christmas tree we carefully picked out—each one bigger than the last—I'd adorn with special new finds like the small feather birds, the sparkling handmade glass icicles, and Samantha's family ornaments. Jim would help with the light stringing, and I would do the rest, which took hours, and then we would listen to Christmas music and Frank Sinatra. We would turn off all of the lights, admire the tree, and drink until we got sleepy.

We'd congregated and welcomed so many in this home—sharing meals, hosting parties, eating and drinking and laughing long into the night. I would miss those big breakfasts we'd served—the smells of coffee, bacon, and pancakes waking the late sleepers. Chanukah, Christmas, Easter, Passover, Thanksgiving, birthdays. The warm summer days and the fall chilling the air, Bailey running in the yard so free and happy—all safely stored in the yearly slideshows I'd made.

One year after the Passover/Easter weekend and a full house, I was walking through the house and slipped with a glass of wine in my hand. I didn't let go of the glass, and it nearly cost me a piece of my finger. Surgery and eight weeks in a splint, that memory wasn't one of my favorites, but it would forever be a part of our story there and the only trip I made to the local emergency room.

Even as I packed, the views from every window were captivating. Sunsets came and went, and the fog would roll across the hills and envelop the house in its dewy grayness until the scenery complete-ly disappeared. Those timeless hills were a regal reminder of how nature conspires to make the largest of human schemes seem so small and insignificant.

I was sitting on the cold, concrete basement floor. Looming above me, boxes, neatly labeled, were sitting on metal shelving. I had left Brooklyn two decades ago with twenty-eight of them, still taped up among the others. Their contents would have to be inspected. Years of the sentimental and the banal—all had to be confronted. Feelings long forgotten, treasures unexplored, pictures and videos, neglected letters and cards, the heartwarming and heartbreaking, yearbooks and artwork, dolls, books, fragments from my childhood...their fates were decided in three words: dump, donate, store.

I would climb this Everest one era at a time.

Alan first. I didn't know how to respect or dissect the remains from his estate; this was complicated. Almost a decade had passed. I found letters between us that needed burning. There were anniver-sary and birthday cards he had given me that made me smile—proof there'd been a softer side to him. Childhood pictures with his sister, Daniel's grandma Sally, and Papa Leo; Alan holding Daniel on the day he was born; baby pictures of them together; our wedding por-trait; and the three of us before we were divorced. I tossed them into the box I began filling for Daniel.

Jim and I lit a fire in the backyard. I started burning papers and old pictures that I wouldn't save. The fire blazed. I said a prayer, like the prayer we say when we mourn. Life goes on. It had before. It would again.

Amy next. Nothing about my sister could be discarded. I would make a box for Ashley, and I would keep a box for me. I looked at her diploma from Smith and touched her graduation cap, its fring-es squashed from years of being in the box. I started to read her journals and her notes to me—my only connection to her. It seemed impossible still that she was gone. I just wanted to call her. I stopped and held a doll that had been hers.

I found my high school diploma and yearbooks. I flipped through their mildewed pages. Teachers, friends, my big, curly lioness hair, and there it was: the senior yearbook quote we were each asked to supply, right below my picture:

"Inside me, there are these walls of flesh and shadow, fire, color, and warmth. Rendering life with each new breath, following in my own time, I have learned the truth of difference."

I reread it many times. The words my wiser-than-16-year-old self wrote was a statement that I definitely didn't fit in.

I found boxes full of thank-you letters and cards. I dumped hundreds of them on the floor, barely remembering some of their authors. So much gratitude and love. What to do with all of that? Would all this mean anything to Daniel if he became the beneficiary of it? I savored every word from anyone kind enough to write to me until I could no longer. It was hard to part with those letters and cards, but I will touch more lives. That won't end.

I found the newspapers from 9/11. Keep. And the wedding photos of Barbara and Bernie, now married sixty-three years. Keep. Pictures of me and Kathy, and all the cards and letters we wrote together and apart. Keep. Every birthday card from Scott. I picked some that made me laugh. Every baby card we received when Daniel was born. Keep. Cards and notes from Ashley. Keep.

I found an envelope with every cashed check I'd written to Bernie to pay him back for the loans he had made me. I counted them, turning them over in my hands. I wondered, *why had I kept them?* There were at least twenty of them—payments made over years, back when banks still returned paper checks. I was mad when I was divorcing that he didn't just give me the money when I really needed it; he took no pity on me. I had to rationalize it; maybe he believed in me and knew I would find my way out of any help I needed. I tore the checks into little pieces and let the confetti fall into a garbage bag.

I had so many books. I started sorting through them. The ones I was willing to part with would be boxed and given to veterans. Hundreds of CDs were spared. I found drawings and artwork I had made in high school and college. When was the last time I'd sat down with a sketchpad? There was a box of writing so heavy I couldn't lift it.

Finally, after two days, I had hauled hundreds of pounds out to the shredding monster and watched as it devoured them. Years of my life documented, now gone.

Numerous trips to Goodwill and the local thrift shop, and eventually bags of clothing for friends were delivered. Our children came and picked out what they wanted. Daniel asked for only one thing. He wanted the doormat. Our doormat had our initials on it. One for each of our three last names. He was sad we were selling the house. I smiled when he made the request. Who else would think of the doormat?

One night, I was alone in the house. I looked at all the things laid out for strangers to pick through. I was letting go of a part of myself. The house could feel my detaching; we had grown close over the years, from those distant and cold first weeks to the warmth and love I knew in its every creak and unevenness. I knew how it sounded and smelled. I knew when it was cold, and how the sun would come through at a certain time of day and make it warm. I knew it would never again feel as it did when we'd lived there. I would mourn the life I had dreamed of on that day I'd put the sheets on the mattress Daniel and I once shared in an apartment where we began again. I was choosing to depart, to give all this away and leave, for no other reason than my belief that something else awaited. I would grieve. But I love beginnings.

Grief is not a straight line. It is not the same for everyone, and it doesn't have a "time's up" ping so that you know you are done. The process can take months or years. Just as you think, "Yes, I have grieved this; I am in acceptance," you discover that, no, you are not done. Not yet... There is more.

I was alone the day my piano left on the back of a rickety old truck. I watched it 'til it made the turn out of the driveway, and then I went back into the house and stared at the empty space where it had been. It was the only time I cried. This precious and beautiful instrument, a symbol of my new life, twenty years prior, still reminded me of what I could create.

My last memory there was made when Jim called me into the master bathroom. I thought he was calling for a towel. It made no sense. We had plenty of towels that hadn't yet been packed. I kept hearing "towel." As I wandered in, he was pointing out the window.

A big barred owl was perched on our back fence. It was mystical. It just sat there in the sunlight, swiveling its head in that way that owls do. I grabbed my phone to get a picture.

I quietly made my way down to the field. I got as close as I could without scaring it. I kept a steady eye on it. I didn't look away, and then, its piercing eyes met with mine. We stared at each other for long enough that I was sure it was there to reveal something. I had never seen a big owl in broad daylight. Our eyes stayed locked, and then it spread its wings and gracefully flew off into the trees. I watched until it disappeared.

When I could no longer see it, I whispered, "Goodbye." I went back inside. My footsteps echoed in the emptiness against the wood floor.

Soon, I, too, would be gone.

KABUKI

When people say I can't do things, I just say nothing.
I don't bother to answer. I just do it and prove them wrong.
~Daniel Dubinsky~

In 2017, Daniel was 26. I'm not sure exactly why I reached out to Dr. Mehta, a geneticist whom we had known since a few weeks after Daniel's birth. It was odd that I emailed her because a part of me really didn't care about the latest in genetic testing. My son was thriving, happy, and healthy. We had hurdled a very long list of developmental differences, and I was content in knowing that my son was neuro-complex but thriving. Our lives had been good—rich with cherished experiences and filled with the best kind of love from family and friends.

Daniel's independent lifestyle in Cambridge had been hard-won, but we'd found our way. Daniel's health was, fortunately, very good. Genetic testing since his birth had consistently produced no specific relational cause for a past that was our "normal."

What more did we need to know? Why did I reach out when I did?

Those actions we take, our attitudes, and the narratives we create define who we become. Would my son's identity change if suddenly, after all these years, there was a known genetic cause for what had always been a mystery? What if there were health issues that had a genetic basis and which we hadn't yet encountered? What if Daniel wanted to have his own children? How would his genetic composition inform that decision?

I talked with my son about visiting Dr. Mehta.

"No interest," he said.

I understood. A part of me had "no interest." After years of traveling in what the medical community refers to as the "diagnostic odyssey," labels and diagnoses would mean nothing now. But what if our wandering, and all we had learned, could somehow benefit him, or another family or science? Would he still feel this way?

Eventually, Daniel conceded to the testing, but not because he had any motive of his own. I suspect he did it for me. The strange thing was that I wasn't even sure he should do it. The world of human genetics is as fascinating and as complicated as the study of the cosmos. To start, one must know what they want to look for and what they hope to find. It is a forensic science based on intuition, clinical observation, patience, time, and available resources.

We hadn't seen Dr. Mehta in years, though I had occasionally kept in touch, mostly because I liked her. She is warm, respectful, and kind. Early on, she was a member of "Team Daniel." She was surprised by my email because she had just been thinking of us. She had recently seen a patient who reminded her of Daniel. Now, with advances in genetic science, she had an idea that might unlock the mystery. As a scientist with a case that had been cold for twenty-six years, she was excited to hear of our interest in pursuing new testing. I was still feeling cautious. The idea of finding a label that could imply limitation hadn't interested me.

At the appointment, I ensured that Daniel would be the one "managing" the conversation. Even though he was an adult, I knew the delicate balance between the "patient" and the fascination of those on the science side of the equation—eager to explore and uncover what might be found in a test tube of DNA with a stranger's name on it. Children who are genetically atypical are "studied," sometimes for years. Seemingly benign tape measurements of their heads and limbs, probing questions, every inch of their body a cause for inquiry...the curiosity, even unintentionally, makes an alien of them.

Outside of the labs and specialists' offices, the identity of a unique child is forged over time and through their experiences. What we are told about ourselves can alter what we believe of ourselves. I was hopeful the conversation would be uncomplicated and sensitive. I trusted that Dr. Mehta knew Daniel and I both had a certain peace—even confidence—in knowing what we already knew. We were oddly comfortable in the unknown. Unanswered questions had become a way of life. Changing the story now would be strange.

When she met with us, she said she felt fairly certain the answer was in Daniel's uniquely shaped eyes. Those eyes had captivated people when he was a baby. Three months later, the report confirmed that Dr. Mehta's instincts were correct. In 1981, Japanese scientists described a set of genetic anomalies they began to see in a group of children and named it "Kabuki Syndrome." It was the shape of their eyes that was the dominant feature. They didn't know exactly what genes caused it or that it existed cross-culturally. Halfway across the world, Daniel and I would become inextricably connected to them. The genetic mutation of KMT2D, which was discovered in 2010 and most commonly associated with Kabuki Syndrome, was identified in Daniel's testing.

Prior to knowing this, while navigating the years of seemingly random complexities, the love I'd felt for my son had never been diminished by medical or educational communities. The faith I'd had in him couldn't have been undermined by science. The individual characteristics that made Daniel unique—his intelligence, sense of humor, imagination, intuition, inquisitiveness, and negotiating skills—didn't differ from what made me unique, such as the color of my eyes, my curly hair, my own sense of humor and intuition, or how my heart takes the lead.

What I discovered along the way was that the greatest limitation for any of us is a broken spirit.

I'd asked Daniel if he wanted to know the results of the tests.

"No interest," he'd replied.

One day, six months later, I mentioned the test results again. I briefly explained that his rarity could be described by science, and there was a name for it. A part of me was sad as there'd been a romance to not knowing.

"Can we talk about this?"

His head down, he nodded and slowly asked me a few questions.

"Does this mean I'll have a short life? Will this make me sick? If I have my own children, would they have this?"

I had wondered about all that, too. I had asked Dr. Mehta.

"No, you will not have a short life because of this."

Pause.

"If you haven't already been diagnosed with something serious, you probably won't be."

Pause.

"You could have children who would not have this syndrome but that is a lengthier discussion."

Silence.

Daniel lifted his head, and then we moved on to baseball.

I wonder when we will discuss it again.

Daniel is Daniel, and we are who we became together. I wouldn't have traded any of what we have lived for any life we could have had. We are just who we are...

ACKNOWLEDGEMENTS

Thank you, Michael Conant and the team at Incorgnito Publishing for believing in the power of telling stories. How we have lived and what we tell about our lives connects, inspires, and creates the discovery that we are not alone.

Jennifer Collins, a writer writes in solitude, but you were my honest witness. You heard my voice calling out from beneath that tangled first draft. Your sensitive and thoughtful editorial guidance helped me shape this narrative into the book it became. You have not only my gratitude, but we are forever bonded in its pages.

Mary Markle, Ashley Wren, Victoria Hone, Lori Ramos, and Marie Pruitt thank you for reading chapters and versions of my manuscript and for your commentary, encouragement and support which kept me filling pages with words.

I am blessed to have many friends. All of them are extraordinary people. Some have travelled with me since I was in high school, and some came into my life later, and every single one of them has an impressive story. I have heard it said, "if you want to know your destiny, look at the company you keep." I never stop noticing how special you all are- and wherever I am headed, the journey has been made richer by you.

There are countless people throughout my career whom I wish to thank. There are those who hired me, mentored me, and worked closely with me. There are brave and talented performers who entrusted me with the care of their chosen profession. I am grateful for the doors that opened and the opportunities that led me to the discovery of my professional potential. While I've served for more than three decades in my industry, I've worked with an exceptional team, I've made special friends. It is said that one friend at work is essential to the quality of one's career. I count among my blessings far more than that and I wish I could name all of you.

Thanks to my colleague Scott Kaufman, for giving me fodder for some of the funniest stories I will ever tell, and for being there- in your inimitable way, good days and bad days. And thank you for being a champion of my writing.

When I gave Joyce Gordon (who was like a mother to me) the completed manuscript of this book, I wasn't sure she would able to read it. I just wanted her to see the dedication. A few days later, I got the last text she wrote to me. She had read he whole book. Days later, she was in the hospital. It was unexpected and yet, I somehow knew she was done. It was an honor to be counted among her family members, but a great honor to know that even before it was published, my book was the last she read. I have yet to say good-bye, nor will I. She was the best laughing and crying partner. My favorite times with her were hanging out in her kitchen, eating and soaking up her stories of courage and love for life. We ate bagels and lox on Saturday mornings and argued about what was in the news. When I was sad, she would say, "We all get a little vial of magic...but we only get so much. It's up to you how you use it, but be careful, because once it's gone, it can't be replaced..." *She* will never be replaced.

Bernie (aka Saint Bernard,) when you hug mom and take her hand, you are holding your 65-years together it is the truest measure of those words, "for better or for worse." You never give up. When I challenged you to give up on me, you both drove me to New York, and left me there, not because you abandoned me, but because this drug infested, dirty, loud, crowded city was my dream. Even if you thought it was crazy, and much too expensive- it was the place where I became who I am. You drove off and didn't look back. You and I have come a long way. "The talk" we've been having about what to do "in an emergency" and where "the important papers" are, has been going on for years, and guess what? You are 90 and you are still here! The money lectures have in part- paid off. It would be nice if you wear those new t-shirts I bought you. You'll be happy to know they were on sale.

Jim, we built this life on a lot of "no's" –ours was a collision in the perfect place in what might have been an imperfect time. Against the odds, we stayed the course. There is no guarantee the second time around things would be any easier, but I trusted we would be better together than we would be apart. I still remember how it felt when you first took my hand in yours. I treasure all those trails we have walked, the suns we've watched set, and the moons we've seen rise. Let's keep colliding, and when we fall, lets promise to pick each other up. Let's keep putting stars in the sky and remember they are there shining down on us- even on a cloudy night when we can't see them. Thank you for believing in me. Thank you for loving Daniel unconditionally. Thank you for reminding me that forgiveness, acceptance and love endure all things.

Kathleena, my co-pilot, thank you for recognizing me when I said you had beautiful eyes, that I was the one with whom you would travel lifetimes and wife-times together. Each time around, we keep getting better. We are here. We are alive, we have each other. Let's grow really old, go to the Grand Canyon, take a '66 Thunderbird and gun it- my dear Thelma. I will forever be your Louise.

Scott Linder, when you were my mentor, it was like a course in race car driving. It was a test of endurance and precision. You taught me to have the confidence to do my job- to be even better at it than I knew I would be, without crashing. You were the first to come visit the hospital when Daniel was born. You are my chosen brother, my project runway, my "Queer eye for the straight girl" forever fashion maven. You are the one that makes me laugh 'til I pee in my pants and calls me out for eating while I talk on the phone. I see reminders of your generosity and good taste in my closet, and I think of how I will love you until I can't remember you. I take some comfort in knowing you'll make sure I am well dressed , that my nails are done and that my hair is colored- what color you'll pick- is up to you – right now, you've got three to choose from. I trust you.

Steven we don't talk much, but I respect and admire you and I wish I had told you more. Forgive me. I should have. I'm happy we have each other. Live free my dear brother. Keep the wind at your back and the sun out of your eyes.

Sam and Kim, you didn't ask for it, but you've both become full time residents of a heart that was not sure how there would be room to love another child, let alone two. Thank you for accepting what might have seemed impossible. Our growing family may be complex, but anything other than that would be boring. Let's just keep making good memories and finding the joy in each other.

Alan, I'm not sure how much you see from the flight deck, but whatever we couldn't find together here on earth, our beautiful son is the is the gift we gave each other.

Amy you are my angel -wherever I go. There you are.

Ashley, my shining star, you will command change and armed with spray paint and milk drops, you'll protest for all that needs righting... the magic you do will forever impact the lives you touch. Thank you for reminding me to keep bending the rules, to keep challenging the status quo, to ask, why not? Carry on my beautiful girl.

Bailey, you are the best. Who else would be so happy to see me when I come in from taking out the garbage? or sit quietly by the door when I accidently leave you outside in the hall?

Daniel, I can't imagine my life without you. You are in every word

I wrote. You are my heart's belonging and the voice of true love. You have taught me that the only thing that matters in life is how you live it. If it's true that we came here to find each other, then we did so to complete each other, and much more.

ROBYN STECHER

Robyn Stecher was born outside of Boston and made in New York. She is a writer and an entertainment industry veteran. She is also the founder of Artemis Rising Enterprises- a coaching and consulting company. Together with her son, they have set out to prove that people are much more than meets the eye—one must see the invisible to do the impossible. She is a certified performance coach and has been a speaker on the subjects of women in business and parenting complex children. She resides in New York City with her husband and Bailey, their rescue dog..

This book is a work of art produced by Incorgnito Publishing Press.

Jennifer Collins - Editor

Robert Cooper - Proof Editor

Star Foos - Artist/Designer

Daria Lacy - Graphic Production

Janice Bini - Chief Reader

Michael Conant – Publisher

October 2020 Incorgnito Publishing Press

Direct inquiries to mconant@incorgnitobooks.com